Cassell's Colloquial Italian

A HANDBOOK OF IDIOMATIC USAGE

Completely revised by
P. J. T. Glendening

Formerly *Beyond the Dictionary in Italian*

CASSELL

Cassell Publishers Ltd
Villiers House, 41/47 Strand
London WC2N 5JE

First edition 1963
Revised edition 1980
Reprinted 1982, 1985, 1989
This edition 1993

ISBN 0 304 07944 8

Printed and bound in Finland

Contents

Preface

Since this book was first published in 1963, as a companion volume to *Beyond the Dictionary in Spanish* (recently retitled *Cassell's Colloquial Spanish*), other languages have joined the series, thereby giving evidence of its utility and popularity, providing as it does a handy, readable key to the living language, supplying information which might otherwise be gleaned only in part and with great difficulty—as well as liability to error—from an ordinary dictionary or other source.

This edition differs from the previous one in that the section called 'Special Vocabularies' has been drastically reduced, the sole survivors being the chapters on 'False Friends' and on 'Disconcerting Genders'. By eliminating these vocabularies far more space has been made available for the basic section, which has been largely rewritten and updated, with the inclusion of numerous new entries.

I wish to make the point that a handbook of everyday usage, such as this, is not the same as a reference book of slang, even though a few common jargon and slang words are in fact explained. And we must be clear about what is meant by 'everyday'. The irrigation engineer, for example, finds *ala mobile* ('lateral', 'flying line') an everyday term. Likewise the hydrologist with *evapotraspirazione* ('evapo-transpiration' or 'consumptive use') and the railway engineer with *armamento* ('track equipment'). But these are not 'everyday' words to the vast majority of people, and would therefore be out of place here. On the other hand, jargon and technical terms in certain spheres of life, such as politics, economics and trade unionism, for example, which impinge significantly on everyday life, have become known to the general public through the press, the radio and TV, and must consequently be considered 'everyday' and thus warrant inclusion in the present volume. Further, no claim is made that none of the words contained here can be found in a general dictionary. Far from it, although it is true that several of the terms included here do not appear elsewhere. However, what is fundamentally meant by going 'beyond the dictionary' is that certain ordinary words and expressions are emphasized, and an explanatory reference is made or background provided to what might otherwise pass unnoticed, or appear odd, obscure or confusing.

I will conclude with some words from the preface to the first edition: it is hoped that this book will be referred to, dipped into, browsed in at odd moments, and not treated as just another dictionary, to be consulted only when an unknown word is encountered.

And now, *in bocca al lupo*, as one says to a student about to sit for an examination, or 'Good luck!'

Miscellaneous Notes

The person reading this book will probably already have a very fair knowledge of the Italian language, of how it is pronounced and so on. For this reason it is obviously unnecessary to start right from scratch; instead, here are a number of pointers to tell you what pitfalls to avoid and what basic things you should do which you might not otherwise think of doing.

Note straight away that Italian is practically a one-country language. It is comparatively rare for foreigners to learn such languages, and the very fact of your doing so puts you many points up in their estimation. I won't claim that you can't put a foot wrong, but if you do, it doesn't matter. They are with you from the start, the Italians, as you are taking the trouble to learn their language. And although in the points which follow I have sometimes drawn attention to common English pitfalls in Italian, I must stress the advice not to bother so much about the possibility of making these mistakes that you never open your mouth. Naturally, the essential thing is to say something, even though it may not be one hundred per cent pure Italian. In quiet, private moments, just try to improve on certain things, but in public think just of expressing yourself, and not of being a perfectionist. Be one, by all means, but not all the time.

Pronunciation. You will certainly have read, or heard it stated, or noted for yourself, that Italian is a 'musical' language, that it has a heavy sing-song accent. That this is in fact so may be obscured if you hear the language spoken by an Italian with a pronounced regional accent (although note in passing that some regional and other accents are extremely musical), but if you tune in to the

Italian radio or listen to the voices of the announcers (or
more especially the announceresses) on Italian TV, you
will immediately recognize the musical accent. Such an
accent in most other European languages tends to sound
effeminate. The stress, falling regularly on the penultimate
syllable, is indeed heavy, and you may emphasize single
words as heavily as you wish, as you may also in English
—but which you may absolutely not do in Spanish, for
example. And although you may have the impression that
Italians are very rapid speakers—and there is no denying
that some speakers of the language are able to utter it at
great rapidity—the fact of there being this heavy stress,
as well as double consonants which have really to be
sounded double, and frequent long vowel sounds, has a
slowing influence on the language. Indeed, some linguists
even claim that Italian is one of the slower European
languages. Certainly it is a mistake to try to skip the
heavy stress, just as it sounds foreign to fail to double
double consonants. Remember, for instance, the difference between *capello* and *cappello*. I do not wish to
exaggerate the importance of this difference in the understanding of the language, as common sense usually guides
the hearer, and the meaning is almost clear anyway, but
using the two words just as isolated sounds, and not in
connected sentences, the doubling of the *p* is all the difference in the world between 'hair' and 'hat'. Shall I sound
the obvious warning at this point? Don't overdo things—
double means double, not treble. I so often hear people
who are perfectly aware of the double sounding of double
consonants, stressing the syllable in question to such an
extent that it never seems to come to an end.

One of the principal English errors in speaking Italian
is the retaining of weak forms. This is, of course, one of
the faults committed by English people in pronouncing
whatever other language they are learning. In Italian it
comes out very readily, perhaps as Italian is also a language with heavy stress. In any group of syllables in English

you will come across a certain number of them pronounced weakly. A weak syllable is one which undergoes
a vowel change from the way the vowel is sounded if
stressed. If the word 'borstal', for instance, had an accented final syllable, we should pronounce it 'al', whereas in
fact, as it is unstressed, we say 'borst'l'. In Italian, however, vowels always retain their pure value, however
much you may lay on the emphasis or however quickly
you may speak. This weakening of certain vowels is a
characteristic you notice even among very practised and
expert English speakers of Italian. You may detect them
saying kjarə'mɛnte instead of kjara'mɛnte (*chiaramente*),
or pɔm'riddʒo instead of pɔme'riddʒo (*pomeriggio*) and
so on. Italians understand what is being said perfectly
well, but it is a nationality-betraying tendency which you
may be fastidious enough to wish to try to avoid.

Remember the pronunciation of the Italian *r*-sound.
Many learners make the mistake of imagining that the *r* is
equally strongly rolled in Italian in all positions—and this
is certainly a mistaken idea—and they then proceed to roll
most strongly those *r*-sounds which come most easily to
the English mouth which, in many cases, are not those
r-sounds which should be most strongly rolled. If, for
instance, you roll strongly the *r* in the infinitive ending of
a verb, you are making a mistake and sound quite un-
Italian. Were it intended that the infinitive *r* should be
strongly rolled, it would be written with a double *r* (certain infinitives do, in fact, have *rr*, and consequent strong
rolling—for example, *porre* and *trarre*). Note such differences as exist between *coro* and *corro*, and *caro* and *carro*.
When there is an initial *r*, many learners find it difficult to
give this sound its correct value; they then, realizing that
the initial *r*-sound should be rolled and being unsuccess-
ful in their attempt, proceed to give the next *r*-sound, if it
happens to be near, the rolling of its life, regardless of
whether it should be long or short. It's a sort of delayed-
action roll, just as Italian learners of English, having

difficulty with the *h*-sound, but being aware that it exists, will not be able to get it out in time for the first word with an *h* but will put it in when the next vowel comes along, as in: ' 'e his 'ere' ('he is here'). Be on your guard.

You will naturally know of the existence of the two *e*-sounds and two *o*-sounds. Confusion here is one of the surest ways for Italians to distinguish even practised foreign speakers of their language. *Pollo*, for instance, has the closed *o*-sound, while *polo* has the open *o*-sound. *Pompa* has closed *o*, *pomodoro* only open *o*'s. *Tortora* has initially a closed *o*, as has *torta*, while *tortura* has open *o*. *Posto* has closed *o*, *posta* the open variety. Regarding the two variations of *e*, note that the closed variety is relatively uncommon, but comes in such words as *bestia*, *essa*, *fermo*, *tegola*. *Telo* ('piece of cloth') is closed, but *tela* ('linen', 'cloth') is open. Lastly, I cannot resist referring to those two famous causes of confusion—*pesce* ('fish'), with initial closed *e*, and *pesca* ('peach'), with open *e*. The plural of 'fish' is *pesci* (closed *e*), the plural of 'peach' *pesche* (open *e*'s). Just to complicate matters, note also *pesca* ('fishing'), which has a closed *e*.

Diphthongs. Three points must be made here. Firstly, when two vowels are written together they do not necessarily form a diphthong—they may well be sounded separately and independently, as in *neonato*. Secondly, diphthongs are always formed with unstressed *i* or *u*. Thirdly, we divide them into two groups, according to whether the stress falls on the first element (*ai, au, ei, eu, oi, ui*) or on the second element (*ia, ie, io, iu, ua, ue, ui, uo*). It must, however, be admitted that the real difficulty lies in remembering whether a vowel is stressed or unstressed. For instance, *pausa* has unstressed *u*, while *paura* has stressed *u*. Thus *pausa* has a diphthong, while *paura* has separately pronounced vowel sounds. Look at *Luigi, lui* and *buio*: *Luigi* has unstressed *u*, *lui* has stressed *u* and *buio* has stressed *u*. Again, *Italia* has unstressed *–ia*, while

Maria and *malattia*, for example, have stressed *i*. These are by no means isolated examples, but are chosen to present the problem to you. The moral is—remember the position of the stress.

Accent. By this word we understand three separate things: stress, as referred to above; the written mark indicating stress (and variation of sound, in some languages, but not in Italian); and the regional or special way of pronouncing a language (the term 'dialect' indicates a variation of vocabulary, grammar and accent from the central language, so that accent in this sense may or may not indicate true dialect; a few sentences will generally soon demonstrate whether Italian, say, is being spoken with a regional accent, or whether a true dialect is being spoken).

Concerning the written accent, you may well be in some doubt as to which one to use and when to use it, as different grammars and dictionaries give different instructions (apart from varying usage with no explanation). Italian rules about it are really quite clear, however. Firstly, there is only one accent, the grave. Then, this accent is written as follows:

a) on words where the stress falls on the final syllable: *caffè, carità, perchè, tribù, università, virtù*;

b) on monosyllables ending in diphthongs: *già, giù, più, può* (but not on *qui* or *qua*);

c) on monosyllables which have one meaning without the accent and another one with it: for example, *da* ('from'), *dà* ('gives'); *e* ('and'), *è* ('is'); *la* ('the'), *là* ('there'); *ne* ('of it' etc.), *nè* ('neither', 'nor').

However, you know what Italians are like with rules—and far be it from me to claim that the clear rules here stated are universally adhered to. In fact, the well-known Feltrinelli paper-back series referred to as *U.E.* (*Universale Economica*) regularly uses the grave accent for *a*, most *e*'s and *o*, while the acute accent is used for the *i* and the *u*, and for such *e*'s as those in *per sé, perché, né* and so on.

In conclusion, note also that such words as *popolo*, *unico* and *veneto*, which are not stressed regularly (regular stress meaning the penultimate syllable, with variations noted above), do *not* take any written accent, except in some dictionaries and guides to pronunciation, which point out that you say *'popolo, 'unico* and *'veneto*. In this respect Italian differs from Spanish.

Diminutives, Augmentatives, Superlatives, etc. The diminutive, although frequently employed, is not so frequent as in Spanish. Most often there is an idea of smallness, quite logically, or of something endearing, pleasant, nice. The augmentative, on the other hand, often gives the idea of something rather or very unpleasant. Over-use or wrong use of the diminutive sounds rather silly, and wrong use of the augmentative either a bit ridiculous or downright rude. In all cases, be careful. For a 'small book', why not say *piccolo libro*, for instance? Don't play about with *librino, libretto* and so on. If you do, you will often be using, not just the wrong word, but a confusing one. *Libretto*, for instance, apart from meaning the 'words' in opera, means 'official book required for workers' (*libretto di lavoro*). I could, but do not intend to, give a list of the various diminutives and the large number of augmentatives. Far better to learn them joined on to specific words, as *casella* ('pigeonhole', *casella postale* being 'box number'), *pochino* ('a little', 'small amount'), *prestino* (as in *È arrivato un po' prestino*, 'He's come a bit early'), *carino* ('nice', 'pretty').

A short time ago I heard someone complaining that every time he ordered a *cappuccino* (coffee with some milk added) in his local 'bar', the barman said *Sì, un cappuccio*, while, when he varied the order and said *Un cappuccio* the barman said, rather disdainfully it seemed, *Va bene, un cappuccino*—which just showed, this man contended, that the barman was determined for him to be wrong. There may be another explanation, but in any case you will find that it is indeed easy to be wrong, so once again, tread warily, but don't let this kind of thing discourage you.

Note the change of certain nouns by the addition of *-one*. The word automatically becomes both masculine and bigger—*scarpa* becoming *scarpone*, for instance, while *librone* comes from *libro*.

How to address and refer to people. You may be bewildered on this fundamental point, as so much contrary advice is given. Regarding how to address people, there is no difficulty about using *tu*, which is used in the same circumstances in which most other languages use their second person singular personal pronoun. Again, addressing children, etc., the plural form to use is *voi*. But here the complications arise, apparently. One book says: '*Voi* is the universal word for the English "you", whether one person or more is referred to.' A second book says: '*Voi*, *Lei* and *Loro* are the three words to translate "you", but as *Lei* and *Loro* present certain difficulties, we shall restrict ourselves here to using *Voi*.' Both are wrong; a third book (*La Lingua Italiana insegnata agli Stranieri*, by Roncari & Brighenti, published by Edizioni Scolastiche Mondadori, Milan) puts the position more accurately; its argument may be summarized as follows:

Voi, plural of *tu*;

Lei, normal form of address in the singular (using third person singular verb form);

Loro, normal form of address in the plural (using third person plural verb form);

Voi, used variously in addressing one or more persons, takes the second person plural verb form and is used in commercial language, among artists and in certain regions of Italy.

Similarly, although many books use exclusively *egli*,

ella and *essa* for 'he', 'she' and 'it' respectively, with the plural forms *essi*, *esse* and *loro*, in actual fact you will almost everywhere and always hear *lui* and *lei* for 'he' and 'she', and *loro* for 'they'. Note that *lei*, meaning 'she', usually takes a small letter, when not beginning a sentence, while *Lei*, meaning 'you', is capitalized. Similarly, plural 'you' takes a capital, *Loro*.

Basic constructions. It is worth while pointing out that you should be quite sure of the ground you are building on before you build. So many people go astray by learning strange words before basic vocabulary, and by trying to use complicated idioms before they know the elementary grammar of the language. I know an Englishman, resident in Italy for 23 years and married to an Italian, whom I heard, during the two hours or so of an evening meal in a restaurant, make mistakes in the grammar of the order he gave the waiter not to bring something, in the 'both . . . and . . .' construction and in giving the date. Which is quite something, after 23 years. You must be perfectly conversant with the basic sentence pattern, constructions, dates and so on. Here is a list.

più . . . (e) più . . .	the more . . . the more . . .
meno . . . (e) meno . . .	the less . . . the less . . .
sia . . . sia . . .	both . . . and . . .
nè . . . nè . . .	neither . . . nor . . .
o . . . o . . .	either . . . or . . .
appena . . . quando . . .	hardly . . . when . . .
più . . . di . . .	more . . . than . . .
meno . . . di . . .	less . . . than . . .

Never be afraid of reading or saying numbers, however complicated they may look. Practise them to yourself. Whenever you read a date, really read it and don't skim over it. Get into the habit of doing this and numbers, both cardinal and ordinal, will soon become easy. Remember that dates take cardinal numbers, except the first of the month, which is the *primo*. For instance, 'the tenth of July' is *il dieci luglio*. On the other hand, kings, popes and so on take ordinal numbers. 'Pope John the 23rd' was referred to as *Papa Giovanni Vigesimo terzo*, and not *Ventitreesimo*, or *Ventesimo terzo*, as here the old form is used. And one last thing, don't be at a loss to know how to ask the time. I have known some quite good speakers of Italian be stumped by this, surprisingly enough. Say: *Che ora è? Che ore sono? or Che ora c'è?*

Idioms. Italian speakers do not use as many idioms as most speakers of English. Certainly, there is less flexibility than in English in forming new words, and new phrases do not crop up so frequently either. English, of course, abounds in verbal idioms, of which Italian has comparatively few. Again, English contains a large number of words which each have a multiplicity of meanings (for instance, 'odd', 'bound', 'point'), of which Italian has relatively few. Idioms proper are sometimes divided into logical and non-logical, the ones whose meaning is immediately (or almost immediately) clear, and those which have to be explained to be understood. There is no hard and fast line of division between the two sorts, of course. Italian has fewer of the non-logical type than English. In short, you have no call to be so highly idiomatic in Italian as you are in English, in the sense of using idioms of the fixed sort (such as 'the proof of the pudding is in the eating', in Italian *se sono rose fioriranno*). Naturally, a few idioms here and there, in the proper context, brighten up the conversation no end . . . but be sure that it *is* the proper context.

Italian - English

A

a (interj).   The daily newspapers in Italy recently reported the case of a worthy gentleman who became somewhat angry at being sent a tax reference number. The cause of his anger was twofold: previously he had been one of the numerous horde of *evasori fiscali* (tax dodgers), and this communication meant that the system had finally caught up with him; and secondly his masculinity had been hurt to the quick by his having been classified as a female. The poor computer, upon being fed his name, had promptly classified him as such because, misguided fellow, he had been in the habit of appending a title (actually no longer in official use) to his name, i.e. *Eccellenza*, and the a-ending had led the machine astray! Very understandable. Of course, the machine had been taught that there are certain male names ending in –a, such as *Luca* (Luke), but this one was obviously not on the list. However, the real point I wish to make here is that the initial *A* sometimes heard before the usually mutilated form of a Christian name is (normally) intended merely to balance the bit knocked off the end part of the name. The stars of Vittorio De Sica's famous film *Bicycle Thieves* are a little boy and his father. And how does the father usually address the boy, Bruno, in the film? *A Brù!*, in point of fact. Likewise, *A Giovà!* means just *Giovanni!* or perhaps 'Hey, Giovanni!' (note the accent on the syllable where the name breaks off). *A Piè!* is 'Pietro', and so on. This form (not one to imitate, though) is also sometimes used more intimately, in softer tones (of sympathy, commiseration, etc.).

abusivo (adj or n).   Yes, 'abusive', but not only of the foul-mouthed variety. It usually refers to someone not authorized to do something. A car-park attendant is a *posteggiatore* or a *guardia-macchine*, but if he is not in possession of an official permit to carry on his profession, he is an *abusivo*. Squatters are also known as *abusivi*.

accendere.   To light (a fire), or to switch on the light, the engine, the television, etc. (*accendere la luce, il motore, la televisione*). The opposite is *spegnere*. If someone approaches you and asks *Mi fa* (or *faccia*) *accendere, per favore*, he is not asking you to set him alight, but to provide a match for his cigarette. A lighter is *accendisigaro* (m), and remember to accent the word on *si*.

accidente (m).   This means 'accident', right enough, although the more usual words by far are *infortunio* and *incidente* (m). *Un incidente stradale*, for example, is 'a road accident'. Note also the plural form (below), used as an interjection.

accidenti! (interj). Italians come out with this word on many occasions, generally to express surprise, annoyance, etc. It is used in just about the same situations where in English various people would say 'Damn!', 'Blimey!', 'My!', 'Crikey!', and so forth. If you drop something and break it, you could well exclaim *Accidenti! Accidenti, che guaio!* is 'My, what a mess!' A euphemism for it is *accipicchia!* while *ammappero!* (accented on the second syllable) is a Romanism for the same thing. Rather stronger is *ammazza!*

accomodare. You can *accomodare* a broken handle, for example, meaning 'to fix', 'to put right', etc. Rather than 'to repair' it can sometimes mean 'to adapt', 'to adjust'. Then again, *accomodare* is much used reflexively, *accomodarsi* (and notice, by the way, the spelling with a single *m*). Here it means 'to come in', 'to take a seat', 'to make yourself comfortable', and so on, when inviting someone in, showing him to another room, asking him to sit down, etc. When (or perhaps 'if' is a better word) you stand up in a bus to give someone your seat, you say *Si accomodi*, or *Prego, s'accomodi*. A rather longer form is *Volete accomodarvi?*

accordo (m). *Un accordo* is 'an agreement'. *Essere d'accordo* means 'to agree'. *D'accordo* is a very common way of indicating that 'It's all right', 'I agree', 'O.K.'. *Si, d'accordo, sono stato un po' brusco, ma adesso tutto va bene.* 'Yes, all right, I was a bit brusque, but now everything's all right'.

accorgersi. 'To realize', 'to notice'. Negatively, 'not to notice or realize, be unaware of'. *Anche il capo se n'era accorto* means 'the boss noticed it, too'. *Lo salutò e lui quasi non se ne accorse*, 'He greeted him almost without the other's realizing it'. *Mi sono accorto troppo tardi dell'errore*, 'I realized the mistake all too late'. *Lo feci senza accorgermene* means 'I did it without noticing'. Another common way of saying 'to realize' is *rendersi conto* (see under **conto**).

acqua (f). Water. *Acqua potabile* is 'drinking water'. The word *acqua* comes into many everyday expressions. If you're talking about something that's gone by, to be forgotten about, you might well refer to it as *acqua passata*. If someone's argument *fa acqua da tutte le parti*, then of course 'it won't hold water'. If someone says to you *Acqua in bocca!* he's telling you to 'keep mum'. *Affogare in un bicchier d'acqua* is more or less 'to make a mountain out of a molehill', and therefore 'to get het up or nervous about something insignificant'.

acquedotto (m). An aqueduct, as the dictionary tells you, when speaking historically. But speaking of urban utilities, this is 'water supply system'.

acquolina (f). 'Little water', in the sense of 'drizzle', perhaps, but of interest mainly in the expression *far venire l'acquolina in bocca*, 'to make your mouth water'.

adatto. A much used adjective for 'suitable, fit, proper'. *L'uomo adatto* is 'the right man' (for the job, etc.).

addirittura. In a literary sense, this may mean 'directly' or 'immediately'. *Da Napoli vado addirittura a Bari*, 'From Naples I'm going straight to Bari'. In normal conversation, however, it means 'absolutely', 'even' or 'really'. *Quella donna non sa niente, addirittura niente!*—'That woman knows nothing, absolutely nothing!' *Questa mattina sono arrivato addirittura prima delle sette!*—'This morning I arrived even before seven!' *Lui ha mangiato quasi un chilo di spaghetti!*—*Un chilo? Addirittura!* 'He ate almost a whole kilo of spaghetti!—What, one kilo? Really!'

addizionali (m pl). 'Fringe benefits'.

addosso. You will come across this word in a number of expressions. For instance, *mettere le mani addosso a qualcuno* is 'to catch hold of someone'. *Come mai posso lavorare con quel tizio addosso?*—'How on earth can I be expected to work with that chap around?' *Avere del denaro addosso* is 'to have some money on you'.

adeguarsi. 'To adjust or readjust' to something, 'to adapt to'. *Bisogna adeguarsi alle nuove esigenze* is 'We have to readjust to the new conditions (requirements)'. The corresponding noun is *adeguamento*, as in *clausula di adeguamento monetario*, 'escalator clause'.

afa (f). Let's start with the corresponding adjective, *afoso*, which means 'sultry, close, muggy' (an often used word in the summer in Central Italy). So *afa* is 'sultriness, mugginess'.

affare (m). This means 'a successful business deal', 'a bargain'. In various contexts it means 'business' in its different applications. Notice the expression *Si faccia gli affari suoi!* 'Mind your own business!' *Un affarone* is 'a real bargain', 'a very profitable bit of business'.

affatto. As is the case with *mica* (q.v.), *affatto* is normally used to back up and strengthen a negative. *Questo lavoro non è affatto difficile* is 'This work isn't at all hard'. *Niente affatto* means 'not at all'. *Lei dice che lui è molto simpatico, ma io non lo trovo affatto simpatico*, 'You say that he's very pleasant, but I don't find him the least bit pleasant'.

affittare. *Affittare un appartamento* is 'to rent a flat'. Stuck on the wall outside the house or flat to let you will find a red, green or yellow notice (the colours being of the luminous variety which catch the eye so readily), on which you will read *Affittasi*. The money you pay for renting a place is called *l'affitto* or else *la pigione* (q.v.).

agente (m).   Depending on the context, he might be any sort of agent, but as like as not he will be a policeman (*agente di pubblica sicurezza*).

agnolotti (m pl).   A sort of 'ravioli', eaten at all times of the year, but traditionally one of the main items in the Christmas dinner.

allenare.   Both this verb and *addestrare* mean 'to train', but there is a difference. *Allenare* indicates personal striving, especially for sport (and 'the trainer' is *l'allenatore*). *Allenamento* is 'training', in the sense of going for a run or practising football, and so on, while *addestramento* is the training a soldier has in drill, or a worker has for his job, etc.

allora.   You know that this means 'then', as opposed to 'now', which is *adesso*. (Spanish speakers, note that it is easy to confuse *ahora* and *allora*.) Apart from this time meaning, *allora* is used, and used again and again, more or less in the same way as *dunque* (q.v.), meaning 'well', or perhaps more with the idea of 'well, then'. There are countless situations where this word can be used. A lady goes into a shop where she has already left an order. Looking at the assistant, she says: *Allora, è tutto pronto?* On a crowded bus, a young lady is standing beside a young man, whose hand inadvertently touches hers on the rail they are both holding for support. Suspecting that the poor chap is getting a bit fresh, the young lady fixes him with a glare and exclaims: *Allora?* 'Well, what d'you think you're up to?' Another example: the teacher has set an exercise, and gives the class a certain time to do it in. When the time is up, he says *Allora, non scrivete più*, 'Now then, don't write any more'. Just one more: some friends have had a bit of a discussion about where to go that evening. After examining each other's suggestions, they say: *Allora, dove andiamo?* 'Well now, where are we going?' *Allora, ha capito?*

alpinismo (m).   Not just climbing the Alps, but any mountains, i.e. 'mountaineering'. The climber concerned is *un alpinista*.

altezza (f).   This is the ordinary word for 'height', e.g. the height of a person, and also a common word for 'depth' (of water). Strangely enough, it is also sometimes 'width', as in speaking of a material. Figuratively, it can mean 'loftiness', while capitalized it means 'Highness' (*Sua Altezza Reale* is 'His Royal Highness'). A common expression is *all'altezza di*, as in *Lui abita in via Bruno Buozzi all'altezza del Cinema Royal*, 'He lives in Via Bruno Buozzi near the Royal Cinema'. It may be variously 'at', 'opposite', 'by', 'outside' or 'in front of' (or, if at sea, 'off'). Lastly, note the use of the expression *non essere all'altezza di*, 'not to be up to something, not to be capable of doing something'.

amabile.   Of wine, this means 'sweet' or 'sweetish'.

ammappero!, ammazza!   See under **accidenti!**

Anagrafe (f). *L'Ufficio dell'Anagrafe*, or simply *l'Anagrafe*, is where you have to go to register births, deaths, marriages, residence and so on. The Registry Office, in other words.

ancora. Here I am referring to the word with the stress on the middle syllable, and not to the noun of the same spelling which takes the accent on the first syllable (i.e. *l'ancora*, 'the anchor'). You will probably be aware of the different meanings of the word. Firstly, we have 'yet' and 'still'. *Non sono ancora arrivati* means 'They aren't here yet'. *Mio fratello era ancora in casa quando sono uscito* is 'My brother was still at home when I left'. Secondly, *ancora* can mean 'even' in the sense of 'still', together with a comparative. 'And her sister is even prettier' would be, for example, *E sua sorella è ancora più carina*. *Ancora meglio* or *meglio ancora* is 'even better'. Thirdly, we have the idea of 'more'. *Ne vuoi ancora?* is 'Would you like some more?' *Ancora due, per favore* is 'Two more, please'. *Ancora un po'* means 'Just a little more'. And fourthly, there is the idea of repetition, of 'again'. For instance, *L'ho visto ancora una volta ieri* means 'I saw him (once) again yesterday'.

andare. This is one of the key verbs of the Italian vocabulary. Of course, it is heard most often in the form *va*. *Come va?* means 'How are things going?' and so on. *Va bene* is equivalent to our 'All right' or 'O.K.'. *Me ne vado* means 'I'm going', from the verb *andarsene*. *Vado a vedere un film* means 'I'm going to see a film', although you should be a bit careful not to overwork the construction *andare a fare qualche cosa*, which is not of such frequent occurrence as the 'I'm going to' construction in English. At night you can *andare a letto*, 'go to bed'. *Andare a piedi* is 'to go on foot', while *andare in bicicletta* is 'to cycle'. *Le cose vanno avanti molto bene* means 'Things are going along very nicely'. Notice especially the form *andiamo*, the Italian equivalent of the French *on y va* and the Spanish *vamos*, not to mention the English 'Let's go', 'come on'. From this we have the noun *andata* (f), of special interest to train (etc.) users. *Un biglietto di andata e ritorno* is 'a return ticket', as opposed to 'a single', which is *un biglietto di sola andata*. *Va bene?*

annoiato. Usually 'bored'. And you are bored because something is *noioso*, i.e. 'boring'. Although there is no hard and fast difference between the two ideas, 'annoyed' is more often than not *infastidito* (because something is 'annoying', i.e. *fastidioso*). *Seccante, seccato*, are usually 'annoying', 'annoyed' (or 'fed up') but again may be 'boring', 'bored'.

antichità (f). If this refers to the things sold in a shop bearing this title, it means 'antiques'. If history is referred to, it means 'ancient times'.

antipasto (m). *Pasto* is 'meal', and what is eaten before the meal (?) is the 'hors d'oeuvres'. The reason for the question mark is the size of some people's *antipasto*, making it hardly possible to call it something prior to and separate from the main meal.

anzi. This is an extremely useful little word. When a statement has been made, *anzi* is the link word with a further statement to strengthen the first one, modify it, change it or contradict it. You may say, for example, *Questo vino è molto buono*. Then you might reflect and conclude that you have understated the case. So you could add: *Anzi, è buonissimo* ('This wine's very good. Indeed, it's excellent'). Or you could say that someone will probably do something, and then change your mind to the extent of saying that he is sure to do it: *Probabilmente lo farà. Anzi, sicuramente*. Or you might tell someone that someone gave you one hundred, then remember the correct figure and say 'fifty' instead. *Mi diede 100, anzi 50. Questa sera fa caldo. Anzi, si va a fuoco*, is 'It's hot this evening. In fact, it's scorching'. If you are reinforcing the first idea, you will tend to say 'In fact', while if you are going rather against it, you will say 'I mean', 'or rather', 'on the contrary', etc.

apertura (f). 'Open door'. *Apertura a sinistra*, in politics, is 'open door (or opening) to the left'.

apolide (m). Accent on second syllable. 'Displaced (or stateless) person'.

apparecchio (m). This refers to all sorts of apparatus, but its special application is to the telephone.

appunto (m). As a noun, this means 'note'. 'To take notes' is normally *prendere appunti*. (Get used to this expression, and don't let yourself say *prendere una nota* if you can help it. Italians do say *prendere delle note*, but *appunti* is colloquial.) Now, the important point here is the use of *appunto* as an adverb, meaning 'just', 'precisely' and so on. *Sono venuto appunto perchè* ... means 'I've come precisely because ...'. *Appunto per questo l'ho detto*, 'That's just why I said it'. *Lei deve pagare.—Sì, appunto per questo sono venuto*, 'You have to pay'.—'Yes, that's the very reason why I've come'. You frequently hear the single word *appunto* as a comment referring to someone else's statement. This shows that the speaker is putting in a 'that's right' or a 'precisely', in agreement.

arbitro (m). Referee. There's no playing about in Italian with different words for different sports, as in English (e.g. 'referee' for boxing and football, 'umpire' for tennis and cricket). No, there's just plain *arbitro* (stress on first syllable).

arco (m). Both 'arch' and 'arc'. It is also 'bow', of the sort used by Robin Hood, and the sort in the sky, too, when there's sunshine (*sole*) and rain (*pioggia*) about together (i.e. *arcobaleno*, 'rainbow'). The violinist's 'bow' is also *arco*. Which reminds me that whereas in English we speak of 'stringed instruments', Italians refer to the fact that such instruments are played using a bow, *strumenti ad arco*.

argomento (m). This is not an argument in the English sense of something to shout about at somebody, bang your fist on the table, or perhaps even go further in the process of getting your point across or defending your view. The Italian *argomento* is more the 'topic of conversation', the subject under discussion. The English 'argument' is rather *discussione* (f), or perhaps *disputa* (f), this being more 'quarrel'. *Luigi ha avuto una disputa con sua moglie riguardante un argomento che ora non ricordo* can be 'Luigi had an argument with his wife about some subject I can't remember now'. 'To argue' may be *ragionare*, *discutere* or *disputare*, according to the context or the tone of the argument. An ordinary talk to someone, by the way, is a *conversazione* (f) or *colloquio*, however elegant these words may sound to the English ear. 'A chat' is more *una chiacchierata*.

aria (f). 'Air', in general, as in English. 'Fresh air' is *aria fresca*. 'To put on airs' is *darsi delle arie*. A much used expression is *campato in aria*, 'to have no basis in reality': *tutto quello che dice sembra campato in aria*, 'everything he says sounds quite unrealistic (or groundless)'. Many Italians, by the way, ascribe small upsets, illnesses, etc., to *un colpo d'aria*, 'a draught'.

arrangiarsi. 'To manage', 'to get by', 'to make shift'. The answer to 'But however will you manage?' could well be *Non ti pre- occupare, mi so arrangiare*, or 'Don't you worry, I can look after myself'. Compare the French *se débrouiller*.

arrivare. This presents little difficulty, really, if you remember that when we say 'to get there', in English, we could often say 'to arrive' just as correctly, which means in fact that to us Italians tend to sound as though they are over-using their verb *arrivare*. *Arrivare con un ritardo di 5 minuti* means 'to arrive 5 minutes late'. *Non ci arrivo*, referring to price, means 'I can't make it' (i.e. 'I haven't enough money'), while it could also mean 'It's beyond me', 'I can't understand'. When a train, for instance, is due to arrive, we say it is *in arrivo*. If you ask for something in a shop, you may be told that they *devono arrivare* (literally, 'they should arrive', i.e. 'they are on order', 'we're expecting them in'). If someone refers to his car, let's say, as *è arrivata*, he means that 'it's had its day'.

arrosto (m). Roast. 'Roast meat' may be either *carne arrostita*, from the verb *arrostire*, or *arrosto di carne*, the latter being the more usual. *Arrosto alla griglia* is a 'grill'. *Arrosto misto* is 'mixed grill'.

articolato. A favourite word of economists and many others nowa- days. If a plan, etc., is *articolato in 4 parti*, it is 'subdivided' or just 'in 4 parts'. Often it means 'well-balanced' or 'well-knit'. It may well be 'systematic' or 'coordinated'. 'Inter-related' is another concept involved. Equally well liked is the corre- sponding noun, *articolazione*. *Una migliore articolazione* *delle fasi di lavoro* would be 'improved coordination of the work phases'. Whatever you do, avoid translating *articolazione* by 'articulation', unless you are speaking about making sounds or moving the body joints.

aspirapolvere (m).   Vacuum cleaner. The verb *aspirare* may be 'to aspire', 'to aspirate' or 'to inhale, breathe in'. The Italian vacuum cleaner, as you can see, 'inhales dust'.

assegno (m).   'Cheque'. A cheque book is *libretto di assegni. Un assegno a vuoto* will, unfortunately, bounce (i.e. it is a 'dud' cheque, literally one that is 'empty'), because the account (*conto*), if any, is *scoperto* ('overdrawn'). An ordinary cheque is *assegno bancario*, while a banker's draft is *assegno circolare*. Note that *assegni familiari* are 'family allowances', while *assegno personale* is 'personal allowance'.

assetto territoriale (m).   Regional planning.

assicurazione (f).   'Assurance' or 'insurance'. In defining the type of insurance, whereas in English we say first the thing being insured against and then 'insurance', in Italian the pattern is to say first *assicurazione*, then 'against' (*contro*) and then the object. For example, *assicurazione contro gli infortuni*, 'accident insurance'; *assicurazione contro l'incendio*, 'fire insurance'. 'Third party insurance' is *assicurazione contro terzi* or *assicurazione RC contro terzi* (i.e. *assicurazione di responsabilità civile contro terzi*). Naturally, 'life insurance' is *assicurazione sulla vita* (or else we would have to say *contro la morte*, obviously!).

assistere.   Something of a false friend, although not so much so in Italian as in some other languages. 'To help' is normally *aiutare*, but *assistere* can sometimes be used. On the other hand, *assistere* frequently means 'to attend, be present at'. *Un assistente* may be a 'lecturer', or just a plain 'assistant'; but an *assistente sociale* is a 'welfare worker'. *Assistenza pubblica* is 'public welfare'.

atletica (f).   'Athletics'. The Italian subdivision into *atletica leggera* and *pesante* does not quite correspond to our subdivision into track and field events. *Atletica leggera* includes all running, jumping, walking and throwing events, while *atletica pesante* includes wrestling and weightlifting. They also speak of *gare di fondo* (long-distance events), the participants in which are known as *fondisti* (singular, *fondista*); and there are also *mezzofondisti*, participants in medium-long-distance events.

attaccabottoni (m).   A chap who buttonholes you and tells you a long, probably doleful and always boring tale, i.e. a 'buttonholer'. Sometimes the word is taken apart and used verbally, e.g. *prima che potessi scappare, lui m'ha visto, e subito m'ha attaccato il solito bottone* ('He saw me before I could get away, and at once he buttonholed me', literally 'he attached the usual button to me').

attaccare. This can be an 'unreliable friend' at times. Admittedly, it does mean 'to attack', which can also be *assalire*. But the usual meanings of the verb are a) 'to stick, fasten', etc., and b) 'to start' (this is a more slangy use of the word). *Attaccare i francobolli* is 'to stick the stamps on'.

atteggiamento (m). 'Attitude', both the way you hold your body, and your mental attitude. Note, however, that *attitudine* (f) means 'aptitude'.

attendere. This is not 'to attend', which is *assistere* or *presenziare*, but rather 'to wait', which to our ears sounds somewhat archaic. Telling someone to wait a moment, you may use this verb, *attenda un momento*, or else the verb *aspettare*, which is certainly more common in normal everyday speech. The adjective *attendibile* means 'reliable'.

attenzione. This is the usual warning to 'be careful'. You can also put it this way: *Stia attento*, 'Look out'. *Stare attento* is used a good deal, in fact. *La polizia deve stare attenta a tutto* means 'The police have to be on the lookout for everything'.

attico (m). If you search the advertisement columns of the Italian papers, hoping to find a suitable apartment, you may think it rather strange that more is asked for an 'attic' than for a luxurious flat—until you realize that *attico* is another of our famous 'false friends', and means 'penthouse', with its connotations of sunshine, views and being far from the madding crowd below. 'Attic' can best be translated into Italian as *soffitta*—and don't say *soffitto*, which of course means 'ceiling'. A *superattico* is the superlative of 'penthouse'.

attirare. Another false friend, but one you are probably aware of. It means 'to attract', while 'attire', as in 'his attire', is usually *vestiti* (m pl), 'clothes'.

attuale. One of the commonest of all 'false friends', meaning as it does 'present' or 'topical', while 'actual' is *reale* or *effettivo*. Likewise, *attualmente* means not 'actually' (which can be variously *realmente*, *in fatti*, and so on) but 'now', 'at present'. *Attualità* are 'topical matters', 'news', etc.

auguri (m pl). The plural of *augurio*, 'good wish'. A much used word, being the stock word for wishing 'good luck', 'best wishes' and so on, ousting all other words. You'd use it to wish luck to someone about to take his driving test (*prendere la patente*), someone embarking on a journey (*buon viaggio ed auguri*), a couple about to get married, and so forth. Nor just when people are *about* to do something, as it is used also to give good wishes on birthdays, saints' days (*onomastici*) and other occasions.
    The verb is *augurare*, meaning either 'to portend, to promise' or 'to wish', e.g. *Vi auguro buon viaggio*, 'I wish you a pleasant journey'. 'I hope so' may be *me lo auguro* (in this case the accent falls on the first syllable).

autista (m).   'Chauffeur' or 'driver', when driving for someone else. When you're driving your own car (or the bus driver driving his bus), the word to use is *conducente*, from the verb *condurre*.

autofinanziamento (m).   This has nothing to do with financing your car; it is the process whereby a company's undistributed profits (*utili non distribuiti*) are used for the company's financial needs, i.e. 'financing by corporate saving', or just 'corporate saving'. Or perhaps 'self-financing'.

autonomia (f).   'Autonomy'. Politically, this denotes the area left of the traditional left, as far as the extremist groups (mainly identified with the *Brigate Rosse* or Red Brigades; a member of this armed movement (*movimento armato*) is called a *brigatista*). Within the area of the *autonomi* ('autonomists') there are many groups with more or less marked differences of ideology, geographical location, etc. This term, as far as the left is concerned, has largely taken over from *extraparlamentare* (q.v.).

autorimessa (f).   Most languages use the word 'garage', and this is certainly to be encountered also in Italian. But the usual word, as signs outside garages will normally advertise, is *autorimessa*.

avanti.   When someone knocks on the office door, this is the call to tell him to enter. *Avanti*, 'Come in'. Apart from this, the word is obviously one of those that you will constantly be having to use. *Non possiamo andare avanti così* means 'We can't go on like this'. *D'ora in avanti* is 'from now on'. In urging someone to go forward, to do something, you would encourage him by saying *Avanti*. 'Further on' is *più avanti*.

azienda (f).   'Business', 'company', 'firm', 'concern'. The corresponding adjective is *aziendale*, which refers to the firm in question or to companies in general. *La politica aziendale* is 'company policy'. Note that a 'farm' is very commonly *azienda agricola*. *Un'azienda avviata* is 'a going (established) concern'.

azzurro (m).   Most foreign visitors to Britain, or foreign readers of our sports news, are initially mystified by references to 'He is a triple blue', and so on—but perhaps Italians are less puzzled than others, as they themselves use the word in a sports context. Their use is however different from the English meaning of 'representative of the university', as in Italian it means 'a representative of Italy', otherwise called *un nazionale* (compare with English 'international'). *Gli azzurri* is often used as a term instead of writing 'Italy' or 'our team'. Confusingly enough, the Naples Football Club, a foremost team in the top division, is known sometimes as 'Gli azzurri', naturally because of its colours.

B

bagnato. I include this word simply because I have so often heard
learners struggling to find the simple word for 'wet'. *Sono
arrivato a casa tutto bagnato* means 'I arrived home absolutely
drenched'.

ballo (m). Yes, the ordinary word for 'dance'. The verb is *ballare*.
It sounds a bit highfalutin to the English ear, perhaps, to refer
to any old dance as a *ballo*, but there it is. On the subject,
ballerina may or may not be the same as the English 'ballerina'.
She may also be a good dancer, not necessarily of ballet, as well
as being that delightful bird, the 'pied wagtail'. Going back to
ballo, this can also give the idea of 'to be at stake', as in *il mio
onore è in ballo*, 'my honour is at stake'. A dance hall is commonly referred to as *un dancing*.

balneazione (f). In these days of pollution, the authorities sometimes find they have to prohibit people from swimming in
waters having a high bacteria count, etc. This, unfortunately,
is frequently the case round the coasts of Italy, latterly, where
tourists may well have seen notices stating that there is a *divieto
di balneazione*, a 'ban on bathing', i.e. 'no swimming allowed'.

banca (f), **banco** (m). Bank, where you keep your money. One of
those few words in Italian that can be used with either a
feminine or a masculine ending. You find, for example, the
Banco di Roma and the *Banco di Santo Spirito*, as against the
Banca Nazionale del Lavoro and the *Banca Commerciale
Italiana*. As *banco* means other things as well, e.g. 'school desk',
the plural 'banks' is always *banche*. Another common way of
referring in writing to a bank is *istituto di credito*.

bandiera (f) **ombra**. 'Flag of convenience', sometimes also *bandiera
di comodo*.

bar (m). Italy possesses a large number of 'bars', which however
are very different from the bars in public-houses. You can
admittedly buy beer in them (most of them, but they have to be
specially licensed, and a number of them are not), but the usual
drink is coffee (see under **caffè**), as well as tea (always made
with a tea-bag), cold drinks ('orange squash', for example, is
spremuta di arancia), and liqueurs (favourite ones are *sambuca*,
made from elderberries, *grappa*, a brandy made from grape
dregs, and various bitters or *amari*). If you are thinking in terms
of the bar of a public-house, where you can go for a glass of
beer, then try a *birreria*, where you may also eat sausages,
goulash, and so on. Bars, more often than not, are standing-up
places, while a *birreria* is a sitting-down place. The man in a
bar serving behind the counter is the *barista* (m) (q.v.).

baraccati (mpl).   People who live in *baracchi*, i.e. huts, hovels. Where there are many such huts together in a district, we have of course a 'shanty-town' or 'bidonville'. There is no precise Italian equivalent of this term. Of course, in Naples you have the *bassi*, and in the big cities of quick, haphazard recent growth you have the slum quarters, but you have to refer to them as *quartieri poveri*, *bassi fondi*, or even *borgate* (see **borgata**).

barba (f).   'Beard'. But *che barba!* means 'what a bore!' *Barbone* (m), apart from being a big beard, can refer to a poodle (also *barboncino*) or to a tramp (beggar).

barista (m).   A man or boy who works in a *bar* (I refrain from saying 'barman' as the two concepts are so different. See also under **bar**). Nothing, of course, to do with a 'barrister', who has no exact equivalent in Italian, so you have to say *avvocato*, who, however, is a 'lawyer', 'counsel', etc.

barone (m).   'Baron'. Not a very important word, you might think. But if you know your Italy, you will realize that in political parlance, a baron is one who directs a centre of administrative, cultural, economic, educational, industrial, etc., power. One who is in a position to dispense patronage, a man of substance and influence and authority. You may speak of *baroni dell'industria*, for instance (leading capitalists), or *baroni delle cattedre* (holders of university chairs or directors of hospitals, etc.), or *baroni bianchi* (those who control the building industry in southern Italy), and so on. The area of the baron's dominion and jurisdiction is known as his *baronia* (f).

batteria (f).   Battery, such as the one in a car, and the drums in music, but also, in sport, a 'heat'. *Ha vinto la prima batteria*, 'He has won the first heat'.

Befana (f).   According to the calendar, this is Epiphany. According to Italian children, *la Befana* is 'the Twelfth Night Witch', armed with a broomstick, and associated with the giving of presents. Present-day custom tends more and more towards giving presents at Christmas, but Italians being so enamoured of buying large and expensive presents for children, *regali della Befana* are not finished yet. In Rome, for instance, the place to visit at Befana is the Piazza Navona, where numerous stalls stand loaded with large and small gifts for children.

bene.   I certainly don't intend to go through all the possible uses of this word, most of which you should be conversant with at all events. Suffice to note some of the most-used expressions, not always to be found in the dictionary, let alone given any stress. *Va bene* means 'All right' or 'O.K.', and *Va bene così?* is 'Is it all right like this?' *Non suona bene* shows that 'It doesn't sound right'. *Speriamo bene* means 'Let's hope it turns out all right', 'Let's hope for the best'. *Due signori molto per bene* are 'two gentlemen, real gentlemen', referring to their gentlemanly characters, or perhaps to their social standing. *Ti sta bene* means 'Serves you right'. *Comportarsi bene* is 'to behave well'. The variations of *bene* are *benissimo*, very frequently heard, *benino* and *benone*. *Benino* is 'quite well', 'pretty well', and *benone* means 'very well', 'very well indeed'. *Benissimo* means 'excellent', 'excellently', 'very good', etc., and it is used by teachers, for example, when a correct answer is given by the student, and in many other circumstances to give praise. You might also often hear the short *be'*. In fact, certain people seem hardly to be able to begin a sentence without first saying *be'*. 'And how did you find the people there?' (*E come ha trovato la gente lì?*) —*Be'*, *non so, ho trovato la gente molto simpatica, insomma* ('Well, I don't know, I found the people very pleasant on the whole'). In addition, we have the series of greetings, *ben arrivato*, *ben tornato* and *ben trovato*. If you arrive somewhere, the person meeting you may well exclaim *ben arrivato* when he sees you. If you have been away for some reason, upon your return you will most likely be met with the exclamation *ben tornato* ('welcome back!'), whereupon you will reply *ben trovato* (or *ben trovata* in the feminine).

beneficio d'inventario (m). *Accettare qualche cosa con beneficio d'inventario* means 'to take something with a pinch of salt'.

benzina (f). Petrol. The Italian *petrolio* corresponds to the English 'oil' (as well, sometimes, as to 'kerosene' or 'coal oil'). *Trovare il petrolio* is the unlikely but true rendering of 'to strike oil'. The two grades of petrol in Italy are known as *normale* (regular) and *super* (premium). You buy petrol at a *distributore* (m) ('petrol pump'), where you are served by a *benzinaio*.

bere. To drink. 'A drink' is *una bibita* or *una bevanda*. *Bibita* is accented on the first syllable.

biancheria (f). 'Linen', either 'bed-linen' (*biancheria da letto*) or 'table-linen' (*biancheria da tavola*). *Biancheria intima* (or *personale*) is 'underwear'.

biancoazzurri (m pl). The Lazio football team. Naturally, this team's colours are white and light blue. Lazio is one of the two First Division teams from Rome. A supporter of the team is a *laziale*, as well as being a *tifoso* ('fan') *biancoazzurro*.

bianconeri (m pl). *I bianconeri* are the Juventus F.C. (of Turin).

bicchiere (m). The glass you drink out of, or 'tumbler'. Don't, whatever you do, confuse it with the glass you look through, which you must be aware is *vetro*, made of *cristallo*. Again, the glass you look into, i.e. the mirror, is *lo specchio*.

bicchierino (m). Diminutive of *bicchiere*, 'glass', but it refers to the contents of a small-sized glass in a bar, i.e. a brandy or liqueur.

So if someone says to you *Posso offrire un bicchierino?* you know what he means.

bicolore. A government coalition of two parties.

bidè (m). We have to be satisfied with the French word in English, *bidet*. In France and in Italy, among other countries, the bidet is a normal household fixture, although a comparative rarity in an English house. The word is therefore more important than it might seem to the person who is not aware of conditions in Italy.

bidone (m). A can, drum, jerry-can, etc. And if you fill a drum with water and sell it as petrol, for example, this action is known as a *bidonata* (swindle). By extension, if a girl makes a date with a boy and fails to turn up, *gli ha dato un bidone*, she has stood him up (compare the French 'poser un lapin'). So to the boy this date was a dead loss, or *bidone*.

big (m). Another English word taken into the language and mis-used. For example, *un big dello sport*, 'a big name in the sports world'; *una riunione dei big*, 'a meeting of leaders (e.g. of the Common Market)'. It is perhaps a shortening of 'big shot', but is not used in a slangy sense.

bilancio (m). This may be 'budget', 'balance sheet' or 'statement of accounts' (or just 'accounts'). The 'budget' is strictly speaking the *bilancio preventivo* ('prior balance sheet'), followed after the event by the *bilancio consuntivo* (or just *consuntivo*). A firm's statement of accounts is its *bilancio*, broken down into the *stato patrimoniale* and the *conto economico* (the 'balance sheet' and the 'profit and loss account'). Note, *en passant*, that the femi-nine counterpart of this word, *bilancia*, means 'scales', 'weigh-ing machine', and, among other things, 'balance' as in *bilancia commerciale* (trade balance) and *bilancia dei pagamenti* (balance of payments). With a capital letter, *Bilancia* is the Zodiacal sign 'Libra'.

bionda (f). A blonde. But if you read in the newspaper that the police (probably the *Finanzieri*, or Customs Police) have im-pounded, for example, *due tonnellate di bionde*, they have not roped in about forty fair-haired maidens, but a couple of tons of cigarettes (smuggled, avoiding customs duties).

birra (f). Beer. *Birra alla spina* is 'draught beer'. *Birra scura* is 'brown ale', while the light variety is *chiara* (or *bionda*). *A tutta birra* means 'flat out', 'at full speed'.

bisognare. 'Must' and so forth, as you will be well aware. You may either use it simply, followed by an infinitive, or with *che*, fol-lowed by a subjunctive. *Per ottenere un grosso successo bisogna allenarsi molto*, 'To achieve real success, a lot of training is necessary'. *Non bisogna dimenticare che è molto lontano*, 'It mustn't be forgotten that it's very far away'. *Bisogna che lui* *vada via*, 'He has to go away'. *Non bisogna esagerare* is 'Now, don't exaggerate'. See also the notes on the expression *ci vuole* under **volere.**

bisogno (m). 'Need'. *Ho bisogno di sonno* means 'I need some sleep'. *Quella ragazza non ha bisogno di nulla* is 'That girl has everything she wants'. *Ne ho bisogno* is 'I need it'. *Chi va in treno non ha bisogno di risolvere il problema della strada* means 'Those who go by train have no call to face up to the road problem'. The most important thing to note is the use of *Non c'è bisogno di . . .*, 'There's no need to . . .'. For instance, *Non c'è bisogno di dire niente*, 'There's no need to say anything'.

bistecca (f). You may think it unnecessary to include such an obvious word. It derives obviously from the English beef + steak. But the point is that in its meaning it has kept the 'steak' part of the word and lost the 'beef' part. Therefore, to say 'beefsteak' you have to add the word for 'beef', i.e. *manzo*. Likewise you can have a *bistecca di maiale* (literally, a 'pork beefsteak'), and so on.

bo', boh. A very much used exclamation, ranging from the quite pretty to the downright vulgar in sound, meaning 'I don't know', 'Who knows?' etc.

bombola (f) **di gas.** A gas cylinder or container. It is quite a common system in Italy to have these gas containers delivered to the house, to provide the gas for the cooker and a gas-fire, perhaps.

borgata (f). The dictionary may tell you that this is 'village' or 'hamlet', but in its modern acceptation it is a district in a city which is drab, lacking in parks and in general amenities and utilities. The *borgate* have normally grown up recently, in a somewhat haphazard fashion, not based on a town plan.

borsa (f). The general word for a 'bag'. A lady's handbag is *borsetta* (and inside it she may have her *borsellino*, 'purse'). Students may have the good fortune to obtain a *borsa di studio*, a 'scholarship' or 'grant'. The *Borsa* (*Valori*) is 'The Stock Exchange', while the *borsa nera* is the 'black market'. In sport, especially in boxing, *la borsa* is 'the purse'.

borsetto (m). When men started carrying handbags, the need was felt for a different word from the lady's *borsetta*; and so they invented the masculine form *borsetto* (yet to be taken up by the dictionaries).

bottega (f). A shop, usually quite a small one. A more common word is *negozio* (m). The word *ditta* is best translated 'firm'. *Un magazzino* (m) can be a 'store', 'storehouse', while *grandi magazzini* are 'department stores'. When you have to tell someone that his trouser zip or buttons are undone, the expression to use is *la bottega è aperta*, 'the shop's open'.

box (m). The English word imported into Italian with the usual change of meaning. It has in fact three ordinary meanings in Italian: 1) 'garage space', 2) 'loose stable', and 3) the 'pits' in motor racing. The English 'box' is normally *scatola* (which also means 'tin' or 'can'). 'Boxing', by the way, is *pugilato* or *boxe* (m).

braciola (f). Chop or cutlet, which can also be *costoletta* (or, popularly, *cottoletta*).

bravo. A false friend. *È molto bravo* refers not to a person's courage, but to his ability, meaning 'He is very clever'. *Bravo* gives the idea of 'good' or 'clever', while the English 'brave' is best rendered as *coraggioso*.

brodo (m). Soup of the consommé type. If it is watery it is called *brodo lungo*, and if strong *brodo ristretto*. Note the expression *tutto fa brodo*, literally 'everything makes soup', signifying 'it all helps', 'all is grist to the mill'.

bruciare. Dictionaries generally list many expressions under *bruciare*, 'to burn', but one that often eludes the lexicographer is *bruciare le tappe*, 'to go ahead like wildfire', 'to get on with a job very swiftly'.

buca (f), **buco** (m). As the dictionary tells you that both these words mean 'hole', you might be tempted to think that they are exact synonyms, which in fact they are not. *Buca* indicates an irregularly shaped hole in the ground, usually fairly deep, or else an opening for a special use, such as *la buca delle lettere*, 'the letter-box'. *Buco*, on the other hand, indicates a narrow opening or a round hole (*foro*), or a hole that goes right through something from one side to the other (*da parte a parte*). So if you have a hole in your pocket, it is a *buco*, as it goes right through the material. Note also the expression *fare un buco nell'acqua*, literally 'to make a hole in the water', meaning to do something absolutely useless, something like 'to knock your head against the wall'.

buffo. Ridiculous, silly, comical. *Forse sembra un po' buffo, ma è successo proprio così*, 'Perhaps you'll think it a bit ridiculous, but that's the way it really happened'. *Mi trovo in una situazione molto buffa* is 'I am in a very stupid predicament'.

bugia (f). A 'lie', 'nonsense', 'rubbish'. Remember to stress the middle syllable. It is more frequently used in the plural, *dire bugie*. Used in replying to someone, *bugie!* is about the same as saying 'Rubbish', 'I don't believe a word of it'. *Balle*, plural of *una balla*, is an alternative. Another one is *frottole* (stress on first syllable). The person who tells lies is a *bugiardo*.

buio (m). An adjective as well as being a noun. Pronounced with the accent on the first syllable, which is pure u, and not diphthongized with the following i. So many people neglect this word altogether and look for another word, such as *oscuro* (q.v.), to mean 'dark'. Both *buio* and *scuro* refer to 'dark' meaning 'lack of light' as in unlit rooms and night, and when referring to a dark, angry look on the face. If you are 'in the dark' about something, you may be *al buio* or more commonly *all'oscuro*. Examples: *È buio*, 'it's dark'. *Questa è la sala da pranzo; è buia, ma tanto ci si vede abbastanza*, 'This is the dining-room; it's dark, but still you can see well enough'. *Lui è completamente al buio di questa faccenda*, 'He's completely in the dark about this business'.

buon giorno. This is of course 'good morning', sometimes used later in the day when we would say 'good afternoon' (*buon pomeriggio* being less common). *Buona sera* may be used anytime after about one o'clock, and therefore equals either 'good afternoon' or (more usually) 'good evening'. *Buona notte* is 'good night'. So much for the easier greetings of this type. But there are several others. Italians are very prone to wish each other something or other. Early on in the day, they may well say *buona giornata*, wishing someone that the day might go well for him. *Buon lavoro* may mean generally 'have a good day's work', or may refer specifically to some task, such as when you deliver a stack of printer's proofs to the proofreader and wish him *buon lavoro* as you take your leave. *Buon divertimento* means 'enjoy yourself', 'have a good time'. *Buon viaggio* is *bon voyage*. If someone is going off on holiday, you wish him *buone vacanze*. Lastly, but not on the same subject, I must mention *buona volontà*, 'goodwill' (not the 'goodwill' you sell with a business, which is *avviamento*, but the will you work away with). This *buona volontà* is very much used in Italian, to denote a person's great willingness.

burino (m). The dictionary states that this means 'peasant' in the Roman dialect. In actual fact, it is a very common pejorative in the sense of 'clodhopper', 'yokel', 'upstart'.

burro (m). Spanish speakers beware. This is the classical Spanish–Italian false friend, meaning 'butter' in Italian (as opposed to 'donkey' in Spanish).

busta (f). Envelope. *Una busta a finestra* is 'a window envelope', while a *busta paga* is a 'pay envelope'. And mind you don't say *busto* instead of *busta*.

bustarella (f). A diminutive of *busta*, 'envelope', and therefore 'little envelope'. But that is not the end of the story. The point is what goes inside this little envelope. The contents are in fact money, and the *bustarella* is slipped to someone to induce him to do what you want him to do, i.e. it is a 'bribe'. 'To bribe' is usually *corrompere*.

buttare. This means 'to throw'. *Buttare via* is 'to throw away'. 'To throw' can also be *lanciare*, but this gives more an idea of precision, and is in fact the word used in those sports where something is thrown. For example, *lanciare il giavellotto* is 'to throw the javelin'. Note also the idiomatic use of *buttare via* and *buttare giù*. (And another thing to note is the common dropping of the final e in the infinitive in such phrasal verbs as *buttar via* and *buttar giù*.) When you say of something that *non è da buttar via*, you convey the impression that it's worth while, that you wouldn't cast it aside, i.e. that it is worth having. Literally, *buttar giù* is 'to fling down'. I call to mind in this context a publicity agent I used to know, who was always making notes of ideas and phrases as they occurred to him—or, as he put it, he always had something to *buttar giù* on paper. Then there is the man who, just before leaving the office to go home for dinner, rings his wife to tell her to *buttar giù la pasta* (put the spaghetti on to cook), so that it will be all ready when he gets home.

C

cadavere (m). 'Corpse'. I am quite amused by the quaint newspaper expressions *giungere cadavere* and *rimanere cadavere*, as in *purtroppo è giunto all'ospedale cadavere*, 'unfortunately he was already dead when he reached the hospital'. *È rimasto cadavere sul colpo*, 'he was killed outright'.

caffè (m). Coffee. You go into a *bar* (often advertised as a *bar-gelateria* or *bar-caffè* or *pasticceria*), order your drink, pay and receive a ticket (*scontrino*) which you present to the *barista* behind the counter (together with a 50-lire tip per person, approximately), telling him what you have already paid for. The system is perhaps a little complicated. Regarding what sort of coffee you want, *caffè e latte* is 'café au lait', *cappuccino* is similar (and much more usual) but somewhat smaller, a *caffè lungo* (or just *un lungo*) is ordinary black coffee with a drop more water than the commoner *espresso* or just *caffè*. If you want your coffee even stronger than the normal (and quite strong) *espresso*, ask for *un caffè ristretto*. Then perhaps you would like something in your coffee? Laced with a tot of spirits (usually brandy), it is referred to as *caffè corretto*. If on the other hand you feel like coffee with just a wee spot of milk in it, hardly enough to make any difference, you might think, then ask for *un caffè macchiato*. This does not really exhaust the list, because the Italians, great coffee-drinkers, love to add their own recommendations when ordering their drink, such as *un caffè bollente* (a really hot cup of coffee), *un cappuccino* *tiepido* (only just warm), *un cappuccino senza schiuma* (without any froth), *un caffè un po' lunghino* (half way between an *espresso* and a *lungo*, if things can be measured to such a nicety), and so forth.

cafone (m).   The original southern Italian 'peasant' has become a general word for 'lout', 'ill-bred upstart', 'vulgar person'.

calcio (m).   Apart from meaning 'calcium', and 'kick', this refers to the national sport, 'football'. A 'footballer' is *calciatore*. *Tirare* is the verb most frequently heard meaning 'to shoot'. *Un calcio d'angolo* is 'a corner kick', *un calcio di punizione* is 'a free kick', and *un calcio di rigore* (or *un rigore*) is 'a penalty'. The equivalent of the First Division in Italy is *Serie A*, after which come *Serie B* and *Serie C*. There are 16 teams in *Serie A*, and 20 in *Serie B*. The league table is called *la classifica*. A team is *una squadra* and a game is *una partita*. If you wish to try your luck on the football pools, you must fill in a *schedina* (13 games, marking them 1, 2 or X, this last being *un pareggio*). The referee is the *arbitro* (q.v.).

cambiare.   To change. The verb also includes changing money, for example, and *cambio* (m) is the word for the 'rate of exchange'.

camera (f).   Of course you realize that this is a 'room', usually a 'bedroom', and not a 'camera', which is *macchina fotografica*. There are many words which can be added to modify the meaning. For example, *camera d'aria* is 'inner tube', *camera di commercio* is 'Chamber of Commerce', and *camera oscura* is a 'darkroom'.

campanilismo (m).   'Local patriotism', 'parochialism', often in an exaggerated form, or excessive support for a local or restricted group as opposed to general community promotion.

campare.   Dictionary-wise, this is 'to live'. But of course you don't *campare* in via Eleonora Duse, for example (this would be *abitare*). *Campare* is more on a par with *vivere*, and the following gives a good indication of its usage: *uno lavora, ma a che scopo? Per campare? Si può campare anche senza ammazzarsi dal lavoro* ('You work, but for what purpose? To live? You can live just as well without killing yourself with work').

camping (m).   To bring to your notice the fairly recent Italian habit of using English words ending in –ing in a slightly incorrect manner. *Un camping*, for example, is 'a camping place' (or site) and *un dancing*, 'a dance hall'.

campo (m).   'Field', physical or figurative. *Campo di gioco* is 'playing-field', 'ground', etc. Italian does not here possess the niceties of English, which reserves different words for places where different sports are played (pitch, court, course, and so on). Italian uses just the all-purpose *campo* (adding *di calcio*, *di golf*, *di tennis*, etc.). *Campo di battaglia* is 'battleground', *campo di concentramento* is 'concentration camp', *campo di visibilità* is the 'range of visibility', and *campo magnetico* is the 'magnetic field'. *Campo* also refers to the type of shot in filming; for instance *campo lungo* is 'long shot', and *campo medio* is 'medium-long shot'. Notice also, and in particular, the use of this word in such sentences as *Lui è un vero esperto in questo campo* ('He's a real expert in this field') and *Non è il mio campo* ('It's not my line of country', etc.).

cancellare. To rub out, erase. The English 'cancel' is often *annullare*.

cantina (f). Originally this was the cellar where wine was produced or stored. By extension, it has come to mean any 'cellar'. In the first meaning, called *cantina sociale*, it is common in names of wine-producing cooperatives or consortia. It may also mean a shop where wine is retailed. Notice that the English 'canteen' (place where you eat) is *mensa*.

capace. *Sono capace di fare questo* means 'I'm able to do this'. *Non sono capace di capire quando lui parla* is 'I can't understand when he speaks'. *Capace* is 'able' rather than 'capable'. It would usually be easier, of course, to use *potere*; however, the *capace* construction is very common. *È capace di tutto*, 'he is capable of doing anything'. Note the impersonal *è capace che* . . .; e.g. *è capace che non venga*, 'he might not come'; *è capace che piova*, 'it might well rain'.

capellone (m). A longhaired person. Derived from *capello* (m), meaning 'hair', which I mention to remind you of the difference between this and the word with a double p, *cappello* (m), 'hat'.

capillare. This adjective, which the dictionary rightly tells us means 'capillary', is commonly used in Italian with the meaning of 'extending everywhere', 'having extensive coverage', as in *una organizzazione capillare di vendita*, 'an extensive sales organization'. It may also mean 'detailed, thorough', as in *un'indagine capillare*, 'a detailed survey, an in-depth inquiry'.

capirai! This exclamation or comment (accented on the last syllable) is really the second person singular, future tense, indicative mood, of the verb *capire*, therefore meaning 'you will understand'. As currently used, according to the circumstances there are many possible meanings. For example, someone tells me that I look dead tired. *Capirai!* I reply, 'I didn't sleep all night with the election results coming in.' Again: I am told by someone that she has to take three different buses to get to the office in the morning; I answer that I have to take four, whereupon she exclaims *Capirai!* ('Just imagine!', 'My!', 'Gosh!', etc.). Another example: Tom and Dick are playing cards in the office, during working hours. Someone peeps in and calls out 'Here comes the boss!' With a smirk, Tom quips *Capirai!*

meaning 'What do I care?' And again, someone says sarcastically to me that I cannot run a hundred yards in ten seconds, and I retort (of course) *Capirai!* meaning 'Of course I can!' Lastly, let's think of the poor chap who has been given his marching orders from his job. *Capirai, mi vuole cacciare via senza spiegazione,* he relates. *Capirai!* I could well repeat, meaning 'Well, get a load of that!' or 'Can you beat that!' or 'Just imagine!' And the list of examples could go on.

capire. To understand. When telling you something, an Italian will very often put in the occasional *Ha capito?* or just plain *capito?*, and you could, if you wish, answer *Ho capito* or just plain *capito.* It is more or less the equivalent of the English 'D'you see?' and 'I see'. *Capire una cosa al volo* means to catch on to it immediately. *Capire l'antifona* (with the accent on the *ti*) is 'to take the hint', i.e. 'to understand the allusion'. *Capire fischi per fiaschi* means 'to get the wrong end of the stick', 'to understand the exact opposite'. Notice the useful little aid to conversation *si capisce.* This means 'naturally', 'of course', 'that is very understandable'. If someone is explaining what he has done or what has been done, you may well find the occasion during a pause to put in *si capisce,* if you wish to be an understanding listener.

capitare. To happen, to happen to. The ordinary words for 'to happen' are *accadere* or *succedere,* when it is an event taking place. *Mi capita a volte di ...* is quite a common construction, meaning 'It sometimes happens that I ...'. Note the emphasis on the first syllable —*cApita.* 'Of course, it *would* happen to me' is *doveva proprio capitare a me!* One of the ways of showing your resignation in the face of unfortunate happenings, etc., is to say (a very common expression) *sono cose che capitano.* And remember: *se capita una buona occasione, non lasciarla scappare* ('if a good opportunity comes your way, don't let it get away').

capo (m). I mention this mainly to point out that *il capo* is 'the boss', 'the leader' (from the gang boss up to the *capo dello Stato,* i.e. 'Head of State'), and also that *cominciare una cosa da capo* is 'to start again from scratch', 'to begin again from the very beginning'. *Un grattacapo* is 'a worrying problem'. The terminus of a bus line is the *capolinea* (m). If something is done *per sommi capi,* it is done 'in brief'. *Da un capo all'altro* means 'from one end to the other'. *Un capo d'accusa* is 'an indictment', 'article of accusation'. If something seems to have neither rhyme nor reason, *non ha nè capo nè coda. Non sapevo dove battere il capo* is 'I didn't know which way to turn'.

capocomico (m). Nothing to do with the chief comedian, or even a minor one, for that matter, but the 'manager' of a theatrical company.

carino. This corresponds pretty much to the English adjective 'pretty'. (Note however that it absolutely cannot be used as the adverb 'pretty' such as in the first line here, where 'pretty much' would be *pressappoco*. Otherwise, as in such things as 'he's pretty mean', 'it's a pretty good film', you would have to say *abbastanza* or, more likely, *molto*, allowing for the fact that English tends to tone things down and Italian just the opposite.) *Carino* also refers sometimes to something not necessarily pretty, but 'nice'. However, *carino* is not done to death to anything like the extent the English 'nice' is. Italian also has *simpatico*, as well as *buono*, *bello*, *grazioso*, etc., according to context. *Carino* usually gives the idea of prettiness, of something sweet. I well remember when our second daughter was about three or four, blonde and full of life, she often used to cause people to remark *che carina!* Now, she also happens to be called Karina. Hence the usual small talk in buses, shops, etc. *Come si chiama la bambina?—Si chiama Karina.—Sì, d'accordo, è molto carina, ma come si chiama?* And so on.

carità (f). Charity. Notice the expression *per carità*, which is approximately the equivalent of 'Oh, no!' or 'For Heaven's sake!'

carne (f). Meat. *Carne in scatola* is 'tinned meat'. *Carne macinata* is 'minced meat'. It also means 'flesh', as in *lo spirito è pronto, ma la carne è debole*, 'the spirit is willing, but the flesh is weak'.

carro attrezzi (m). This is an ordinary 'breakdown lorry', or else the truck that comes along and tows away cars parked in *zone vietate*, 'forbidden areas'. It is an *autogru*, a 'crane truck', complete with policeman (*vigile*), to give it the requisite authority. Once your car has been towed away, you have to pay both the fine for improper parking and the haulage and storage cost, quite apart from all the trouble you are put to.

carrozza (f). 'Coach', not the sort run by Wells Fargo in the old days, which is *diligenza* (f), but the railway carriage sort and the sort drawn by horses round Rome, for example (the Rome *carrozze* being also known locally as *botticelle*). On the railways, *carrozza letto* is 'sleeping car'.

carrozzella (f). 'Invalid chair' or 'wheelchair' (otherwise *sedia a rotelle*).

carrozzina (f). This diminutive of 'coach' means 'pram'.

carrozzino (m). A motorcycle 'sidecar'.

carrozzone (m). The dictionary will point out that, speaking of circuses or gypsies, this means 'caravan', but will almost certainly omit to mention that popularly it means an entity, especially a public body, the management and manipulation whereof gives rise to illicit gains, i.e. a 'bandwagon'; e.g. *il carrozzone clientelare partitico*, 'party bandwagon'.

carta (f). Paper (but never a newspaper, which is *un giornale*). Here is a list (*elenco*) of some of the more important sorts of paper:

> *carta asciugante*, blotting paper
> *carta carbone*, carbon paper
> *carta da bollo*, stamped paper, official paper
> *carta da imballaggio*, packing paper
> *carta da scrivere*, writing paper
> *carta igienica*, toilet paper
> *carta intestata*, headed paper
> *carta protocollo*, foolscap paper
> *carta straccia*, waste paper

Another way of saying *carta da bollo* is *carta bollata*, and this sort of paper is very much in use, as it is prescribed by official bodies when you make a request for almost anything, such as a work permit (*permesso di lavoro*). The stamp duty is 1,500 lire, and you would ask in a shop (a tobacconist's with a sign outside indicating such things are authorized to be sold) for *carta da bollo da millecinquecento*.

cartotecnica (f). Paper products.

cascare. A colloquial equivalent of *cadere*, 'to fall'. 'To be taken in by something' is *cascarci*, e.g. *quell'idiota c'è cascato!* 'the fool fell for it!' *Non ci casco* is 'You can't catch me!' *Cascare dalle nuvole* is 'to be flabbergasted'. *Casco dal sonno* is 'I'm dead tired'.

casistica (f). In philosophy 'casuistry', but usually 'case-history'.

caso (m). 'Case', in most cases. *In caso di bisogno* is 'in case of necessity'. *In tale caso* means 'that being the case', 'in that case'. *Il caso è che* ... means 'the point is that ...'. *Lui ne prese uno a caso* is 'He took one of them at random'. *Con me, non é il caso che tu ti senta a disagio*, 'With me you don't have to feel uneasy'. *Non ci ho fatto caso* means 'I didn't notice it' or 'I didn't pay any attention to (or take any notice of) it'. Note especially the expression *caso mai* (see **mai**), meaning 'just in case'. *Per caso* means 'by chance', 'by any chance'. *L'hai visto, per caso?* 'Have you seen him by any chance?' *Stavo li seduto per caso*, 'I was sitting there just by chance'. *In ogni caso* is 'at any rate'. *In questo caso* is 'in this case'. If there are two alternatives, two possibilities, then *i casi sono due*. For instance, *o gli parli tu o gli parlo io* (either you speak to him or else I will). Notice also the reference to *force majeure* in the words *un caso di forza maggiore*, which is clearly 'a case of something beyond control'. In my experience, this expression is overworked as an excuse, including many things which could quite easily have been avoided. *Come vedete, è un caso di forza maggiore*, 'As you can see, it's completely beyond my control'. Well, often it isn't, or wasn't.

cassa (f). Apart from being 'case' or 'chest', this refers to either 'cash' (as *pronta cassa*, 'ready cash') or 'cash-desk' (e.g. *pagare alla cassa*, 'pay at the cash-desk'). It is also the 'till' itself. It means 'bank' (i.e. 'savings bank') in *cassa di risparmio*, and 'fund' for instance in *Cassa per il Mezzogiorno* (Development Fund for Southern Italy and the Islands). A 'safe' is *cassaforte* (f). There is much talk these days of the *cassa integrazione*, i.e. the fund to reimburse workers stood off work, covering a certain percentage of wage losses and for a certain period. A sort of unemployment benefit, although limited to those 'temporarily' stood off, and not for the 'real' unemployed.

cava (f). As you are motoring along an Italian road, you may catch sight of a sign pointing away, saying '*cava*'. This is by no means an archaeological or geographical sight, but merely a 'quarry'. A 'cave' is *caverna* (or perhaps *grotta* (q.v.)).

cavallo (m). 'Horse', of course, even the 'gift horse', not to be looked in the mouth variety (*A caval donato non si guarda in bocca*). In the plural *cavalli* refers to a machine's horse power. The only snag is (luckily, only a very slight snag) that the Italian *cavallo* is a metric animal (equal to 0.9863 HP). It is abbreviated as CV, meaning *cavallo vapore*, and is equal to 75 kg per metre per second, while the HP is equal to about 76. Still, a very minor difference. Note that *cavallo di razza* is 'thoroughbred'.

cavare. Passing by some of the dictionary definitions, we come to the word 'get'. Now *cavare* is nothing like so comprehensive as our famous 'get', but corresponds in a number of ways. The paper tells us that so-and-so has had an accident, but that *se la caverà* ('he'll pull through, get better again'). *Cavare soldi allo zio* is 'to get money out of uncle'. If you can't get the hang of something, you may say that *non riesco a cavarne nulla*. If someone is in a fix, we hope that he'll *cavarsela*, 'get out of it'.

cavolo (m). 'Cabbage'. But more than this. *Non capisce un cavolo* means 'He doesn't understand a blind thing'. *Che cavolo vuoi?* is 'What the devil do you want?' *Non me ne importa un cavolo* is 'I don't give a damn'. Just *cavolo!* means 'Hell!', 'Damn it', etc. I should add that, although considered a 'low' word, when used in this way, it is actually a milder alternative to *cazzo*, one of the most vulgar Italian expletives (don't use that word!). One last thing: *salvar capra e cavoli* is just about the same thing as 'to have your cake and eat it', only the English expression refers to an impossibility while the Italian one means reconciling two very difficult (but not absolutely impossible) alternatives.

Celere (f). This may be a feminine word, but there's nothing very feminine about the ways of the Riot Squad, referred to here.

cena (f). The evening meal, that is, supper or dinner. *La Cena di Leonardo* is the way Italians refer to what we call Leonardo da Vinci's 'Last Supper'.

centralino (m). 'Telephone exchange' or 'switchboard'. The operator is called the *centralinista*.

centro (m). Of course, 'centre'. *Fare centro* is 'to hit the nail on the head'. The term *centro direzionale* was invented some years ago in Rome, by a group of architects intending to set up a series of these 'centres' containing head office blocks, centres of representation, etc., as the hubs of areas of new city development—'business centres', but more than just 'business'; however, they have yet to prove themselves, that is, to grow into something more than just large blocks of offices. *Centrosinistra* is a government formula based on a political and parliamentary alliance of the parties of the left and of the centre, dating effectively from the first Moro government of 1963. Other government formulae include *centrismo*, *centralità* and *centralismo*. *Centrismo* is based on cooperation among moderate parties. *Centralità* is a neologism introduced by the then DC party secretary, Forlani, to indicate the overriding central function of the majority party (i.e. the DC party). *Centralismo* refers to a political system controlled by a single source of power.

certo. 'Surely', in the sense of 'certainly', 'of course'. *Posso chiedere un favore?—Certo* ('May I ask a favour?—Of course'). The adjective *certo* occasionally has a rather nostalgic ring about it, as in *ricordo bene certe serate*, 'I well remember certain evenings ...'; *certe risate!* ... 'the laughs we had! ...'; *certe ragazze!* ... 'oh those lovely girls'.

chiacchierone (m), ... **ona** (f). One who prattles or chatters a lot. The verb is *chiacchierare*, and the word *chiacchiere!* means 'rubbish' because it is 'idle gossip', 'prattle'.

chiasso (m). Noise, din, row, racket. For example: *Lei faceva più chiasso possibile per non sentire il rumore della strada*, 'She made as much row as she could so as not to hear the sounds from the street'.

chiodo (m). Nail, which you hit with a hammer (*martello*). The nails on your fingers are *unghie* (f pl). *Avere un chiodo fisso* means 'to have a bee in your bonnet'. *Piantar chiodi*, literally 'to plant nails', means 'to incur debts'.

ci. Your elementary studies will have shown you the varied meanings of *ci*. There are the following: here; there (place); there (with verb 'to be'); it; us; ourselves; each other, one another. It is imperative to be fully conversant with these various applications of the word if you are to speak the language well. *C'è* means 'There is' and also the question form 'Is there?' What's more, when asking whether someone is at home, on the telephone or in person, you say, for example, *C'è Massimo? Ce ne sono* means 'There are some (of them)'. *Ci sto molto bene* means

'I'm doing very well here', 'I'm getting on fine'. *Ci siamo* may be 'Here we are', or as a question *Ci siamo?* it asks' 'Are we agreed then?' apart from 'Are we there?' *Ci risiamo* is 'that same old story again', 'here we go again'. *Non ce l'ho* means 'I haven't got it'. *Ci vediamo*, literally 'We see each other', is used to signify 'Be seeing you' or 'So long'—or, as in *Ci vediamo spesso durante l'estate*, 'We often meet during the summer'. *Ci penso io* sounds reassuring, but they are often fateful words. The promise is that 'I'll take care of that', 'Leave it all to me', 'Don't worry', but as often as not it is a signal for you actually to start worrying. If someone tells you that he doesn't believe something, he may say *Non ci credo*, 'I don't believe it'. *Che c'entra Massimo in tutto ciò?* 'Where does Massimo come into all this?' *Non c'entra*, or *che c'entra?* 'that's got nothing to do with it', 'that's beside the point', etc.

For *ci vuole* ('is needed') see **volere**. Lastly, note the expression *C'è da fare una cosa*, meaning 'There's something to be done'. *C'è da pagare mille lire* is 'There's 1,000 lire to pay'.

ciao. 'Cheerio'. Very familiar and in very general use. Less informal is *Salve*. Italians learning English will often say 'Goodbye' when passing you in the street. This is because they say *Ciao* (or *Addio*) in like circumstances in Italian, while we, of course, say 'Hello'. So remember, *ciao* may be either 'hello' or 'goodbye', according to circumstances. Bear in mind though, that it is familiar style. *Arrivederci* and *Arrivederla* are more suitable for 'goodbye' in most cases, until you are sure just which form to use—and, of course, this is quite simple, as it is really just a matter of repeating back to people what they themselves use to you.

ciclismo (m). Cycling. One of the national sports of Italy. There is great interest in the famous 'Tours' every year and in the time and speed track events. The '*Tour de France*' is the *Giro di Francia*, and there is the national *Giro d'Italia*. The overall leader during the *Giro di Francia* wears the coveted *maglia gialla* (yellow jersey) and the overall leader in the *Giro d'Italia* wears (and, by extension, is called) the *maglia rosa* (pink jersey). The distance cycled in one day of the tour is a *tappa*, that is, a lap in the sense of a part of the total distance. Otherwise one lap, being once round the circuit, is a *giro*. 'To sprint' is *scattare*, and when the winner and those near him arrive, the main body of runners-up, usually all in a lump, is called *il plotone*. 'A track' is *una pista*. 'A cyclist' is *un ciclista*.

cin cin. This sounds very dated to the English ear, but is nevertheless the regular equivalent of 'cheers' when having a drink. Another possibility is *salute*, but *cin cin* is more widely accepted.

cioè. 'That is to say', or 'namely'. For example: *Per molti abitanti della città, e cioè per tutti quelli che abitano vicino alla stazione,* *il problema è grave,* 'For many inhabitants of the town, that's to say, for all those who live near the station, the problem is a grave one'. *La domenica e negli altri giorni di festa, la città ospita trecentomila persone, e cioè ha una popolazione sei volte più numerosa di quella invernale,* 'On Sundays and other holidays the town houses three hundred thousand people, that is, it has six times the population it has during the winter'. *Il cane lappeggia, cioè prende l'acqua con la lingua,* 'The dog laps, that is, drinks water with the tongue'.

clergyman (m).   Not the man, in fact, but what he wears, a clergyman's going-out clothes. The clergyman himself is usually *pastore anglicano.*

clientelismo (m).   'Patronage', referring to the persons gravitating around a public figure or body, tied to him or it more by a system of favours than by reasons of ideological or other affinity. This system has one of its most widespread and traditional applications in the practice of 'recommendations' (see also **sottogoverno** and **raccomandazione**). The adjective is *clientelare.*

coincidenza (f).   Is it just a coincidence that, apart from meaning 'coincidence', this means 'connection' in the sense of one train connecting with another?

colf.   Not a real word, but a made-up one from *collaboratrice familiare,* i.e. 'family collaborator'. The old word for a woman who was employed to do the housework was *donna di servizio* (or *tuttofare,* if she did all the chores). With a view to raising the status of this type of work, however, the official denomination is now as stated above.

collegio (m).   Usually, 'boarding school'. When the English 'college' is another name for a 'school', the Italian is *scuola. Collegio* may of course be 'public school', in so far as this type of school is a 'boarding school'. A university college would be *istituto universitario* or *istituto di studi superiori. Collegio elettorale* is 'constituency'.

colpo (m).   May be a 'blow' in the physical sense or in the figurative sense. *Mi ha dato un colpo* could be 'it gave me quite a turn'. If someone does something just to make an impression, you say *L'ha fatto per far colpo. Un colpo di telefono* is 'a phone call': *Vuoi che ti dia un colpo di telefono domani?*—'Would you like me to ring you tomorrow?' *Colpo di stato* is of course *coup d'état,* and there was once talk of a *colpo di stato strisciante,* one lying latent, ready to burst forth and to take over the reins of power if conditions are right (helped along by the so-called *strategia della tensione,* the strategy based on keeping the country in a state of tension).

combinare.   According to the dictionary, 'to combine' when used transitively, and 'to be agreed upon', when intransitive. Actually, it is a much used verb, generally with the meaning of 'to arrange', 'to do', sometimes perhaps in rather a bad sense. *Cosa hanno combinato loro due adesso?* 'And what have those two been getting up to now?' *Combinare i soliti guai* is 'to get into trouble as usual'.

combinazione (f). 'Combination' or 'coincidence'. *Guarda che combinazione!* is 'What a coincidence!'

come. I don't intend to say very much about this adverb, as you will doubtless already be able to manipulate it reasonably well. Note the expression: *Come no*, meaning 'Of course'. *Posso usare la sua matita un attimo?—Sì, come no.* 'May I use your pencil just a moment?'—'Yes, of course'. Then note the exclamation: *Com'è bella!* 'How beautiful she/it is!' Note also the use of *Come?* instead of *Che dice*, for 'What?' or 'What did you say?' Remember that when you want to say 'as if', *come se*, you must use the subjunctive. *Lui comanda la gente come se lui fosse il capo*, 'He orders the people about as if he were the boss'. And lastly, I would point out the common use of *come* to mean 'as soon as', 'when'; e.g. *come videro il cane, scapparono*, 'when (the moment) they saw the dog, they took to their heels'.

commedia (f). This can be misleading, as the Italian *commedia* is not only what we call a 'comedy', but a 'play' in general. However, when you know enough Italian to go to an Italian theatre, if possible, you will already certainly know enough to realize this.

commercialista (m). 'Business consultant'.

commercializzare. 'To market' a product. *Commercializzazione* (f) is 'marketing'.

commozione (f). Apart from 'emotion' (and not 'commotion', which is *confusione*, *agitazione* or sometimes *tumulto*), *commozione cerebrale* means 'concussion'.

comune (m). The municipality, sometimes referred to as the commune. The mayor is called the *sindaco* (accented on the first syllable). The city (town) council is called the *giunta municipale*. Its seat in Rome is the *Campidoglio* (Capitol).

comunicativa (f). Some people have it, others haven't. And it is of such importance in language learning and practice. It is the ability or gift of establishing friendly contact or of putting things across (whether teaching or otherwise). Most languages do not have a common word for this. In English we have 'communicativeness', which cannot exactly be called a common term. The Italian word, on the other hand, is in common use, and this itself is an indication of the importance attached by Italians to friendly personal relations. *Lui ha comunicativa, ha buona comunicativa, ha scarsa comunicativa* = 'he has the gift of putting things across', 'he is very good at putting his meaning across', 'he is bad at getting things across', and so on.

comunque. One of those extremely common words used in all sorts of circumstances. It means 'however', 'anyway', 'in any case', 'at any rate', 'still'. It is usually an alternative to *in ogni modo*. *Ha promesso di venire. Comunquei non ho troppa fiducia in quello che dice, quindi non aspetterò per molto tempo*. This is 'He has promised to come. However, I don't bank too much on what he says, so I'm not going to wait very long'. *A che ora viene?—Non so ancora. Comunque viene senz'altro.* This would be: 'What time is he coming?'—'I don't know yet, but he's sure to come, anyway'. One more example: *Ho perso molti soldi oggi. Comunque ne ho ancora abbastanza per mangiare* ('I've lost a lot of money today. Still, I've got enough left to (be able to) eat'). Overhearing other people's telephone conversations sometimes, I am always struck by the large number of meaningless or semi-meaningless *comunque's* bandied about.

concussione (f). Extortion, or graft with intimidation. The English 'concussion' is *commozione cerebrale*.

conferenza (f). One meaning in Italian coincides with the English 'conference', but the other meaning, to be careful about, is 'lecture'. The Italian *lettura* is, of course, 'reading'.

confetti (m pl). Sugared almonds. Small amounts of these, in pretty packs, are distributed to friends, relatives, etc., when a wedding is due to take place. The English 'confetti' are *coriandoli*.

confezione (f). The original Italian meaning was in line with the English word 'confection', but it has taken after French latterly and the word now means 'ready-made clothing'. English 'confectionery' is *dolciumi*, the confectioner's is generally *pasticceria*, and the confectioner is *pasticciere*. Another meaning of *confezione* is 'packaging'.

conflittualità (f). This is a trade union and political neologism, dating from the *autunno caldo* ('hot autumn') of 1969. The leaders of the unions (CGIL, CISL and UIL) wished to express thereby the need not to grant any let-up to the industrialists. This *conflittualità* may be *strisciante* (ongoing all the time, in a low key), *a singhiozzo* (i.e. 'hiccup fashion', now and again, and again, etc.) and *permanente*. It therefore amounts to 'continuous unrest'.

confronto (m). Comparison. *Confrontare*, 'to compare'. The English 'to confront' is usually *affrontare*, and may also be *trovarsi di fronte* (*a qualcuno*). *Non c'è nessun confronto* is 'there is no comparison'.

congiuntura (f). Strictly speaking, this means 'economic situation' or 'state of trade', but it has taken on almost catastrophic overtones and come to mean something like 'economic crisis', so that it seems superfluous to add *sfavorevole*. In actual fact, one has to judge from the context whether 'economic situation' is intended, or whether 'adverse economic situation' or even 'slump' (*congiuntura bassa*). There is also the adjective *congiunturale*, which again may mean 'economic' (i.e. pertaining to the economic situation) or 'critical', 'adverse', etc.

consultazione (f). This may well be 'consultation', and *libri di consultazione* are 'reference books', but the word has also come to mean 'election', from the expression *consultazione elettorale*. Otherwise, a 'general election' is *elezioni generali*. The plural *consultazioni* means the talks between the President of the country and ex-presidents, prime ministers past and present, and so forth, during a *crisi di governo* (government crisis) (see **crisi**) which follows the resignation of the cabinet, with a view to deciding who shall have the mandate to try to form the next government.

contestazione (f). The legal meaning is 'objection', but the modern meaning is 'protest against the constituted authorities'. *Contestare* is therefore 'to protest against' (authority), and the protester is a *contestatore*.

contestuale. This is said of something that occurs at the same time as something else, i.e. 'simultaneous'.

continente (m). 'Continent', but also 'mainland'. Therefore *sardi* (Sardinians) and *siciliani* (Sicilians) travelling to the mainland are going *al continente*.

contingenza (f). The 'cost-of-living bonus' is called *indennità di contingenza*. When prices rise by over a certain amount, wages go up in step (i.e. a 'threshold agreement'). These rises are decided upon and applied on a quarterly basis. The 'units' or 'triggers' of increment are called *scatti* or *punti di contingenza*.

conto (m). The bill. To ask the waiter to bring the bill, you say *Fa' il conto* or *Mi faccia il conto*. The tip you may leave the waiter, by the way, is called *la mancia*. *Fare una cosa per conto suo* is 'to do something by (*or* for) oneself'. *L'ho fatto per conto mio*, 'I did it on my own (off my own bat, on my own initiative, for myself)'. *Fare i conti con qualcuno* means 'to settle with someone', or 'to reckon with someone'. *Rendersi conto di qualcosa* is 'to realize something'. In accountancy, the *conto economico* is the 'profit and loss account'. In a bank you may have a *conto corrente* (current account) or some sort of *conto vincolato* (deposit account). *A conti fatti* means 'all things considered', 'all in all'. *In fin dei conti* is 'in the end', 'when all's said and done'.

contravvenzione (f). A 'fine'. If you are *in contravvenzione*, you are 'liable to be fined', i.e. 'committing a minor offence'.

controllare. This is a verb to beware of. The usual meaning of it is 'to check', not 'to control'. In English we control people, including ourselves at times, and also vehicles and other machines, as well as controlling animals, the ball in such games as cricket and football, and our thoughts. *Tutto sotto controllo*, 'everything under control'. But we do not go upstairs 'to control' whether the children are asleep, or ring the railway station 'to control' train times, for example. The verb *controllare* would, however, be the correct one to use in Italian, as in other languages, in these and similar circumstances. The corresponding noun is *controllo*, which can be 'check' or 'control' in English according to what is said.

controproducente. This adjective means 'producing an adverse effect', and therefore sometimes 'negative'.

convenire. Here we have a multiplicity of possible meanings. It can mean 'to call to court', 'to bring a case against'; 'to acknowledge'; 'to establish'; 'to meet (together)'; 'to agree (on)'; 'to be necessary'; 'to be better to', and so on. In practice, the last-named meanings are the important ones. *Conviene farlo subito* is 'It would be best to do it right away'. *Non mi conviene* is 'it's not worth my while'. *Conviene che tu te ne vada*, 'You had better go'.

convento (m). This is in fact a 'convent', but in the old meaning of the term, for friars or for nuns as the case may be. Thus it is more often than not 'monastery' in present-day terms.

convitto (m). A 'boarding school' or, at university level, a 'college hostel'.

coppa (f). Cup, in the sense of an award. In a motor-car, the oil sump is known as *la coppa dell'olio*. The cup you drink out of is, of course, *una tazza*. As a cooked meat, *coppa di testa*, often shortened to just *coppa*, is 'brawn', while as a synonym of *capocollo*, *coppa* means a sort of salami.

corno (m). Horn. Now, Old Nick has horns, and the way to make this sign, meaning the devil, is to fold in the thumb and the two inside fingers of the hand, holding the two outside fingers outstretched, and pointing at the ground. This is to ward off the evil eye, to stop anything bad from happening, something like touching wood (but in Italian we have also *tocca in ferro*). Or you may point the outstretched fingers and jab in the direction of someone, to wish him evil (a nasty thing to do). This action is called *fare le corna* (see also **scaramanzia**). Now, *fare le corna* exists with another meaning, too, which seems something of an obsession with Italian film makers, *inter alia*. If the wife does it to the husband, it means 'to make a cuckold (of him)', 'to cuckold (him)', in which case *lui porta le corna* (he is a cuckold), i.e. *è cornuto* (*Cornuto!* is a much resented insult, by the way). Either way round, we have the verbs 'to betray' and 'to be unfaithful'. *Non me ne importa un corno* means 'I don't give a damn'.

corrente (f).   In the house, you have two sorts of *corrente*, the one that blows through the cracks (draught) and the one that gives you light (electricity). *Manca la corrente* means 'the electricity has been cut off'. Then we have the figurative use of the word, very widespread these days in politics, indicating the factions within a party. Note in conclusion the expression *essere al corrente di* . . ., meaning 'to be acquainted with . . .', 'to be well informed about . . .'.

corsia (f).   On an *autostrada* ('motorway') etc., this is a 'lane'. In sport it is also a 'lane' of a running track. In a hospital it is 'ward'. Otherwise it is 'gangway' or 'passage'. In some cities there are *corsie preferenziali*, marked by thick yellow lines on the road. These are special lanes reserved for buses and taxis.

cosa (f).   'Thing', as you must be very well aware, and used by Italians with a great variety of meanings, as in English, although not quite to such an extent. Naturally, all languages make great use of such a basic word as 'thing'. Note that 'something' may be either *qualche cosa* or else *qualcosa*. The important point to make here is the use of the word *cosa* to replace *che?* or to supplement it as in *che cosa?* when asking a question. *Cosa ha detto?* is perfectly normal for 'What did you say?' *Cosa vuole?* 'What does he (*or* do you) want?' and so on. Note, too, that Italians frequently add *una cosa* after the verb *dire*, as in *Ditemi una cosa*, 'Just tell me', and also after the verbs *sapere*— *Sa una cosa?* more or less 'Would you like to know something?' —and *sentire*, 'to hear'. For example, *Senta una cosa*, which means 'Just listen to this'. As indicated above, 'thing' is used more in English than is *cosa* in Italian, and this is largely explained by the fact that Italian has the word *roba*, which corresponds roughly to the English 'things' or 'stuff'. For further explanation, see under **roba.**

così.   'In this way', 'like this'. *Si fa così* means 'You do it like this', or else 'You go like this'. *Così così* corresponds to the French *comme ci, comme ça*, 'so so'. *Basta così* means 'That's enough', 'It's all right like that' or 'That will do'. As a question it is just as common. *Basta così?* 'Is that enough?' 'Is it all right like this?' and so on.

No, non è mica così gives the idea of 'No, it's not at all like that'. 'And so on', 'and so forth' can best be rendered in Italian by *e così via*. *Non voglio dire così* is 'I don't want to say that', 'That's not what I want to say'. *Non direi così* is 'I wouldn't go so far as to say that'. *E così via*.

coso (m).   I don't know what your particular word is for something whose name you have temporarily forgotten or which escapes you for the moment. 'Just now I saw old what's-his-name', 'Hand me the thingummy, will you' and so on. Just as many English speakers overdo this, so do many Italians. *Ho parlato*

con coso riguardante coso would not be thought an extra-
ordinary thing to say by some people. At best *coso* is a useful
word when you really do forget a name for the moment, but
to many people it is a taboo word.

costume (m). If, you might say, *costume* means 'custom' or 'usage',
which it indeed does, and also 'costume' and even 'fancy
dress', which is also the case, what sort of police are the *squadra
del buon costume*? Well, basically *not* the sort to see that you
are properly dressed, although this could come into it, as a
state of undress would attract their attention as would also
ladies' clothing flaunted on men (*travestiti*, 'transvestites'), because, you see, this is the 'vice squad' (known as *il buoncostume*).
Legally, *costume* means '(public) morality'. In the plural it is
'morals' or 'behaviour', or a person's 'ways' or 'habits'. *Una
persona di strani costumi* is 'a person with strange ways'. *Una
donna di facili costumi* is 'a woman of loose morals'. Note also
the word *malcostume* (m), which is 'immoral behaviour',
'immorality', and also 'general corruption' as in *malcostume
politico*. Therefore, with this word you will have to be on
your guard, with your eyes open for the context. A sociologist,
for example, studying the *costumi* of a group, has in mind its
'behaviour', while obviously a *costume da bagno* has nothing
to do with morality in the bath!

crisi (f). Apart from economic crises and international political
ones, Italy has its full share of small everyday crises of ordinary
living, and of government crises. In English, we tend to avoid
the actual word 'crisis': economic slump, shortage, depression;
attack or fit of nerves; and so on. But the Italians use it liberally:
*crisi economica, crisi petrolifera, la crisi del 1932, una crisi di
pianto, una crisi di nervi*, etc. In Italian political language, a
crisi indicates the void that occurs when a government resigns
and which lasts until the next one is formed. There are three
types: 'guided' (*guidata*), when the objective is defined in
advance; 'veiled' (*mascherata*), when the whole occurrence is
cleverly masked as a ministerial reshuffle; and 'extraparliamen-
tary' (*extraparlamentare*), when the government resigns without
there having been a vote of no confidence in the House.

croce (f). A cross. 'The Red Cross' is simply *La Croce Rossa*. When
tossing up, one says *testa o croce?*

cucchiaio (m). Spoon (tablespoon). A teaspoon is *cucchiaino* (adding *da tè* or *da caffè*, if you wish). A 'spoonful' is *cucchiaiata*.

cucina (f). Kitchen, but also the 'stove' or 'cooker'. And it is also
'cooking' or 'cuisine'. *Cucina casalinga* is 'good, plain cooking'.

cupolone (m). *Cupola* is 'dome' and *cupolone* is therefore 'big
dome'. *Il Cupolone* is St Peter's.

curare. The basic meaning of this verb is 'to take care of', 'to look after'. In the publishing field, this still applies and so means 'to edit' (and *a cura di* ... means 'edited by ...'), while in the medical field it means 'to nurse', 'to give treatment to', but not (necessarily) 'to cure', which is usually *guarire*. *Casa di cura* is 'nursing home'. A medical *cura* is 'course of treatment', perhaps 'cure' if qualified by another word, such as in *cura dimagrante*, 'slimming cure', or else 'care' or 'nursing' when general medical, etc., attention is intended. If someone tells you *curati di te*, you are being advised to 'look after yourself', and not to cure or treat yourself.

D

dagli, dai. Much like *su*, as a word of encouragement. 'Come on!', 'Cheer up', and so forth. At a boxing match you would expect a shouted *dagli* to mean 'let him have it', and you'd be right. Two boys may be in a hurry, and one of them, starting to run, turns to the other one and says *dai, corri*. On the whole, *su* is milder than *dai* or *dagli*. Moreover, *dai* can be used to express your disbelief, perhaps; for example, if someone tells you he cannot pay you because he has no cash, and you suspect this not to be true, you could well say *dai* (depending on your terms with him, of course).

dattero (m). Date, of the sort you eat. 'The date', meaning the day of the year, is, of course, *la data*. And a 'date' with a girl or boy friend is *appuntamento* (doesn't sound very romantic, does it?). 'Out of date', meaning past the time of expiry, is *scaduto*.

dattilografa (f). Typist. Accented on the third syllable. The verb 'to type' can be *dattilografare*, although in speaking it is more common to say *scrivere a macchina*, or (and this is the more usual alternative) *battere a macchina*.

davvero. Really, indeed. *Ti ha piaciuto davvero il film?—Si, davvero*. 'Did you really like the film?'—'Yes, truly'. *Dice davvero?* 'Are you telling the truth?' Naturally, it may be used as a question or as an indication of disbelief, according to tone.

debole (m). 'Weakness' in the sense of 'weak *or* soft spot'. Accent on the first syllable. *La signora Rossi aveva un debole per le persone distinte* means 'Mrs Rossi had a weakness for distinguished people'. You could also say 'have a partiality for' or 'be partial to'. *Lei ha un debole per lui* means 'She has a soft spot for him' or 'She is rather keen on him'. As you will know, *debole* is an ordinary adjective meaning 'weak', 'feeble' and so on. There is an alternative noun, *debolezza* (f): *per quella sua* *debolezza delle cose francesi,* 'through that weakness of hers for things French'.

decade (f). This is 'decade', meaning a ten-year period, as in English usage, and also sometimes a ten-day period, which is correct again in English but not as much used as in Italian. *Decade* is accented on the first syllable.

decidersi. 'To decide, make up one's mind'. *Lei si è decisa già?* is 'Has she made her mind up yet?' *Deciditi!* means 'Make up your mind!' This is all quite straightforward, and put in to remind you that quite often an English expression, commonly used, has a simple English equivalent, which itself is near to the Latin and therefore usually near to the Italian word. So here, instead of translating 'make up your mind', think of 'decide', and there you are.

decina (f). Ten. Naturally, the cardinal number is *dieci*, but it is common in Italian to say *una decina, una quindicina, una ventina, una trentina, una cinquantina,* instead of just *dieci, quindici, venti, trenta, cinquanta.* Sometimes, however, the . . . *ina* form refers to approximately that number, e.g. *una decina* may be 'about ten'.

decollo (m). Speaking of aircraft, this means 'takeoff'. In Italian, as in English, however, it has extended its meaning away from the aeronautical field. It has in fact ousted the words *ascesa* and *ripresa* in popular economic language. That is, they speak of the economic *decollo* ('recovery') of a depressed area, part of the *Mezzogiorno* (q.v.), for example.

definitiva. *In definitiva,* a very much used expression, means 'in conclusion', 'after all' (*dopo tutto*) or, sometimes, 'to come to the point'.

delitto (m). Not a 'delight' (which is *delizia* or *diletto*), but one of the words for 'crime'. The other ones are *crimine* (m), *reato* (m) and *criminalità* (f). (*Crimine* is accented on the first syllable and *reato* on the middle one.) *Reato* and *delitto* are the words used in a strictly legal sense, and both may range from the less serious ('misdemeanour') to the more serious ('felony'). Such a title as *Le causalità della criminalità* may sound complicated, but is really only 'Causes of Crime'. *Il corpo del delitto* is 'corpus delicti'.

delusione (f). Disappointment. You will also find the word *disappunto,* but Italians have more *delusioni* than *disappunti.* The corresponding adjective, also a bit of a false friend, is *deluso. Lei era rimasta delusa da . . .* means 'She was disappointed by . . .' Note that a 'delusion' is *una illusione* (f).

dente (m). Tooth. *Non è pane per i miei denti* means 'It's not my cup of tea'. 'To have a tooth out (or filled)' is *farsi cavare (o otturare) un dente.* In cooking, *al dente* is a very common term used with respect to spaghetti and suchlike. *Gli spaghetti? Mi piacciono al dente.* 'Spaghetti? I like it just on the point of being done, that is, with a solid feel between the teeth'. (I notice that dictionaries usually call *al dente* 'underdone', but it is just a slight fraction, and an intentional one; if the spaghetti is really underdone, you would say it is *troppo al dente.*)

di.   With attached article, this of course becomes *del, dei* and so on. This is not going to be a treatise on the many and various ways of using the word *di.* I wish to point out the partitive use—corresponding to English 'some', 'any'. *Mi dia del burro* is 'Give me some butter'. *Ha delle olive?* asks 'Have you any olives?' In practice, there is often a substitute for both singular and plural. Instead of *Mi dia del burro* you often hear *Mi dia un po' di burro,* for example. And, whereas you could say *Ho visto dei soldati,* you would in fact probably say *Ho visto molti soldati* or *un gruppo di soldati.*

difficile.   No difficulty about this, it is just 'difficult' or 'hard'. Except that Italians commonly use it also with the meaning of 'unlikely'. For example, *È difficile che io esca di sera* means 'I seldom go out in the evening' (i.e. it is unlikely that I will go out in the evening). *È difficile che lui venga domani* is 'he is unlikely to come tomorrow'. Note the use of the subjunctive.

diplomato (m).   The adjective *diplomatico* means just what you would expect it to mean, 'diplomatic' (or 'tactful'). The false friend lurks in the noun *diplomato,* he in fact being someone with a diploma, a diploma-holder. A *diplomatico* is a 'diplomat'. Note that *un diploma di laurea* (see **laurea**) is 'degree'—and note also that diploma is one of those masculine words ending in –a.

direttissima (f).   You will sometimes see in the newspapers (although not too often, the speed of justice being what it is) that someone is being tried in a *processo per direttissima,* which means that he is being given a 'summary trial'. (Although this procedure is not, as is common elsewhere, reserved for minor offences: quite the contrary, in fact.) Not to be confused with the masculine *direttissimo,* which means 'fast train' (see **espresso**).

direttivo (m).   A collective noun meaning 'leaders', as in *direttivo del partito, del sindacato* ('party (union) leaders').

direttore (m).   I put this in to remind you that a *direttore* is far more often a 'manager' than a 'director'. For instance, *direttore d'albergo, d'azienda, di banca, commerciale, di fabbrica, generale, del personale, tecnica* are all 'managers' (hotel, factory, bank, sales, works, general, personnel and technical, respectively). The Italian list grows longer, too (*direttore di un giornale, d'orchestra, di una scuola, di una prigione*) whereas at this point the English word list diversifies (editor, conductor, headmaster and prison governor, respectively). The English 'director' of a company may be *amministratore* (often the *amministratore unico*) or a *membro del consiglio d'amministrazione* (member of the board of directors), otherwise called *consigliere*. The 'director' of a film is *regista* (m), while the 'art director' is *scenografo*, with the accent on the *og* part.

direttrice (f). Is the female counterpart of the males listed above.

dirigismo (m). 'Government controls', 'State planning'. *Dirigismo economico* is 'planned economy' (whereas 'economic planning' is *programmazione* (or *pianificazione*) *economica*, and 'economic policy' is *politica economica*).

dirottare. In the old days, merely 'to change course'. Nowadays, normally 'to hijack'. A 'hijacking' is *dirottamento* and the 'hijacker' is *dirottatore* (or alternatively *pirata* (m) *dell'aria*).

disastro (m). This is a 'disaster', right enough. It's also a common way of referring to a 'flop', something that didn't come off very well. *È un disastro!* is 'It's terrible!' Note also in this context that *tremendo* (q.v.) refers to something bad, unless it is specifically stated that the size is intended.

disavanzo (m). If something is left over (food, money, etc.), you say that it *avanza* (*avanzare*, 'to be left over, remain'). Thus we have *avanzo*, 'remainder', and *avanzi* (e.g. 'savings'). By adding dis- to form *disavanzo*, we turn the idea round, and find ourselves lacking instead of having some over, i.e. there is a 'deficit' (*un deficit* also exists).

disco (m). A gramophone record. *Disco della frizione* is 'clutch disc'. *Un disco volante*, if you believe in such things, is a 'flying saucer'.

discorso (m). Speech, conversation, talk. *Cambiare discorso* means 'to change the subject'. *Ti dispiace cambiare discorso?* is 'Do you mind if we change the subject?' If you are talking about something, and someone says something off the point, you could say *Questo è un altro discorso*, 'that's another question'. *È quasi impossibile avere un discorso con lui* means 'it's almost impossible to talk to him' (because his point of view is so different, etc.). *Che discorsi!* is 'What nonsense!'

discussione (f). This is more often 'argument' than 'discussion'. However, to English ears, an ordinary Italian conversation, with perhaps four or five people all talking at the same time, may well sound like an argument, or even a quarrel!

disegno (m). This is usually 'drawing', but may also be 'design' or 'pattern'. *Un disegno di legge* is a 'bill'. Industrial or project designing is usually *progettazione* (f). A 'preliminary design' is *progetto preliminare*, and a 'final design' is *progetto definitivo*.

disgrazia (f). Usually an 'accident' or a 'mishap'. Unfortunately, *una disgrazia non viene mai sola*, 'troubles never come alone'. The noun referring to a person, *un disgraziato*, is frequently heard and corresponds to the English 'wretch', in the sense of some poor, unfortunate person, as well as in the sense of some 'miserable wretch'. So, too, with the adjective, also *disgraziato*. Notice that the English 'disgrace' is more often than not *una vergogna* (literally, 'a shame'). 'Disgraceful' is likewise *vergognoso*.

disoccupazione (f). 'Unemployment'. 'Unemployed persons' are *disoccupati*.

dispetti (m pl). *Dispetto* exists in the singular ('spitefulness', etc.), but the word heard most often by far (in mothers' mouths, usually, when talking to small children) is *dispetti*, as in *Non fare dispetti!* ('Don't be naughty', 'Don't play about', 'Don't play tricks', 'Don't annoy me', etc.). If someone is *dispettoso*, he is 'annoying', 'cheeky', and so on.

dispiace. The opposite of *mi piace* ('I like it') is not *mi dispiace* but *non mi piace*. *Mi dispiace* means 'I'm sorry', 'Excuse me'. Then there is the very important use of this word in asking someone whether he minds (doing) something. *Lei dispiace se apro la finestra?*—'Do you mind if I open the window?'

disponibile. 'Available' or 'free' in the sense of 'vacant'. That chair that no one is sitting on at the next table may well be *disponibile*, if you're wanting one. It is also a very much used word referring to a person's willingness and/or readiness. *X si è detto disponibile per una svolta*, 'X has stated he will support (is in favour of) a change'. The corresponding noun is *disponibilità* (f), 'availability' according to the dictionary, although this is not always the best word to use (we have 'willingness', 'readiness', 'goodwill', 'support', and so on). In the economic sense, *disponibilità* means 'liquid assets', 'available funds' or 'cash'.

disposto. *Non sono disposto a lasciarmi prendere in giro* means 'I'm not prepared to let myself be tricked'. *Siamo disposti a pagare la metà* is 'we're prepared to pay half'. *Lui è ben disposto verso di noi*, 'He is well disposed towards us'. *Lei è disposta a credere la loro storia*, 'She is inclined to believe their story'.

distributore (m). This may be 'distributor', but these days what is more often referred to is a *distributore automatico* ('slot machine', 'automatic vending machine'), or the place where you fill up the tank of your car, i.e. the 'petrol pump'.

diva (f). *Diva* is really a 'goddess', but is used to refer to a 'star' of stage or screen. The male counterpart is the *divo*.

diventare. To become, to get, to grow. *Lei è diventata molto magra* means 'She has got very thin'. *Diventare pazzo* is 'to go crazy', while *far diventare pazzo* is 'to drive crazy'. There is also the form *divenire* (less usual): the past participles of the two verbs are *diventato* and *divenuto*, respectively.

diverso. Just to remind you that this adjective can mean 'different' just as much as it means 'various' or 'several' (as in *diverse volte*, 'several times'). English speakers of Italian tend to use the word *differente* a bit too much, overlooking that *diverso* is not infrequently the best word to use. *Sembra molto diverso adesso* is 'It (he) seems very different now'.

divertirsi. 'To enjoy, amuse oneself'. *Mi sono divertito molto ieri al teatro* is 'I enjoyed myself very much at the theatre yesterday'. *Si diverte a giocare a carte* is 'he enjoys playing cards'. *Divertiti!* means 'Have a good time!' The corresponding noun is *divertimento*. To a friend going off to the cinema, for example, you could say *Buon divertimento*—'Enjoy yourself'. If something is *divertente*, rather than enjoyable it is 'funny, amusing, entertaining'.

divisa (f). Strictly speaking, a 'foreign bill of exchange', but by extension, also (and usually) 'foreign exchange' (i.e. *valuta*). It also means 'uniform', as in *divisa di gala*, 'full dress uniform'.

doroteo (m). A member of the *Dorotei*, a faction of the Christian Democratic party. The name derives from the convent of the Sisters of St Dorothy (*le suore dorotee*) where some party leaders held a meeting in March 1959, and drew up a plan to seize the reins of party leadership from Fanfani—a plan which was crowned with success.

dorso (m). Back. With reference to swimming, this is the 'back stroke'.

dottore (m). Not just a medical doctor, but any graduate who has taken his doctorate. If you look at a list of the heads of various offices, departments, etc., do not be surprised to see that many of them are 'doctors'. *Dottore* (or more often *dottò*) is also used as a mark of respect (?) in addressing very many people who are neither medical doctors nor any other sort.

dritto. This may be another form of the adjective *diritto*, meaning 'straight', 'straight up', 'straight along', 'upright', or a colloquial adjective and corresponding noun with the idea of 'smart', 'clever', 'slick'.

drogheria (f). Don't try to call this a 'druggery' or anything fancy like that. Different books will tell you different things for a *drogheria*, and it is really quite hard to pin it down precisely, but the nearest translation would be a 'general store'. If you say 'grocer's', you have a case, as you can buy certain eatables in certain *drogherie*, but it is generally stretching the point a bit. You can purchase the following in a *drogheria*: cotton wool, toothpaste, soap, detergents, shampoo, brooms, brushes, herbs, coffee beans, perfume, dried fruit, and so on—so perhaps you can make up your own mind what translation you would like to give the word. At any rate, you do not get drugs and medicines there. For these you would of course go to a *farmacia*.

due passi (m pl). *A due passi* means 'only a short distance away'. *Siamo a due passi dal teatro* is 'We're only a few yards from the theatre'. Otherwise you can *fare due passi* (or *fare quattro passi*), if you wish to 'go for a short walk', 'have a bit of a stroll'.

dunque. As a noun, in the expression *venire al dunque*, it means the 'crux', 'the crucial point', 'the decisive moment'. Otherwise, and very commonly, *dunque* is a conjunction meaning 'so, well, then'. *È tardi, dunque facciamo presto* means 'It's late, so let's hurry up'. *Eccola dunque arrivata!*—'So here she is then!' *Dunque, sì o no?*—'Well, then, yes or no?' I should point out that some people who appear not to like pauses in their flow of words, and having to ponder on something, fill in the time by saying *Dunque . . . dunque . . . dunque . . .* (this may mean 'Now, let's see . . . let's just see . . .' etc., or it may not even mean that).

E

ecco. Every learner of Italian should be aware of the first meaning of *ecco*, 'here . . . is', in the same way that *voici* and *voilà* are used in French. *Eccolo* in the usual way means 'Here he is' or 'Here it is'. If someone or something is espied in the distance, then *Eccolo* is 'There he is' or 'There it is'. In conversation, *ecco* is very frequently used. *Non mi ricordo come si chiama quella ragazza.—Si chiama Eleonora o qualche cosa così, non è vero?—Sì, ecco, adesso mi ricordo che si chiama Leonora.* ('I can't remember that girl's name'. 'It's Eleonora or something like that, isn't it?' 'Yes, that's it, now I remember, it's Leonora.') Again, *È un animale che somiglia molto a un cavallo, con strisce; anzi, assomiglia a una zebra, ecco.* 'It's an animal that ˃ ery closely resembles a horse, with stripes; or rather it resembles a zebra, to be more precise.' Another example: *Siete un bugiardo, ecco quello che siete!* 'You're a liar, that's what you are!'

You will notice that *ecco* is often put at the end of a sentence, to confirm something (something like 'mark you', or the Welsh 'look you'), or even as an afterthought. *Non si può dire che non è giusto, ma, insomma, come dire? . . . non è sempre corretto, ecco.* ('You can't say it's not right, but all the same, what should I say? . . . well, it's not always correct, you see.')

Just one or two further examples: *Come, non basta così? Dunque, le do ancora due, ecco. Va bene così?* 'What, isn't this enough? All right, I'll give you two more, look. Is that all right now?' *Avete una camicia grigia?—Ecco una camicia di colore più o meno grigio* ('Have you a grey shirt?' 'Here's a shirt of a more or less grey colour'). And finally a few expressions using *ecco*:

Ecco tutto, That's all
Ecco fatto, That's that
Eccolo che arriva, Here he comes
Ecco di che si tratta, That's what it's about
Eccone abbastanza, That's enough of that

edicola (f). Bookstall, kiosk, news stand. Accented on second syllable.

educato. This adjective does not always necessarily refer to one's school education. In fact, it very likely points to one's manners, meaning 'polite, well-mannered'. 'Education' in the school sense is rather *istruzione* (the Ministry of Education is indeed called the *Ministero di pubblica istruzione*), and 'educated' can therefore be *istruito*. According to the context, however, it may also be *educato*. *Educazione* (f) also has the two ideas; it is either 'education' or 'upbringing', or it may mean *buone maniere*, good manners. *Insegnare l'educazione a qualcuno* is 'to teach someone manners'. Someone with bad manners is referred to as *maleducato*.

eh. The man has been waiting in the *bar* for a long time, and the *barista* asks him if he is expecting someone. The man tells him that his girlfriend should have turned up half an hour ago. The *barista* commiserates: *Se non fanno aspettare non sono contente*, he says. *È come se fossero meno donne se non arrivano in ritardo . . . Eh . . .* answers the man. ('They're not satisfied unless they make you wait . . . It's as though they were less womanly unless they turn up late' . . . 'Dead right', answers the man). All this, to underline the fact that the much used *eh* often means 'yes' with emphasis. *Hai fame?—Eh!* . . . ('Hungry?—I'll say I am!'). *Canta bene quella ragazza?—Eh!* . . . ('Does she sing well, that girl?'—'And how!').

elemento (m). Apart from meaning 'element', this is commonly used to mean 'radiator' (i.e. heating element in a central heating system) or 'pupil', 'student', 'employee' in schools, firms, etc. (e.g. *Lui è un ottimo elemento* = 'He's an excellent student, employee, worker', etc.).

elenco (m). The normal word for 'list', which may also be *lista*. *L'elenco telefonico* is 'the telephone directory'.

elettricità (f). Electricity. In common speech, people usually call it *la corrente*. Note that a 'switch' is *interruttore*, but although *girare* means 'to turn', you cannot put the two words together to mean 'turn the switch on'. In fact the whole actions of turning the light on and off are expressed in the verbs *accendere* and *spegnere la luce*, respectively. A 'power station' is *centrale elettrica*. The 'electricity bill' is called the *bolletta della luce*.

entrare. 'To enter'. Remember that Italian has the construction 'to enter into a room', that is, *entrare in una stanza*. The corresponding noun is *entrata* (f), which may refer to an entrance in the sense of a door or to one in the sense of the going in, or else the entrance which refers to the money you pay to go in. In book-keeping, *entrate e uscite* are 'revenue and expenditures'. Note particularly the expression *non c'entra*, meaning 'that's beside the point'. *Voi non c'entrate* is 'This is no business of yours' (see also under **ci**).

entro. This preposition means 'in', 'within' when followed by a number, e.g. *entro tre settimane*, 'within three weeks', and 'not later than', 'by the end of', when followed by a noun, e.g. *entro questa sera*, 'by the end of this evening'.

eppure. 'Yet', 'still', 'nevertheless'. *Disse che non veniva, eppure è arrivato proprio adesso* means 'He said he wouldn't come, and yet he's just arrived'.

equo canone (m). *Equo* (accented on the first syllable) means 'fair', 'just', 'equitable'. *Canone* (also accented on the first syllable) usually means 'rent' or 'fee'. The reference here is to a 'fair rent'. A law establishing a system for calculating a fair rent was passed in late 1978.

esercizio (m). 'Exercise', as in *fare dell'esercizio*, 'to take some exercise', and 'practice', as in *sono fuori esercizio*, 'I'm out of practice'. *L'esercizio finanziario* is 'the financial year'. Notice that 'the army' is *l'esercito* (accented on the second syllable).

esonerare. Although sometimes 'to exonerate', this usually means 'to relieve of', especially in the sense of removing someone from office. So if you read that someone has been *esonerato*, he will have been dismissed, probably because of suspected or proven misdeeds.

esperienza (f). This may be 'experience', as in *Lui lo sa per esperienza*, 'He knows it from experience', or it may be 'experiment' (which is also *esperimento* or *prova*).

espresso (m). As a noun, this may refer to coffee, of course, or to a 'special delivery letter', or to a 'fast train', strictly speaking called *direttissimo*, which according to the Italian classification is second on the list after the very fastest or *rapido*, and preceding the *diretto* and the *accelerato* (which is a real false friend, being in point of fact a 'slow train'!). Which means that the English 'express train' is *rapido*, while, as stated, the Italian *espresso* is a neologism for the more correct *direttissimo*, or 'through train'. Now, another thing. If you do something *espressamente*, you are doing it for a specific purpose, and not necessarily quickly, at all. As in restaurants this is the idea given by *piatti espressi*, do not go ordering something from this part of the menu because you are short of time; quite the contrary, it means that such dishes have to be prepared explicitly or expressly for you, perhaps calling for quite a wait on your part.

evadere. Normally, this means 'to escape, make one's escape'. *Evadere dalla prigione* is 'to break out of prison'. Commercially, *evadere la corrispondenza* is 'to clear the correspondence' (and *evadere una lettera* means 'to forward a letter'), while *evadere un ordine* is 'to execute an order'. In bureaucratic practice, *evadere una pratica* is 'to deal with a piece of business'.

eventualmente. One of the classical false friends between English and Italian. Our 'eventually' means *alla fine, finalmente, infine*, while *eventualmente* is 'if', 'possibly'. *Eventuale* is 'possible' or 'any': *una vostra eventuale risposta dovrebbe arrivare entro la fine del mese*, 'Your answer, if any, should arrive not later than the end of the month'.

extraparlamentare. 'Non-parliamentary' or 'outside of parliament'. And which parties, or more often so-called *gruppuscoli* (from the French *groupuscules*), i.e. 'small groups', are outside of parliament? In particular, the extremists (left of left and right of right). Thus *extraparlamentare*, noun or adjective, is normally best translated 'extremist'. The term *autonomo* (q.v.) has recently more or less replaced *extraparlamentare*, covering the majority of left-wing groups.

F

fabbrica (f). A factory. Do not of course call this a *fattoria*, which is a 'farm'. 'A fabric' is *un tessuto, una stoffa*.

faccenda (f). *Una faccenda* is 'a matter', 'a bit of business', etc. It can be translated 'thing' or even 'story' according to the expression as, for example, *No, questa è un'altra faccenda*, 'No, that's quite a different story'. *Faccende domestiche* are 'household duties' or 'chores'. *Non capisco niente di questa faccenda* is 'I don't understand a thing about this business'. *Una brutta faccenda* is 'a bad business'.

faccia (f). Face. *Faccia tosta* is 'cheek, nerve, brazenness, effrontery'. *Ci vuole una bella faccia tosta per fare una cosa simile*, 'It takes some nerve to do such a thing!' *Non guardare in faccia nessuno* means 'to be no respecter of persons'.

fagiolo (m). Bean, usually kidney bean or similar. Stress on first a. If you want to say 'broad bean', say *fava*. French (green) beans are *fagiolini*. *Fagioli di spagna* are runner beans. A common dish is *fagioli all'uccelletto*, consisting of beans cooked in a sort of gravy. Bean soup is *zuppa di fagioli* and, when served in restaurants where it is a speciality, it can be counted on to provide the connoisseur with an exquisite and very plentiful meal in itself, second to none. Then note two common expressions: *andare a fagiolo*, 'to suit right down to the ground', and *capitare a fagiolo*, 'to arrive, happen, just at the right moment *or* just when needed'. E.g. *Questo mi va proprio a fagiolo*, 'This is just the thing for me'.

fare. *Fare* more often means 'to make' than 'to do', although it can mean either. And apart from these two basic meanings, there are several expressions, which deserve to be stressed, where *fare* corresponds to another verb in English.

    fare attenzione, to be careful
    far caldo (freddo), to be warm (cold) (of weather)
    far colazione, to have breakfast
    fare il conto, to get the bill ready
    far fare qualche cosa, to have something done
    fare finta, to pretend
    far fuori, to kill, 'bump off'
    far male, to hurt
    fare una passeggiata, to go for a walk
    fare una visita, to pay a visit
    non poter fare a meno di, not to help doing something

Here are a few examples in sentences: *Non avevo ancora fatto colazione*, 'I hadn't yet had breakfast'. *Lei ha fatto finta di non capire niente*, 'She pretended not to understand anything'. *Non potei fare a meno di sentire tutta la conversazione*, 'I couldn't help hearing the whole conversation'. *Cameriere, mi faccia il conto, per favore*, 'Would you please bring me the bill, waiter'.

If you wish to be informed of something, you could for example leave instructions for someone to 'let me know when he arrives'. This would be *Mi faccia sapere quando arriva, per piacere*. If you are not bothered one way or the other about something, you may well say *mi fa lo stesso*. If something makes you sick, nauseates you, you would be using a very common, albeit slangy, expression if you said *mi fa schifo*. *Farla finita*, to cut it out; e.g. *falla finita!* 'Cut it out!' *Fare orecchi da mercante*, 'to turn a deaf ear'. *Far furore*, 'to be all the rage'. *Questo fa proprio per me*, 'this is just the thing for me'. *Faccio come mi pare*, 'I do just what I want to'. And lastly—although it would be possible to go on and on about this verb, in the same way that you could go on and on with the English verb 'get', note the construction *fare meglio a (non) fare una cosa*, 'had better not do something', e.g. *farebbe molto meglio a non toccarlo*, 'you had far better not touch it'.

fastidio (m). 'Bother', something that puts you out or upsets you. The adjective is *fastidioso*, meaning 'irksome', 'upsetting', 'off-putting' or 'tiresome', perhaps also 'fussy'. *Mi dà troppo fastidio* means 'It annoys me too much'. *Le dà fastidio?* asks 'Does this bother you?' The verb *infastidire* means 'to molest', 'to annoy'.

fasullo. 'Bogus, sham'; 'false'; 'phoney'. *È una situazione fasulla*, 'it's a phoney situation'. *Quella tavola Luigi XV è fasulla*, 'that Louis XV table is a fake'. *Guarda questa moneta. È fasulla!* 'Just look at this coin. It's a fake!'

fattoria (f). This is the usual word for a 'farm'. Don't confuse it with 'a factory', which is *una fabbrica* (q.v.).

fattorino (m). Nothing to do with little farm boys or anything like that. This means 'messenger', boy or man; an errand-boy is also *fattorino*.

fava (f). Bean, of the broad variety (otherwise use *fagiolo* (q.v.), *fagiolino*). In English we 'kill two birds with one stone', but in Italian they say *prendere due piccioni con una fava*.

favore (m). You can use this word, or *piacere*, to mean 'favour'; but the point I'd like to stress here is that you should not overdo the *per favore* business. I've heard Englishmen in shops asking for several articles, saying *per favore* after each item (and sometimes before it, too!). This sounds strange in Italian. Be polite, by all means, but check yourself from doing *per favore* to death. *Per favore!*

fegato (m). 'Liver', you might think, and that's that. But remember that Italians think a great deal about their livers, and a good many of them, doctors included, immediately blame it on the liver if they have some malaise or other, and at once vow to cut out coffee, etc. So the liver is a subject of conversation, and in like manner it has a variety of secondary meanings. *Avere fegato*, for example, means 'to have pluck, guts'. *Lui ha un bel fegato!* is 'He's certainly got a nerve!' *Mangiarsi il fegato* (*per la rabbia*) indicates 'to be seething (with anger)'. *Fegatoso*, mind you, means 'liverish', 'bad-tempered', and *not* 'plucky'.

femmina (f). The nurse comes out of the labour ward, sees the expectant husband, and says: 'It's a girl!' Well, in Italian she wouldn't say *è una ragazza!* but *è una bella femminuccia!* (likewise for a boy the word would be *maschio* or *maschietto*). *Femmina* of course means 'female', and can be used for animals to denote the female of the species, if you wish to stress this fact. *Un elefante femmina, una tigre femmina*, for instance, are a 'cow elephant' and a 'female tiger'. Otherwise we have *elefantessa*, although no corresponding word for *tigre* in the masculine (this being one of the animals of female gender, such as *volpe*, 'fox'). To stress that you mean a 'male tiger', you would have to say *una tigre maschio*.

fermare. 'To stop', sometimes 'to arrest or detain', and also 'to fasten'. A bus-stop is *una fermata*, and it is a request stop if it is *facoltativa*. If a child runs too far ahead, the mother, maid, etc., with it will call out: *Ferma! Fermarsi* is 'to stop'. *L'auto si fermò con una frenata*, 'The bus braked to a stop'. *Fermarsi di* *botto* means 'to stop short'. Remember to distinguish between this verb and *firmare*, which is 'to sign'.

Ferragosto (m).   This is the August bank holiday. The fifteenth of August, the feast of the Assumption, is the specific day of the holiday, although it is quite common for the whole week to be taken as a holiday. It is usual for all shops to close on the fifteenth, and in fact many shops close for the summer holidays for a week or two during this period. This is a general holiday throughout Italy and visitors to Rome will find it almost dead, while those who visit the seaside resorts will have to fight to find a place.

ferro (m).   Iron, both the metal and the household appliance. 'An electric iron' is *un ferro da stiro elettrico*. The verb 'to iron' is *stirare*. *Essere ai ferri corti con qualcuno* means 'to be daggers drawn with someone' (or at least 'at loggerheads'). The equivalent of our 'touch wood' is *tocca ferro!* If someone is *sotto i ferri*, he is on the operating table, and the surgeon is wielding his *ferri chirurgici*, or surgical implements. *Un ferro da calza* is 'a knitting needle', and *lavorare ai ferri* is 'to knit'.

fetta (f), **fettina** (f).   These words mean 'slice', used for meat, bacon, bread, etc. A slice of bread quickly fried or just heated with oil and garlic, a very popular tit-bit, is called *bruschetta*. *Tagliare a fette* means 'to slice up'.

fiammifero (m).   The sort of 'match' that you strike (usually called *svedesi*, 'Swedes'). Note, however, that the sort of matches frequently used in Italy are tiny ones called *cerini*, minute waxed sticks which take some people some time to get used to. A close second in popularity are book-matches, usually referred to by their registered trade name—*fiammiferi Minerva*. Note, too, that the 'match' played between two teams is *una partita*.

ficcare.   *Ficcarsi* is 'to hide oneself somewhere'. The basic idea of *ficcare* is 'to stick *or* thrust something somewhere'. You can stick your nose into someone else's business (*ficcare il naso negli affari altrui*), stick your hands into your pockets (*ficcare le mani in tasca*) and so forth. *Ficcare* is also 'to pack things in a suitcase', e.g. *Giulia ficcava della biancheria e alcuni oggetti da toilette nella sua valigia*, 'Julia stuffed some underwear and some toiletries into her case'. *Un ficcanaso* is a 'busybody'.

figura (f).   Just to remind you that this does not primarily refer to the 'figure', but to the 'appearance' in general. And note the very popular expressions, *fare una bella figura* and *fare una brutta figura* which mean respectively 'to cut a good figure' ('to keep up appearances', more or less, but rather stronger), and 'to let yourself down, to make a bad impression, to lose face'. In Italy, it is important to present a façade, to have people think that you are making the magnificent gesture, doing the right thing and so on. You should avoid *fare una brutta figura* or even worse *una figuraccia*, creating a bad (terrible) impression. I must say, however, that this fear of making a *brutta figura* and the desire to make a *bella figura* are not so pronounced as at one time. Husbands (some of them) push the baby out in the pram, people carry their own shopping home, and so on, and there is generally more openness about things.

figurarsi. 'To 'imagine', 'to fancy', 'just think'. *Figurati che l'avevo scambiata per sua sorella!* 'Just think, I mistook her for her sister!' Someone comes up to you and inquires: *La disturbo?* and you politely answer *Si figuri!* ('Not at all'). A friend asks you: *Ma pensavi di farlo davvero?* ('Were you really going to do it?'), and you could answer: *Ma no, figurati!* ('What do you think', 'of course not'). *Che cosa voleva?—Figurati cosa poteva volere!* ('What did he want?'—'You can just imagine what he wanted!'). Notice the form *figuriamoci! Nemmeno il Milano poteva battere la Lazio, figuriamoci poi la Salernitana!* ('Not even Milan was able to beat Lazio, so what chance does Salernitana have?') (or 'as for Salernitana . . .', or 'so just imagine what Salernitana could do!').

fila (f). A 'row', 'line'. *Per cinque giorni di fila* means 'for five days running'. A row of trees, bushes, etc., would be *filare* (m). The verb *filare* may be 'to spin' or 'to run, go away', 'to make off' (*Fila!* or *Fila via!* is 'Off with you!'). It can also mean 'to be going steady with someone': *filano da quattro anni*, 'they've been going out together for four years'. Again, regarding an argument or reasoning, it means 'to hold water', e.g. *per un certo verso il ragionamento fila*, 'in a manner of speaking (from one point of view) the argument holds water'. *Un discorso filato* is 'a well-reasoned speech or argument'. Instead of *di fila* you may say *filati* as in *cinque giorni filati*. *Zucchero filato* is 'candy floss'. *Filato* is otherwise 'yarn'; *filato casalingo* is 'homespun yarn'. *Una stella filante* is 'a falling star' or, made of paper, a 'streamer'.

filo (m). 'Wire', the sort made of metal, or 'thread', 'yarn'. *Filo diretto* is 'direct line' (or perhaps 'hot line'). *Per filo e per segno* is 'thoroughly', 'in detail'. *Prendere il treno per un filo* is 'to catch the train by the skin of your teeth'. If *rimane ancora un filo di speranza*, 'there is still a faint hope'. *Parlare con un filo di voce* is 'to speak in a very weak voice'. *Dare del filo da torcere a qualcuno* means 'to lead him a merry dance', 'to give him a lot of trouble', 'to be a hard nut for him to crack'.

finanziere (m). According to context, he may be a 'financier' or a member of the Customs Police Force (with many ordinary police duties in Rome, for example).

finestra (f). Of course, 'window'. I would just remind you that 'shop windows' are something else, i.e. *vetrine* (f pl). The window of a car or in a train is *finestrino* (note that it has turned masculine). The dire alternative, *o mangiar questa minestra o saltar questa finestra*, is 'To choose between the devil and the deep blue sea'.

firma (f). I stress that this is 'signature', the verb 'to sign' being *firmare*. 'A firm' or 'business' is *una ditta*, *un'azienda*. 'Dry land' or 'terra firma' is *terraferma*.

fiscalizzazione (f). There is an occasional hue and cry in the press about this. Simply, firms have to pay *contributi* (*oneri sociali*), i.e. 'social charges' to the State for their employees. In times of difficulty, they find this a big burden and can apply to the State to take over the charge; this is known as *fiscalizzazione*. The trade unions are against this practice, as of course it means putting the onus on the general taxpayer instead of the firms concerned.

fisco (m). The 'Board of Inland Revenue', 'Treasury' or 'Exchequer'. The body responsible for applying the *legislazione* (f) *fiscale* or 'revenue laws'.

fisico (m). This noun may mean 'physicist' or 'physique', 'constitution'. *Lui ha un fisico di ferro*, 'He has a very strong constitution'. 'Physics', the subject, is *fisica*.

foglia (f). 'Leaf', the sort that grows on trees. The masculine counterpart of this word, *foglio*, means 'sheet of paper'. And note that the 'sheet' you put on the bed is *un lenzuolo* (plural *le lenzuola*, f pl. Don't use the m pl form given in dictionaries as an alternative). *Mangiare la foglia* means 'to size up a situation in a flash', 'to smell a rat' (and not really, as several dictionaries state, 'to take the hint', which is, rather, *capire l'antifona*). For example, if a confidence man (*truffatore*) tries to trick someone, and the man in question realizes this, he has *mangiato la foglia*. Similar expressions are *subodorare un inganno* (or just *subodorare* something), i.e. 'to suspect a trick', and *non cascarci*, 'not to fall for it'.

fondo (m). 'Bottom' or 'end' of something. *Il fondo marino* is 'the sea-bed'. *In fondo al corridoio* is 'at the end of the corridor'. *Andare fino in fondo* means 'to get to the bottom of something', 'to see it through to the very end'. If you own a *fondo*, you have a 'farm', while *fondi rustici* means 'landed property'. Of course, *fondo* also means 'fund', as in the *Fondo Monetario Internazionale*. The *fondo cassa* is the 'cash in hand'. *In fondo* is a common expression, giving the idea of 'when all's said and done', 'at heart' or 'fundamentally'. *Ma, in fondo, è una brava ragazza* means 'But she's really a good girl, basically'.

forchettata (f). Derived from *forchetta*, 'fork', this means 'forkful'. Not a very useful or much used word, you might think. But remembering the popularity of spaghetti in Italy, and the eating thereof with a fork, the utility of this word becomes more obvious. The surprising thing is sometimes the amount contained in a forkful. The fork is placed in a small quantity of spaghetti, which is rolled or twirled against the side of the plate (not in the middle!), and the resultant bundle placed in the mouth. It is sometimes said that from start to finish there should be no *soluzione di continuità* (no interruption) between the pasta on the plate and the pasta in the mouth and the tummy (i.e. keep it all going, one forkful after the other, until the platter is clean). This naturally takes long practice.

formaggino (m).   We all know that *formaggio* (French speakers beware of the order of the second and third letters) means 'cheese', but note that *formaggino* is 'processed cheese'.

forza (f).   Strength or force. The point of including this word is to indicate how much it is used in everyday speech to encourage people. At a football match, for example, you may hear the shout, *Forza, Roma!* meaning 'Come on, Rome!' 'Play up, Rome!' And it isn't a word to be merely shouted. You often hear the spoken encouragement being given to people. Notice in this context the use of *su* and *dai* (q.v.). Another point worth mentioning is the use of the expression *per forza*. This means 'have to', 'must', 'necessarily'. *Devo venire questa sera per forza* is 'I *have* to come this evening'. *Lui deve pagare domani, non è vero?* means 'He should pay tomorrow, shouldn't he?' and the answer might be *Sì, per forza, perchè se no, non possiamo partire*, 'Yes, he *must*, otherwise we can't leave'.

Note the expression *a forza di*, 'by dint of': *a forza di pregare ha ottenuto quello che voleva*, 'by asking so much she managed to get what she wanted'. *Gliel'ho fatto capire a forza di schiaffi*, 'I made him understand with the flat of my hand'. *Bella forza!* are ironic words, spoken when someone has made a great show at doing something which really required little effort: 'How clever!', 'That was dead easy!' *Forza pubblica* is the 'police'. *Forza maggiore* is something that tickles me. It is, of course, *force majeure*. I conjure up ideas of earthquakes, acts of war, and suchlike, yet when some Italians apologize for not having kept a promise, for example, adding that it was because of *forza maggiore*, you can bet your boots it was forgetfulness, or the film took longer than he had thought and he didn't have enough time, or some such trivial thing. (See also under **caso**.)

fotografo (m).   Remember to stress the second syllable. And remember, too, that it means the person, 'photographer', not the 'photograph', which is *fotografia* (*fotografia istantanea* is 'snapshot'). 'Camera' is *macchina fotografica*. A 'press photographer' is *fotoreporter*, *fotocronista*. *Un fotoromanzo* is 'a picture-story'.

fregare.   The first meaning of this verb is 'to rub'. However, this is one of those words adopted by the lower strata of society and given the double and contradictory treatment of mystification and diversity of clear meaning. You can pin it down to several clear-cut meanings, yet the adept users of this word will still smile a wicked smile and keep something back from you. *Fregare* can be used in the expression *Me ne frego*, corresponding to the French '*Je m'en fiche*', 'I don't give a damn'. Then, in slang, *fregare* can be 'to pinch, to steal, to knock off'. 'To cheat' is another possibility. *Mi hanno fregato!*—'They've cheated me!' *Mi hanno fregato il libro!*—'My book's been stolen!'

fresco.   Remember that, regarding the temperature, this means 'cool', although otherwise it is usually 'fresh'. However, *vento fresco* is 'strong breeze' (Beaufort Scale 6).

froscio (m).   A homosexual. Sometimes called a *finocchio*, which really means 'fennel'. In some places, one can see the words *potere ai frosci* chalked up on walls ('gay power').

fumetti (m pl).   Strip cartoon. *Un fumetto* can be 'a cartoon' in a paper (a film cartoon is *cartone animato*), or 'a comic' (which is also called *un giornaletto*). Popular cartoon characters are *Paperino* (Donald Duck), *Topolino* (Mickey Mouse), *Braccio di Ferro* (Popeye) and *Pippo* (Goofy).

funzione (f).   'Function', but the important thing is the common use of *in funzione di*, which is not usually 'as a function of'. *Era là in funzione di direttore di lavoro*, 'he was there as works supervisor'. It sometimes means 'depending on'. The verb is *funzionare*, 'to work, operate, function, act'. *Non funziona*, 'It's not working'. *Funziona così*, 'it works like this'.

fuoribordo (m).   An outboard motorboat.

fuoriclasse (adj and m). As an adjective, 'outstanding', 'exceptional'; as a noun, 'ace', 'champion'.

fuoriserie (adj and f).   As an adjective, 'custom-built', 'made to order'; as a noun, 'custom-made car', 'special-bodied car'.

furbo.   This adjective indicates that someone is 'smart', 'crafty', 'clever', 'cunning', 'artful'. *Non fare il furbo* is 'Don't try to be clever'.

fusto (m).   Not a very useful word, this, you'll probably say to yourself. The dictionary says that it means 'barrel, cask'. The colloquial application is otherwise, however. A *fusto* is the sort who likes to show off his muscles to everybody. He'll make a point of wearing a short-sleeved shirt, and an open collar to show the hair on his chest, and he'll stand on a bus even if there's plenty of room to sit, because he wants to hang on the rail and show his biceps and so on. There was a film called *Il Grande Fusto*, 'The Great He-Man'.

G

gamba (f). Leg. In Italian you are not able to 'pull the leg', that is, to use the word 'leg' in the expression that conveys this idea, which is, in fact, *prendere in giro* (i.e. 'to take round'). Notice the very much used expression *in gamba*, which may mean 'in fine form', 'on the ball' (*Oggi mi sento proprio in gamba*, 'I feel in really good form today'), or be used as a compliment, meaning that you know what you're about, that you know how to put things across, that you are really good at your job, etc. *È una ragazza molto in gamba* means, to stretch the translation a bit, 'there are no flies on her', 'she knows her onions'. *Sentirsi in gamba* may also be 'to feel well again' after an illness, 'to be fully recovered'. Note the expressions *correre a gambe levate* ('to run at full speed'), and *darsela a gambe* ('to take to your heels'). I must also mention that if you are wishing to refer to a 'leg of chicken' in a restaurant or shop, forget about *gamba* and give it its right name, *coscia* (literally 'thigh').

gara (f). Match, event, contest, competition. *Una gara femminile* is 'a ladies' event' and *gara maschile* is 'men's event'. In business, *indire una gara* is 'to call for tenders'.

gatto (m). 'Cat'. The she-cat is *gatta*, and *gatta ci cova* means 'there's something fishy going on', 'there's something in the wind'. *Ho altre gatte da pelare* means 'I have other fish to fry', 'I have more important things to see to'. *Mi sono preso una gatta da pelare* means 'I've really let myself in for something'.

gazzella (f). If an animal is intended, it is naturally 'gazelle'. Otherwise it will be a 'Carabinieri patrol car'.

gemelli (m pl). 'Twins', 'cufflinks' or (capitalized) 'Gemini'. The point to notice is that in Italian *gemelli* may also be used where we use 'triplets', 'quads', 'quins' and so on. 'Triplets', for example, are *tre gemelli* or *gemelli nati da un parto trigemino*, 'children born of a birth of triplets', if you could say that.

geniale. Here is another one of the words which can easily be confused. This adjective means 'of genius', 'ingenious', while the English 'genial' is *gioviale, cordiale*.

gentile. 'Kind', 'polite'. *È stato molto gentile da parte tua fare ciò* means 'It was very nice of you to do that'. *Vuoi essere così gentile di chiudere la porta?*—'Would you be so kind as to shut the door?' *Troppo gentile*, 'That's so kind of you'. *Gentilezza* means 'kindness', 'favour'. *Quella donna è d'una gentilezza estrema*, 'that woman is kindness itself'. *Fare una gentilezza a qualcuno* means 'to do someone a favour'. *Fammi la gentilezza di uscire*, 'Would you please go out?' *Per gentilezza* is 'please'.

gergo (m). 'Slang'; *gergo sportivo, professionale* is 'sports, business jargon'. *Gergo della malavita* means 'cant' (i.e. underworld slang). Italian underworld slang is characterized by its regional differences. For example, in Rome 'police' are called *madama*, in Milan *pula*, in Naples *giusta*, in Palermo *brigghio* or *zaffa*, in Venice *pua* or *madama*, in Turin *pola* or *vola*, in Bari *acqua*, in Genoa *vola*, in Aosta *fum*, in Florence *bianca-nera*, in Bologna *questurein* and in Foggia *polenta*. Just to impress on you how difficult it is to understand such talk, here is an extract: *due gratta col violino sottobraccio* (two thieves with submachine-guns under their arms) *sono andati a bombardare una contessa carica di polenta* (went to break open a safe full of gold). *Mentre usavano lo splendor sono arrivate le madame avvertite da un soffia* (As they were using the oxyacetylene flame, up came the police, tipped off by an informer). *Uno s'è dato e l'altro, pizzicato, ha cantato alla belva dove abitava la mina dell'apostolo* (One got away and the other one, arrested, confessed to the chief of the Flying Squad where his accomplice's mistress lived).

gettone (m). Token coin. If you wish to make a phone call, or travel on the *Metropolitana*, you buy a *gettone* (at certain bars and newspaper kiosks, or from machines for that purpose), and use the slotted token in the apparatus. *Gettone di presenza* is 'attendance check'.

già. As you must know, this means 'already'. *Il treno è già arrivato* means 'the train has already arrived'. But you will hear this word a lot more than you might think, as it is very often used to mean 'Yes, that's right'. *Quella ragazza è una civetta irrecuperabile.—Già!* ('That girl's a terrible flirt.'—'Yes, she certainly is', or 'You can say that again'). In this way it is often used double—*Già, già*—to enhance the effect.

giallo (adj and m). As an adjective this means 'yellow', of course. As a noun, however, it refers to a detective story or film, a 'thriller'. *Ho visto un giallo stupendo ieri sera* means 'I saw a wonderful detective film last night'.

giallorossi (m pl). Literally, the 'yellow-reds'. These are the colours of the Rome Football Club, and members of the team are called *i giallorossi*.

ginnasio (m). Watch this false friend. The word means 'secondary school', 'grammar school', 'high school'. The place where you do gymnastic exercises, the English 'gymnasium', is *una palestra*.

girare. To turn, used transitively. *Girare l'angolo* is 'to turn a corner'. Intransitively, it means 'to turn (itself) round'. *Mi gira la testa* means 'My head's in a whirl'. *Lui ha girato abbastanza* gives the idea that 'He's knocked around quite a bit'. The corresponding noun is *un giro*, 'a turn'. *Andare in giro* is 'to go round'. *Stare in giro* means 'to be around'. *Il capo sta in giro* means 'The boss is about'. A *giro* (or *giretto*) often refers to a trip or tour. *Vado a fare un giro per la città* is 'I'm going to have a walk round the town'. *Mio cugino sta facendo un giro in Francia* means 'My cousin is making a tour in France'. On top of all this we have the well-worn phrase *prendere qualcuno in giro*, 'to pull the leg, to take the Mickey'. *Ci sta prendendo in giro* is 'You are pulling our legs'.

The famous *'Tour de France'* is called, in Italian, *Il Giro di Francia*, while the Italian 'tour' is *Il Giro d'Italia*.

giudice popolare (m). *Giudice* means 'judge', but a *giudice popolare* is not one who lets everybody off scot free, enjoying popular acclaim, although he may sound like it. He (or she) is, in point of fact, a 'juryman', 'member of the jury'. I see in today's paper that the *giuria popolare* has been appointed (by drawing lots, i.e. *per sorteggio*) for an important trial due to take place shortly. There are six members, with four reserves (*supplenti*).

giusto. This adjective means 'just', 'fair', 'suitable', 'fit' and 'proper'. You often hear people using it to say 'That's right'. *Sì, è giusto*, 'Yes, it's quite right'. It may also be an adverb, in the following way: *giusto in questo momento*, 'just at this moment'. *Giustissimo* is also frequent, 'absolutely right'.

gomma (f). This is the material 'rubber'; a 'tyre' (also known as *pneumatico* or *copertone*); a 'rubber' or 'eraser' ('ink rubber' is *gomma da inchiostro* and 'pencil rubber' is *gomma da matita*); and last but not least 'chewing gum' (in full, *gomma da masticare*). I would like to go back to the 'tyre' meaning. 'A flat tyre' is *gomma a terra*, and this term sounds rather sinister to some ears. For example, someone parks his car by the roadside (especially a car with foreign plates), and goes off for a time. He returns, climbs in and sets off—only to find he has a flat tyre. Never mind! Here are a couple of helpful fellows waiting to help. Out climbs the driver, in goes the hand of one of the two, out comes the briefcase, and away flee the two thieves (who had of course been responsible for puncturing the tyre while the driver was away).

gommone (m). 'Rubber dinghy' (*canotto pneumatico*).

governante (f). She may be either 'housekeeper' or 'governess', so you have to know what her functions are before you can tell.

grana (f). Colloquially, this means 'trouble', and in slang (but a very common term) it is 'money'. *Grane in vista* means 'trouble ahead'. *Piantare una grana* is 'to cause trouble' (and one who is always causing it is *un* (or *una*) *piantagrane*, i.e. 'a nuisance' or 'a trouble-maker'). *Cercare grane* or *andere in cerca di grane* means 'to look for trouble'. *Quel lavoro gli ha dato un sacco di grane*, 'that work has given him a whole lot of trouble'. *Lei ha un sacco di grana*, 'she's got tons of dough'. *Grana* also means 'Parmesan-type cheese' (*parmigiano*). In this case it is masculine, because it refers to *formaggio*.

granata (f). The Torino F.C. The local 'derby' in Turin is between *Torino* and *Juventus*.

grazie. As pointed out in the case of *per favore* (see **favore**), you can easily overdo using this. English speakers tend to thank a great deal, and the word *grazie* is sometimes out of place in Italian. An unexpected *grazie*, in a shop for example, often receives the comment *grazie a lei* (with the stress on the *lei*). However, if you do use it too much, or rather, more than is normal, you are of course erring on the right side. To qualify *grazie*, you may say *tante grazie, grazie tanto, molte grazie, grazie molto* or *grazie mille*; I personally think *grazie tanto* is the best combination for 'Thank you very much'.

grazioso. This may be 'graceful' (or even 'gracious' in literature), but in ordinary speech it is 'pretty'.

grinta (f). Just to make sure, I've just looked this word up in several different dictionaries, finding that one of them ignores the word altogether, while all the others give let's say the old (and still existent) meaning, i.e. 'grim or sinister countenance', but (with one exception) they make no reference to the modern, wider meaning of a term that originated in sports jargon. The only one of these dictionaries to mention it is an Italian-French one (and the French word given is '*poigne*'). The idea is one of tenacity, resoluteness, doggedness, perseverance, pluck. The adjective is *grintoso*, i.e. 'game, dogged, resolute, determined, tenacious'. *Quella ragazza va a cavallo con molta grinta* would be 'That girl rides very gamely' or 'She is a plucky (or dogged) rider'.

grosso. The general meaning of this adjective is of course 'big'. *Avere il fiato grosso* is 'to be out of breath'. *Un pezzo grosso* is 'a big shot'. *Grosso modo* means 'broadly speaking'. *Un mare grosso* is 'a very rough sea'. *Un grosso guaio* is 'big trouble'. *Questa volta l'hai fatta grossa!* means 'This time you've been and gone and done it!'

grotta (f). Notice the different ending from the English 'grotto'.

guaio (m). A 'mess', a 'spot of bother', 'trouble', a 'difficulty', an 'embarrassing situation'. *Un bel guaio* is 'a nice mess'. *Passare per un brutto guaio* is 'to be in a spot of serious trouble'. *La ragazza è nei guai* is 'the girl's in trouble'. *Ho perso la mia cartella: è un guaio*, 'I've lost my briefcase, so I'm in trouble'. *Ostia ha i suoi guai, ma offre ai Romani la comodità di avere il mare a due passi* ('Ostia has its drawbacks, but it offers Romans the convenience of having the seaside on their doorstep').

guarda, guardi. Without going into all the niceties of the verb *guardare*, note that it is extremely common to start a sentence with this word *Guarda, se lo dici un'altra volta, mi arrabbio*, 'Look, if you say that again, I'll get angry'. Many people use it as a sort of introductory word in their answers, before going on with the answer proper. *Che pensa lei, signora, della situazione politica?—Guardi, la politica non mi interesa affatto*, 'What do you think of the political situation, madam?—Look, I'm not the slightest bit interested in politics'.

guarda un po'. 'Just look' or 'just imagine'. *Guarda un po' quell'uomo*, 'Just look at that man'. *Sapete che Luigi ha lasciato la moglie?—Ma, guarda un po'!* ('Did you know that Luigi has left his wife?—Well, just imagine!'). See also under **poco**.

guasto (m). 'Breakdown, failure'. Lifts, telephones and slot machines which are out of order will have the word *guasto* on a card placed on them. Some of them seem to have one permanently. *Guastafeste* (m or f) means 'spoilsport', 'party bore', etc.

guida (f). 'Guide', in the sense of one who accompanies visitors round the town, and also 'guide book'. *Una scuola (di) guida* is 'a driving school'. *Guidare* is 'to drive'. *Lui non sa guidare* means 'He can't drive'. *La patente di guida* is 'the driving licence'. *Rosanna sta prendendo lezioni di guida* is 'Rosanna is taking driving lessons'. Another thing to note is that *la guida telefonica* is 'the telephone directory', otherwise called the *elenco telefonico*.

I

idraulico (m). A rather high-sounding name, perhaps, for 'plumber'. Otherwise known as the *stagnaio*.

ignorare. Sometimes a misleading word, meaning 'not to know', 'not to realize' as well as 'to ignore'. *Lei non ignorava che lui aveva lasciato Milano in compagnia di Luigi* means 'She was not unaware that he had left Milan together with Luigi'. 'To ignore someone' is more usually *far finta di non vedere qualcuno*.

imbroglio (m). This can be a 'mix-up', 'tangle' or 'scrape', or 'difficulty', but summons up in the minds of most Italians the idea of 'trick' or 'fraud'. The verb is *imbrogliare*, generally meaning 'to swindle', 'to cheat', 'to defraud'. *Imbroglione* is 'trickster', 'cheat'.

imbucare. Don't go getting involved with *andare alla posta con questa lettera* or things like this. Just put the letter in the hole, as they say in Italian. *Vado a imbucare queste lettere* means 'I'm going to post these letters'.

immondizia (f). 'Rubbish', 'refuse' or 'garbage'. 'Garbage' more in the sense of 'what is swept up', rather than 'filth, muck', is *spazzatura* (f). The 'dustman' is the *spazzino*. *Gettò il sasso su un mucchio d'immondizia* would be 'He threw the stone on to a heap of rubbish'.

impegno (m).   If you decide to *assumere un impegno*, you are making a commitment, just as *mancare a un impegno* is 'to fall short of one's commitment' (also *venir meno ai propri impegni*). Other words possible for this idea are 'engagement' and 'undertaking'. If you make a sort of loose arrangement, but leave yourself quite free to back out without letting anyone down, we say that this is done *senza impegno*, i.e. on a non-committal basis, not binding you. On the other hand, if you work or do something *con impegno*, you are doing it with 'zeal', 'care', 'diligence', etc. The adjective, and a very common one, is *impegnativo*. This may indicate that much effort is required (it is 'demanding', 'exacting' or 'difficult'), or perhaps that something is 'binding'. Then we have the verb *impegnare*, or the more usual *impegnarsi*, and special interest attaches to the past participle *impegnato* used adjectivally. *Lui non può venire adesso, perchè è impegnato*, 'he cannot come just now as he is busy'. Or it very frequently means 'committed', 'serious', e.g. *lui è un attore impegnato*; *letteratura impegnata*; *teatro politicamente impegnato*. *I paesi non impegnati* are 'the non-aligned countries'.

impiantistica (f).   Normally, given that electrical, sanitary, air-conditioning, etc. systems or plants are *impianti* (*elettrico, sanitario, dell'aria condizionata*), these—called collectively *impiantistica*—are our 'utilities'. Often, too, the word refers to the construction of such plants, i.e. 'plant engineering'.

impiegato (m).   *Impiegati* are not necessarily always 'employees', who in Italian are strictly speaking *dipendenti*. Nor is every *impiegato* a clerk. 'Office worker' is probably the nearest equivalent. In business administration the category (*classe impiegatizia*) is called 'the white-collar class', sometimes 'clerical grades', as opposed to the 'blue-collar class', which includes *operai* and *manovali* ('workmen' and 'labourers'). The use of *colletti bianchi* and even of *colletti blu* is creeping into the language, but usually in political articles in magazines, not in administrative use.

importare.   *Non importa* means 'It doesn't matter'. *Mi importa un fico secco* means 'I don't care two hoots'. For this last expression we also have *Me ne infischio*, while across the borderline into slang we have *Me ne frego*, from the verb *fregare* (q.v.).

imposta (f).   Until recently there was a multitude of taxes in Italy, but the recent tax reform (*riforma fiscale*) has grouped and simplified things a great deal, and there are now just four major taxes, whose acronyms are the following: IRPEG, IRPEF, ILOR and IVA. IRPEG is *imposta sul reddito delle persone giuridiche* (income tax on corporate entities), IRPEF is *imposta sul reddito delle persone fisiche* (income tax on individuals),

ILOR is *imposta locale sui redditi* (local tax on income) and IVA is *imposta sul valore aggiunto*, i.e. the value-added tax (VAT).

impresario (m).   The only time this may be translated 'impresario' in English is in the sense of a theatre manager. Otherwise we have 'contractor', 'producer', 'undertaker' (*impresario di pompe funebri*), and various 'managers'.

incavolato.   'Angry', 'furious'.

incensurato.   In law, *essere incensurato* means 'to have a clean record'. It is also a noun, as in *è un incensurato*, 'he has a clean record'. The logic is that such things are only usually spoken about when the person in question has, in fact, committed some sort of offence, which makes him therefore a 'first offender'. Such offenders are frequently given a *condanna condizionale* or 'conditional discharge'.

inchiostro (m).   Ink. *Inchiostro di china* is 'Indian ink'—and note that this doesn't mean, literally, 'Chinese ink', as China is *Cina* in Italian, and the corresponding adjective *cinese*.

incidente (m).   The usual word for 'accident' (see **accidente**).

incisivo.   This adjective is quite an 'in' word, in the sense of 'resolute', 'vigorous', 'effective'. *Azione incisiva* is 'vigorous action' (and therefore 'effective'). *Una politica incisiva* is 'a resolute policy'.

indifferente.   When you really don't mind one way or the other, or else you politely wish to convey this impression, this is the word to use. 'Would you rather go to the Fiamma or the Fiammetta?' —'It's all the same to me', *Per me è indifferente*. It does not give the same impression of lack of interest as the English word.

indirizzo (m).   As you will know, this means 'address'. But it is also a fairly frequently used word with the meaning of 'direction', 'trend', 'guidelines' or 'general lines'. *L'indirizzo politico* (e.g. of company) is 'policy'. *Indirizzo produttivo* is 'type of farming' or 'land use'. Note that *indirizzario* means 'mailing list'.

industria (f).   'Industry'—but not always. It is often used to mean a single plant or factory.

ingannare.   To deceive, hoodwink. *Ingannare il tempo* is 'to while away the time'. *L'apprenza inganna* is 'you can't judge by appearances'.

ingorgo (m).   An 'obstruction'. Usually refers to traffic, *ingorgo del traffico* being a 'traffic jam'. *Un ingorgo pauroso* is 'a terrible traffic jam'.

iniezione (f).   Quite straightforward, as a word: 'injection'. I mention it in order to emphasize that as a practice it is extremely widespread in Italy. Injections are prescribed by doctors at the drop of a hat. And suppose you have nobody in the house to give you one? Never mind, ask your *portiera* (concierge) or the lady next door; as likely as not, she will do it for you, or if not, she will know someone who will.

inno (m). Although *inno* is 'hymn', *inno nazionale* is 'national anthem'.

inquadramento (m).   Many trade union claims (*rivendicazioni sindacali*) are about *inquadramento*, i.e. in this sense 'worker classification' or 'staff classification' (*inquadramento del personale*). Collective labour agreements are normally subdivided into two parts, concerning the economic side and the general conditions (*la parte economica* and *la parte normativa*). The economic side deals with payment, based on worker categories, and hence the importance of *inquadramento*. In the military sense, *inquadramento* is 'organization'. Rarely, is it, as several dictionaries state, merely 'division into squares'! Note that 'job classification' is *classificazione del lavoro* (or *classificazione delle posizioni*).

inqualificabile.   I put this adjective in as it is an example of a word that could *almost* be transliterated—'unqualifiable'—but just wouldn't make sense. The usual translation is 'disgraceful', 'despicable', or 'contemptible'.

inquietante.   This adjective does have an (almost) exact counterpart in 'disquieting', although 'worrying' is more usual. But then a problem arises when we have, for example, *una bellezza inquietante*. 'Disquieting'? No, it won't do. It is in fact 'a devastating beauty'.

insaputa (f).   *All'insaputa di qualcuno* is 'without someone's knowledge'. *A mia insaputa* is 'unknown to me', 'without my knowing' or 'behind my back'.

insolazione (f).   The usual meaning of this is 'sunstroke' (also called *colpo di sole*).

insomma.   One of those words put in to prop up a sentence, often with little or no meaning. Something like the English 'anyway'. Actually, the dictionary meanings of 'on the whole' and 'in short' are also often adhered to. *Aveva la piega impeccabile ai calzoni, i guanti bianchi, l'ombrello nella mano, l'aria, insomma, di un uomo distinto*, 'He had impeccably creased trousers, white gloves, an umbrella in his hand, in short, the look of a distinguished gentleman'. *In questo contesto è la parola giusta, insomma*, means 'in this context it's the exact word, in point of fact'. *Sì, è vero, ma non si dice, insomma* is 'Yes, it's true, but you don't say it, you see'. *La parola 'dai' si usa più che altro per incoraggiare qualcuno, insomma per farla fare più sforzi, ecco*, 'The word "dai" is used more than anything else to encourage someone, that's to say to make him try harder, you see'. *Sì, ma, insomma* . . . 'Yes, but, anyway . . .'. *Come vanno le cose? —Be'*, *insomma* . . . 'How're things?'—'Well, you know . . .'.

intendere. This is not the usual word for 'understand' (which is of course *capire*). I wish to stress only the expressions *s'intende* ('of course') and *intendiamoci bene*, 'Now let's get this quite straight', 'Let's put this point quite clearly', 'Don't let's misunderstand each other', 'Mind you, of course . . .'. Remember the past participle is *inteso*.

interessamento (m). 'Interest' in something, or 'concern' for something. If I want something done in an office, and an acquaintance who works there helps me to get it done, I will of course thank him, for his *interessamento*. Not quite 'interest' or 'concern' here. 'Trouble' is probably the best word. At a different level of language, we could also speak of his 'good offices'.

interurbana (f). A long-distance telephone call or 'trunk call'. Much easier in these days of subscriber trunk dialling (STD), i.e. *teleselezione* (f).

intervento (m). Surgically, an 'operation'. As a general political or economic term, often 'intervention', but, referring to specific actions, 'measure' or 'project'. In computer language, again, *intervento manuale* is 'manual control'.

invece. This may be either 'instead of' (when followed by *di*) or 'on the contrary', 'on the other hand'. You will hear it rather more than you might imagine, with the second meaning. For example, *Aveva l'intenzione di venire domani, e invece è venuto oggi* ('He intended to come tomorrow, but he's come today instead'). It often corresponds to the English 'though' at the end of a sentence, or to the word 'actually'. *Dopo aver promesso di fare tante cose, ha invece lasciato l'ufficio senza fare niente*, 'After promising to do so many things, he left the office without actually doing anything'. *Lui dice che è molto urgente; io dico che non c'è urgenza, invece*, 'He says that it's very urgent, but I say there's no hurry, though'. *Bianchi ha giocaio bene. Rossi invece ha giocato molto male*, 'Bianchi played well. Rossi, on the other hand, played very badly'.

investimento (m). Commercially, an 'investment', but out on the road, a 'crash, collision'. *Subire un investimento* is 'to be run into'. *Investire* is the verb in both senses. 'Investment credit' may be translated as *agevolazioni per nuovi investimenti* (literally, 'facilities for fresh investments').

ipotesi (f). 'Hypothesis', naturally, as in *ipotesi di lavoro* ('working hypothesis'), but as often as not it corresponds to 'case'. It is also 'supposition' or 'assumption'. *La vostra ipotesi è inesatta*, 'Your assumption (or supposition) is incorrect'. *Facciamo un'ipotesi*, 'Let's suppose that . . .'. *Nella migliore delle ipotesi*, 'at best'; *nella peggiore delle ipotesi*, 'at worst', or 'if the worst comes to the worst'. *Se, per ipotesi, lui dovessi . . .*, 'Supposing that he should . . .'. Remember to place the accent on the second syllable. This is a common Italian word, believe it or not.

istanza (f).   'Request', 'application', 'petition'. *Tribunale di prima istanza* is 'court of first instance', and *tribunale di seconda, di ultima istanza* is 'court of appeal, of final appeal'. I must also mention that *istanza* is a rather hazy in-word with politicians, meaning especially 'request', but also 'demand, aspiration, impelling necessity'. They try to weave the word into every possible context.

iter (m).   If you put in your bill to a large organization, you cannot expect to be paid the same day. The bill has to follow the established 'iter' (i.e. 'itinerary'), to be authorized, signed, initialled, registered, stamped, stamped again, filed, and all the rest of it. So the *iter* is the established path of action, be it administrative, bureaucratic, judicial, legislative or parliamentary.

IVA (f).   The equivalent of VAT, the value added tax. IVA stands for *imposta sul valore aggiunto*.

L

laboratorio (m).   Not only 'laboratory', but also 'workshop'.

laico.   This adjective (accented on the first syllable) is more often 'secular' than 'lay'. The neologism *laicizzare* means 'to secularize'. *Una scuola laica* is 'a non-denominational school'. Political parties independent of church control are called *partiti laici*. Naturally, when opposition to the church or to religion is very pronounced, *laico* can easily take on the meaning of 'anti-clerical' or 'anti-religious'.

lampadina (f).   This may be a 'small lamp' (diminutive of *lampada*, 'lamp'), or 'torch', but you will find it nearly always means 'electric light bulb'.

lampone (m).   'Raspberry'. Nothing at all to do with *lampo*, which means 'flash' or 'lightning', or 'blitz' as in *guerra lampo*, 'blitzkrieg'. Note that a 'zip fastener' is *chiusura lampo* (and note that the feminine *chiusura* has no effect on *lampo*, which does not change its ending). 'Raspberry' in the sense of a rude noise is *pernacchia* (f).

lanciare. 'To throw'. Other words meaning 'to throw' are *gettare* and *buttare*. More precision and strength is usually implied with *lanciare*, as for example when it is used in sports. When in English there is a particle following 'to throw' (e.g. 'in', 'out', 'up'), the corresponding verbs are *gettare* or *buttare* (the latter far more commonly used colloquially). The noun 'throw' is *lancio* (m). Notice the following names of sports: *lancio del disco, del giavellotto, del martello, del peso* ('discus', 'javelin', 'hammer' and 'putting the shot', respectively). I suppose I had better mention the following words, too, as they are so frequently used these days: *lanciafiamme* (m) 'flamethrower', *lanciamissili* (m) 'missile launching pad', *lanciarazzi* (m) 'rocket-launcher', and *lanciasiluri* (m) 'torpedo-tube'.

largo (adj and m).   A familiar false friend, this adjective, meaning 'wide', as does the French '*large*'. Note the position of *largo* before a measurement, e.g. *il fiume a questo punto è largo 100 metri*, 'at this point the river is 100 metres wide'. The English 'large' is normally *grande*. The noun means variously 'width', 'largo' (in music) and a sort of town square (resembling a *piazza*).

lasciare. 'To leave' or 'to let' (in the sense of 'allow'). Therefore *lasciare* closely follows the meanings of the English 'leave'. *Lascimi stare* is 'Let me be'. *Lasciare stare qualche cosa* means 'leave something alone'. As in many other languages, 'to drop' takes the form of 'to let fall', *lasciare cadere*. *Lasciò cadere il giornale e tornò a passeggiare nel parco*, 'He dropped the paper and went on with his walk in the park'. Note particularly the idiomatic use of *lasciare perdere*, corresponding to the English 'Let it go at that', 'Forget it', 'Don't go on about it', and so on.

lastra (f).   The dictionary tells us that this means 'slab' (of stone), 'plate' (metal), and so on, and also 'plate' in the photographic sense. Extending this meaning, we find it means 'X-ray plate' and by further extension, the 'X-ray [photograph]' itself. *Ho dovuto pagare settanta mila lire per le lastre*, 'I had to pay seventy thousand lire for the X-rays'.

latte (m).   'Milk'. Note that the gender is masculine, as in French as opposed to Spanish (*la leche*). *Latte condensato* is 'condensed milk'. *Latte detergente* is 'cleansing milk'. In the summer, a popular drink in 'bars' is *latte di mandorla*, 'milk of almonds'. *Latte scremato* is 'skimmed milk' (and part-skimmed milk is *latte parzialmente scremato*). Perhaps you think it unnecessary to mention this fact? The point is that in Italy, because traditionally it is supposed to be more healthy, which is of course nonsense, milk with the cream removed actually costs more than the integral product! 'Full cream milk' is *latte intero*. 'Milk Distribution Centre' is *Centrale* (f) *del Latte*.

laurea (f).   Academic degree. 'To take one's degree' is *prendere la* *laurea*, and the reflexive verb *laurearsi* is 'to obtain a degree' (shall we be pessimistic and mention the verb 'to fail one's examination'? It is *essere bocciato*). The general word for passing an exam is *essere promosso*. *L'Università dove si era laureato qualche anno prima* is 'The university where he had obtained his degree a few years earlier'. A *laureando* is one in the final year at university prior to taking his degree. *Un laureato* is 'a university graduate'. *Essere laureato in legge* is 'to have a degree in law'.

lavabo (m). The accent is on the middle syllable. This means 'washbasin', and sometimes also the room where the washbasin is situated. Another word for 'washbasin' is *lavandino*, which however various dictionaries tell us is regional, to be avoided, or a synonym for 'kitchen sink'.

lavaggio (m). 'Washing' (but not the 'laundry' sense of 'washing', which is *bucato* (m)). *Lavaggio a secco* is 'dry cleaning' and *lavaggio del cervello* is 'brainwashing'.

lavanderia (f). 'Laundry'. *Lavanderia a gettone* is 'launderette'.

lavare. 'To wash'. Remember to use the reflexive form when you mean 'to wash yourself', i.e. *lavarsi*. *Mi sono lavate le mani* is 'I washed my hands'. *Lavare i piatti* is 'to wash up'. *Lavare a secco* is 'to dryclean'. Note that 'dishwasher' may be *lavapiatti* or *lavastoviglie* (both masculine). A 'washing machine', on the other hand, is *lavatrice* (and feminine).

lavata (f). 'Wash'. 'To have a good wash' is *darsi una bella lavata*. *Una lavata di capo* means 'a ticking-off'.

lavativo (m). This has three colloquial meanings. First, instead of *clistere* (m), it means 'enema'. Second, referring to one who shirks work it means 'lazybones'. And third, with reference to an unbearable person, it means 'a pain in the neck'.

lavello (m). A very sound, usually very thorough Italian–English dictionary tells us that this word means 'blacksmith's tempering bath'. Not terribly important, one might think. In actual fact, it is quite a common word, meaning 'kitchen sink' (other dictionaries which recognize this word seem to be unsure as to whether the meaning is 'sink' or 'washbasin'. As stated, it is 'sink', a synonym for the more staid and less used *acquaio* (m)).

lavoro subordinato (m) or **lavoro dipendente**. However humble or menial you may think this sounds, it just means 'employment' (i.e. you are in the employ of another person or body).

leggina (f). 'By-law'.

lentiggine (f). 'Freckle'; and the adjective 'freckled' is *lentigginoso*. Quite straightforward in meaning, although certain dictionaries complicate things by giving translations such as 'lentigo' and 'lentiginous'! (Stress the second syllable of *lentiggine*.)

lenzuolo (m. singular, but f. plural, *le lenzuola*). 'Sheet' (the sort you put on the bed). 'A sheet of paper' is *un foglio di carta*.

lettura (f). Not altogether straightforward, as it means 'reading', from the verb *leggere*, 'to read'. 'A lecture', on the other hand, is *una conferenza*.

leva (f). This may mean 'lever' or, figuratively, 'stimulus'. But many young men associate it automatically with military service, as it means 'call-up', 'conscription'. *La leva del 1980* is 'the 1980 call-up', 'the conscripts of 1980'. *Mio figlio è di leva* means 'My son is of call-up age'. The word is particularly in use in Italy where there is still conscription.

libreria (f). A 'bookshop', not to be confused with 'library', which is *biblioteca* (f). It is also used for 'bookcase'.

libro (m). This, of course, means 'book'. I intend to mention only three variations, all coloured. *Libro bianco* is (or rather, should be) the equivalent of our 'white paper'. *Un libro giallo* (or just *un giallo*) is a 'thriller' or 'mystery story'. And *libro nero* is 'black list'. To go back to *libro bianco*, it was originally a public report issued by a parliamentary commission, with government authority, namely a 'white paper'. In recent years, however, individual parties have taken it upon themselves to issue reports on given topics calling them *libri bianchi*. Thus a *libro bianco sul petrolio* issued by the Republican Party would be considered by us as a Republican Party Report on Oil, and not a white paper.

lievitazione (f). Nothing to do with 'levitation', although it does refer to things going up. Namely rising prices. Strictly speaking, it is a good dictionary word for 'rise' in the baking sense, but in point of fact it is nearly always used in the economic sense, *lievitazione dei prezzi*. You might think that *aumento* (m) is a better, more serviceable word; unfortunately, however, *lievitazione* is in fashion.

lift (m). 'Liftboy'. An example of an English word being adopted after part of it has been lopped off. (Our 'lift' in the same sense as the American 'elevator' is *ascensore* (m).) Other examples are *camping* and *night*, meaning 'camping-ground' and 'night club', respectively.

lì lì. 'On the point of', 'just about to'. *La ragazza era lì lì per piangere* means 'The girl was on the verge of tears'.

lingua (f). 'Tongue', meaning both the thing you have in your mouth and 'language'. *Avere qualche cosa sulla punta della lingua*, as you would be right in guessing, is 'to have something on the tip of your tongue'. *Non aver peli sulla lingua* means 'to be very outspoken'. You will probably have read the much-quoted refrain *Lingua toscana in bocca romana*, referring to the 'best' Italian. Well, Italians are not so familiar with this saying as some English books would have us believe, and at any rate they dispute its validity. *Lingua toscana*, yes, but *bocca romana*?

liquidazione (f). This, the dictionary tells you, may be 'clearance sale' (*vendita di liquidazione*), which it is, or the 'winding-up' of a company, or 'liquidation', all equally correct. But mention of this word conjures up another image to the mind of the average Italian. Under Italian law, a *liquidazione* is payable to an employee upon termination of his employment, at the rate of one month's pay for every year worked, and pro rata for shorter periods (based on the highest wage or salary paid during the term of employment). We can therefore call it 'final settlement' or 'severance pay'. I have also seen it referred to as the 'golden handshake', but this is stretching the point somewhat, except for the sometimes monstrously high *liquidazioni* paid to certain *superburocrati* ('high-ranking civil servants').

litigare. 'To quarrel'. This denotes one stage further than *discutere*, which sometimes means 'to argue' and which may involve raised voices, to put it mildly. 'Altercation' or 'quarrel' is *litigio* (m).

logico. 'Logical'. 'And that's logical enough', you'll say. However, you would not normally say 'That's logical' anything like so many times as an Italian says *è logico*. The Italian often uses it to mean 'That's right' or 'Of course'. Quite often the point in question is not at all a logical one, but will be referred to as *logico*, just the same.

lotteria (f). 'Lottery'. As in Spain, Italy runs State lotteries. There are four of them a year, named *Lotteria di Merano, di Monza, di Agnano* and *di Capodanno*, held more or less quarterly. The actual 'draw' is called *l'estrazione* (f).

lottizzazione (f). In urban development, 'lotting', i.e. the division of a development area into lots and providing it with the requisite utilities and infrastructure. The corresponding verb is *lottizzare*. This word is also used in a political sense, *lottizzazione del potere*, indicating the distribution of positions and offices on boards of directors and in particular in *sottogoverno* (q.v.) posts, thereby reflecting the distribution of ministries to the various parties forming the coalition. Thus, *lottizzazione dei posti* is more or less 'allocation of posts or jobs' (based on patronage), or 'jobs for the boys'.

lubrificazione (f). 'Lubrication'. Likewise, *lubrificante* (m) is 'lubricant' (or just plain 'oil'). I include these words to remind you of the extra syllable in the Italian versions.

luce (f). 'Light'. 'To put the light on' is *accendere la luce*, and 'to turn the light off' is *spegnere la luce*. Of a bridge, *luce* is the 'span'.

lucidare. 'To polish', i.e. to make *lucido*, or 'bright'. A 'floor polisher' is *una lucidatrice*; it is quite a common appliance in Italian homes, where there are so many floors of marble and tiling.

lucido. As mentioned above, this means 'bright'. Speaking of the mind, for example, it means 'lucid' or 'clear'. As a noun it means 'polish' (*lucido per le scarpe* is 'shoe-polish'), and also 'tracing'. *Carta lucida* is 'tracing paper'.

lunario (m). 'Almanac'. But I include this word only for the expression *sbarcare il lunario*, meaning 'to make ends meet'.

lunatico. A false friend. This Italian word is an adjective meaning 'moody', 'crotchety', while the English 'lunatic' is *pazzo* or *matto* (q.v.). Note that 'lunatic asylum' is *manicomio*, and the 'lunatic fringe' is *gruppo di estremisti fanatici*.

lungo. Just to point out the position of *lungo*, 'long', before a measurement, and not after it as in English, e.g. *questa strada è lunga 10 chilometri*, 'this road is 10 km long'. Similarly with *alto*, 'high', and *largo*, 'wide'.

lungomare (m). 'Seafront' or 'promenade', in the sense of what you walk or drive along by the sea. A promenade in the sense of 'a stroll' is *una passeggiata*. If the promenade is along the banks of a river it is not a *lungomare* but a *lungofiume*, i.e. *lungo* plus the name of the river. Rome, for instance, has the *Lungotevere*, i.e. the roads and walks along by the River Tiber (*il Tevere*). Similarly, Florence has its *Lungarno* (*lungo l'Arno*). Compare also *lungolago*, the 'lakeside' or 'lakefront'.

lunotto (m). The 'rear window' in a car.

lupo (m). 'Wolf', strictly speaking. Yet the word is far more common than the very small number of wolves left in the country would appear to warrant. This is because an alsatian dog is called *cane lupo*, or just *lupo* for short (the dictionary will give you its more formal denomination, *pastore tedesco*). The words *in bocca al lupo* are said to someone about to take an examination, etc., meaning 'good luck'.

lustro (m). If you know the Latin '*lustrum*', this should give you no difficulty, otherwise you might be mystified by being told that for example someone has been in office for *tre lustri*. This is in fact fifteen years, which means that a *lustro* is a 'five-year period'. Note, *en passant*, that the adjectival 'five-year' as in 'five-year plan' is *quinquennale* (*piano quinquennale*).

M

ma. *Ma* means 'but', of course, but it is used rather more in Italian than is 'but' in English. Apart from the fact that it is so frequently used alone (accompanied by an expressive look and/or gesture), it is also used in the combinations *ma si*, *ma no*, *ma che* (*macchè*)*!*, etc., meaning respectively 'oh, yes, it is', etc.; 'oh no, it's not', 'not at all', 'never', etc.; 'what's all this?', 'you don't say', 'come off it', and so forth.

macchina (f).   'Machine', quite obviously, and referring of course to whatever machine is specifically indicated, such as *macchina da scrivere, da cucire*, etc. ('typewriter', 'sewing machine'). However, *una macchina* will usually refer to 'a car', for which it is the sole normal colloquial word. Note, by the way, that 'camera' is *macchina fotografica*, while the Italian *camera* is 'bedroom', 'room'.

macello (m).   Although dictionaries will tell you truthfully that this means 'slaughterhouse', this is only half the story. Colloquially, in parts of Italy, and especially Rome, *macello* refers to any sort of 'shambles'. *Che macello!* 'What a mess!' 'What a shambles!' This can refer to the shambles someone makes of his work, or the shambles the children make of their play-room, or the shambles the car makes of the drive in wet weather, or the shambles politicians make of negotiations, and so on.

magari.   Why so many dictionaries don't say so I can't imagine, but *magari* has two clear meanings: 'perhaps' and 'if only'. Meaning 'perhaps', it is just about the same as *forse*, the usual dictionary word, while the other meaning is the same as the Spanish '*Ojalà!*', 'If only it were', 'I wish it were', etc. *Cosa faresti se avessi cento milioni lire?* 'What would you do if you had a hundred million lire?' *Magari!* 'I just wish I had!' Coming into contact with the Italian of everyday use after having studied from books outside Italy, this is one of the words most likely to strike you, as it crops up again and again.

magazzino (m).   A false friend. It means 'store', 'large shop', and never the English 'magazine' which you read, which is *rivista* (q.v.) in Italian (sometimes referred to as *rotocalco*, which is really the 'rotogravure printing process', but is extended to mean a product of this process, namely 'illustrated or glossy magazine'). Note that *grandi magazzini* are 'department stores' (the main chains of department stores in Italy being UPIM, Standa, Rinascente and MAS).

maglia (f).   A knitwear garment (apart from being 'stitch' or 'mesh', according to the context). It frequently means therefore 'vest', or the 'shirt' or 'jersey' worn by athletes. *Lavorare a maglia* is 'to knit' (*ago da maglia* is a 'knitting needle' and *fatto a maglia* is 'knitted'). *Maglietta* may be 'jumper' or 'vest', but is perhaps most often 'T-shirt'. *Maglieria* may be 'knitwear', 'knitted garments', or the place where things are knitted, i.e. 'knitwear factory'. *Maglione* (m) may be 'pullover' or (for athletes) 'sweater'. *La maglia gialla*, the 'yellow vest' or 'yellow jersey', is the garment of honour worn by the cyclist leading the field (in overall position, including all stages) in the '*Tour de France*' (*il Giro di Francia*). The leader of the *Giro d'Italia* ('*Tour d'Italie*') wears and is known as *la maglia rosa* ('the pink jersey').

mai. This means 'never', of course, but it is also used in a number of circumstances when it cannot be a translation of 'never', but rather perhaps of 'ever'. *Non è mai troppo tardi*; this is regular and means 'It's never too late'. An expression you hear hundreds of times is *Come mai?* 'However . . . ?' 'How on earth?' *Come mai non ha finito il lavoro?* 'Why on earth haven't you finished the work?' *Ho visto che ha cancellato il suo nome—come mai?* 'I've noticed that you've crossed your name off—why on earth have you done this?'

Mai più means 'never again', as you would expect. *Non si sa mai* is 'You never know', 'You never can tell'. *Mai e poi mai!* is 'never!' uttered with emphasis. *Più (meno) che mai* is 'more (less) than ever'. 'Hardly ever' is *quasi mai*. *Caso mai* is a very frequent combination, meaning 'in case', 'just in case'. *Ti consiglio di prendere l'ombrello, caso mai dovesse piovere*, 'I'd advise you to take an umbrella, in case it rains'. *Non avrai bisogno di niente, ma ti lascio il mio numero di telefono, caso mai*, 'You won't need anything, but I'll leave you my phone number, just in case'.

malavita (f). The 'underworld' of criminals as a general concept, or the 'criminals' themselves (individually *malviventi*). Occasionally referred to as just *la mala*. *La nuova mala* indicates the new class of brutal, aggressive, trigger-happy criminals.

malcostume (m). Either 'immorality' or 'graft, corruption'. Opposed to *buoncostume* (see under **costume**).

male. This can be 'evil' or 'badly', with several variations. Note that *mi fa male* means 'it hurts me'. *Non c'è male* corresponds to our 'not so bad' in answer to the question *come va?* When someone says *sono rimasto male*, he means 'I was disappointed'. *Di male in peggio* means 'from bad to worse'. *Non è male* means 'it's (he's, she's) not bad'. The question *che male c'è?* asks 'what's wrong with it?' (i.e. 'why shouldn't I do it?'). *Meno male* (see under **meno**) means 'just as well', 'thank heavens', and so forth, according to the circumstances.

mamma mia! Whoever in English would exclaim 'My mother!'? In Italian, however, it is a common utterance, in a variety of tones according to the feeling. And Italians are not necessarily content to say it just once. Some people repeat the expression to give added emphasis, or as a further outlet for their feelings.

mammismo (m). Two ideas are involved here. One is the tendency of certain adult men to exaggerate the need for maternal protection. The other is the inclination of certain mothers to interfere too much in the lives and activities of their children even when they are grown up. I will not try to go into the psychological background here, but would just point out that this 'mummyism' is a fairly common phenomenon in Italy.

mancanza (f). *Sentire la mancanza di qualcuno* is 'to miss someone'. *In mancanza di meglio* corresponds to the French *'faute de mieux'*, i.e. 'for want of something better'. At all events, this word indicates the idea of something lacking, as in *mancanza di tempo*, 'lack of time', *mancanza di educazione*, 'bad manners' (that is, 'lack of good manners').

mancare.   You will be aware that the basic meaning of this verb is 'to be lacking'. *Manca uno dei libri* means 'One of the books is missing', for instance. *Ne mancano almeno cinque* means 'At least five are missing', or else 'We are short of five at least'. Another example: *Una notizia che, se non è sensazionale, per lo meno non manca di originalità*, 'Some news which, although perhaps not exactly sensational, is at least not lacking in originality'.

Non ci mancava che questo is the equivalent of 'this is the last straw'. *Venire a mancare* is, in my view, a quaint way of saying 'to die': *Angela è venuta a mancare improvvisamente* means 'Angela suddenly died' (and to make things more complicated still, they sometimes say *venire a mancare all'affetto dei suoi cari*, literally 'come to be lacking to the affection of his/her dear ones').

Notice the construction *mancare poco* which means 'to come near to', 'to have nearly done something'. *Mi manca poco a concludere questo lavoro* means 'I'm very near to finishing this job'. *Poco mancò che fosse licenziato* is 'He came very near to being dismissed'.

In expressions of time, *mancare* usually shows the number of minutes to the hour. *Mancano cinque minuti alle dieci* means 'it's five to ten'; but it may sometimes show the number of hours, etc., yet to go until something happens, e.g. *mancano tre ore alla partenza*, 'they are (or we are, the train is, etc.) leaving in three hours'. *Mancare a un appuntamento* means 'not to turn up for an appointment', and *mancare di parola* means 'not to keep one's promise'. Then, in conclusion, we have the polite answer *ci mancherebbe altro*, meaning 'it's no trouble at all', 'it's a pleasure', and so on. For example, if someone has been at my place and is just leaving, I may well offer to see him to the bus stop (*Ti accompagnerò alla fermata dell'autobus*), whereupon he may answer *ci mancherebbe altro*, i.e. 'oh, no, don't put yourself out'; or he may say something such as *non ti voglio scomodare* or *non c'è bisogno* ('I don't want to disturb you' or 'there's really no need'), thereby giving *me* the cue to say *ci mancherebbe altro* ('oh, it's no trouble', 'it's a pleasure', etc.).

mancia (f).   In a country where tipping is so widespread, this is an essential word. *Una mancia* is 'a tip', in the sense of 'a gratuity', as indicated. Otherwise 'a tip' can be *un consiglio*, 'a piece of advice'.

mannaggia. 'Damn it!' Sometimes with the addition of *la miseria*, i.e. *mannaggia la miseria!* 'Oh, hell!'

mano (f). Need it be pointed out that it is *LA mano?* (plural *le mani*). *Stringere la mano a qualcuno* is 'to shake someone's hand'. *A mano a mano*, or more commonly *man mano*, means 'gradually'. *Man mano che* means 'as' as in *man mano che arrivavano, si sedevano*, 'they sat down as soon as they arrived', or *man mano che i giorni passano*, 'as the days go by'. A person described as *alla mano* is 'easy to get along with', 'cordial', etc. If a place is *fuori mano* it is 'off the beaten track'. In driving, you should of course *tenere la mano* (i.e. drive in the permitted direction), and not go *contro mano* (i.e. in the forbidden direction). In painting (e.g. woodwork, walls, etc.), *una mano* means 'a coat of paint'.

marciapiede (m). 'Pavement'. Note that *pavimento* is 'floor'. A 'parquet floor' is *pavimento a parquet*. *Battere il marciapiede* means 'to walk the streets'.

marinare. In the context of the kitchen, this means 'to pickle', but a schoolboy will tell you that it means 'to play truant', i.e. *marinare la scuola*.

marmellata (f). 'Jam' (the sort you eat). Remember that the English 'marmalade' is much more narrowly defined than the Italian word. Strictly speaking, 'marmalade' is *marmellata d'arance* in Italian. Note also that the traffic type of 'jam' is *ingorgo* (q.v.).

mascalzone (m). 'Scoundrel', 'blackguard'. The 'dirty trick' such a person is likely to play is *una mascalzonata*.

maschio (m). A 'male'. A male child is *un maschio* or *maschietto*, while a baby girl will be referred to as *una femmina* (q.v.) or *femminuccia*. *Maschio* is also an adjective meaning 'male', 'manly' or 'masculine' (but 'masculine' gender is *maschile*).

materia (f). The meaning I wish to stress here is that of 'subject', 'subject matter'. *È stato promosso in tutte le materie* means 'he has passed every subject'.

matto (adj and m). The adjective means 'mad', 'insane'. *Matto da legare* is 'stark, staring mad'. 'To drive someone round the bend' is *far diventare matto qualcuno*. 'A lunatic' is *un matto* (or *un pazzo*). *Andare matto per qualcosa* is 'to be mad about something', i.e. 'to be terribly fond of it'. *Roba da matti!* means 'quite crazy!'

menare. This has the primary meaning of 'to lead', either as in *questo sentiero mena al villaggio*, 'this path leads to the village', or as in *menare una vita tranquilla*, 'to lead a quiet sort of life'.

Two idiomatic uses of this are seen in *menare qualcuno per il naso*, literally 'to lead someone by the nose', meaning more or less 'to lead someone up the garden path' and *menar il can per l'aia*, literally 'to lead the dog about the threshing floor', indicating really 'to beat about the bush', 'not to come to the point'. And here I should point out the difficulty of finding equivalents to idiomatic expressions. As I have just stated, and as dictionaries will (sometimes) tell you, *menar il can per l'aia* means 'to beat about the bush'. But a rider must be added: while the English expression is of very common use, the Italian one is not, and you will meet many an Italian who has never heard of it. So, although they are 'equivalent' expressions in a dictionary sense, they are in fact by no means equivalent in use and context.

Secondarily, *menare* means 'to move swiftly', and by extension 'to lash out' (with hand, foot or tongue). *Menare le mani* is 'to lay about one', *il cane mena la coda* means 'the dog wags its tail'. *Menare un colpo* means 'to land a punch', and *menare calci* means 'to lash out with the feet', 'to land kicks'. By extension again (and this is the meaning perhaps most commonly heard in the Rome area) we have 'to hit', 'to beat up'. *Mo' ti meno* is something one often hears one boy saying to another, i.e. 'Now I'm going to bash you!'

menefreghista (m and f).   Someone who doesn't give a damn. The attitude in question is known as *menefreghismo*. Derived from the verb form *me ne frego*, 'I couldn't care less'.

meno.   There are several expressions using this word. *Più o meno* means 'more or less', and is used as much as English speakers use this expression or Spaniards use '*más o menos*'. *Almeno* or *per lo meno* mean 'at least'. *A meno che ...* means 'unless ...'. *Vengo senz'altro, a meno che non ci sia qualcosa da fare urgentemente* is 'I'll come for sure, unless something has to be done urgently'. *Meno male* is an expression which is used a very great deal meaning 'just as well', 'luckily', 'it's a good job', 'fortunately'. For example: *Piove ancora?—No, ha smesso proprio adesso.—Meno male, perchè non ho portato l'ombrello* ('Is it still raining?'—'No, it's just stopped'.—'A good job too, as I haven't brought an umbrella').

Fare a meno di ... often means 'to do without something'. *Possiamo fare a meno di questo, mi pare* means 'We can do without this, I think'. When something cannot be helped or avoided, once again we have the word *meno*, as in this example: *Non ho potuto fare a meno di sentire quello che dicevate*, 'I couldn't help hearing what you were saying'.

mensa (f).   The meaning you will most frequently come across is that of 'canteen', such as a 'factory canteen'. The Italian *cantina* (q.v.), on the other hand, is usually 'cellar'.

mensilità (f).   A 'monthly payment'. The important thing to note here is the *tredicesima mensilità* (or just *la tredicesima*), which is a payment which employers have to make by law at the end of the year, i.e. in addition to the December salary, another month's salary has to be paid. Being approximately Christmas time, it is sometimes called the 'Christmas bonus'. Several employers also pay a *quattordicesima mensilità* (and even a *quindicesima*, and at the outside a *sedicesima*!).

mente (f). 'Mind'. *Avere in mente una cosa* means 'to intend to do something'. *Venire in mente* means 'to come to mind, to occur to you'. *Mi saltò in mente di fare così* means 'I felt a sudden urge to do it'. *Mente* sometimes refers to the 'master mind' behind an idea, an organization, etc.

meridionale (m and f, and adj). 'Southerner' or 'southern'. Often, unfortunately, used with some degree of condescension, when people from northern Italy refer to those from the south of the country (Sicily, Calabria, Apulia, Basilicata, Campania, etc.). *È un meridionale*, 'he's a southerner'. The opposite is *settentrionale*, but the word is far less used than *meridionale*. The corresponding nouns meaning 'south' and 'north', both masculine, are *meridione* and *settentrione*.

messa (f). There are two distinct meanings of this word: 1) the church mass, and 2) 'placing, putting', etc., used however only in certain expressions, the ten most important of which I would say are the following: *messa a dimora*, 'planting out'; *messa a fuoco*, nothing to do with fire, but 'getting in focus' (also figuratively); *messa in piega*, 'set' (of the hair, after a shampoo); *messa a punto*, with a variety of meanings, the foremost being 'tuning up' (of a motor) and 'outlining of the situation'; *messa a terra*, 'earthing' (in electricity; and note also the use of *massa* to mean 'earth' in electricity); *messa in moto* or *in marcia*, 'starting up' (an engine); *messa in opera*, 'installation'; *messa in orbita*, 'placing in orbit' (a space vehicle, etc.); *messa in scena*, 'mise-en-scène'; and *messa in vendita*, 'putting up for sale'.

Regarding the first meaning, 'mass', as you may know or can otherwise well imagine, an easy mistake for an Italian to make in English is to say 'to go to mess' on Sunday; and I will take the opportunity of pointing out that the word 'mess' in Italian is *pasticcio*, *pizza* or *macello* (q.v.).

messaggero (m). 'Messenger'. The important thing to note is that one of the largest Italian daily papers is the Rome '*Messaggero*'. Thursdays and Sundays are the big days for advertisements, if you are looking for a room or a flat, or want to buy or sell something, and so on.

metà (f). 'Half'. I would point out two things in particular. One, the similarity to the word *meta* (f), meaning 'aim, goal, target' (no written accent and with the stress on the first syllable), and two, that this word is a *noun*, and is not to be confused with *mezzo* (q.v.), which *inter alia* means 'half' as an adjective. So, 'to cut in half' is *tagliare a metà*; 'halfway between Florence and Siena' is *a metà strada fra Firenze e Siena*; 'halfway through the month' is *a metà del mese*; while for example 'a half truth' is *una mezza verità*, and 'a half portion' is *una mezza porzione* (see also under *mezzo*). Note that while in English we say 'my better half', in Italian they say just 'my half', *la mia metà*.

metro (m). This, you know, means a 'metre'. *Metro quadrato* (*cubo*) is 'square (cubic) metre'. And by extension, *un metro* is the 'ruler', etc., used to measure with (for 'tape measure', use *metro a nastro* or perhaps *rotella metrica*). It is also a 'yard-stick', e.g. *non si possono giudicare tutti con lo stesso metro*, 'you can't judge everyone by the same yardstick'. And, finally, it means 'underground (railway)', being the masculine abbrevia-tion of the feminine *metropolitana*. In this case it has a written accent on the last syllable. The Rome *Metropolitana* runs from the Central Station out to Ostia. Actually, only part of its length is under ground, as it traverses a long stretch of open country before coming to the seaside. Work has also been going on for some years to construct a proper city network, now nearing completion.

mettere. Meaning, as you know, 'to put, place', and so on, this verb naturally comes into very common use. Note the past participle *messo*. I would refer to the expressions quoted under *messa*, e.g. *mettere a fuoco*, 'to focus, bring into focus'; the verbal forms are, naturally I think, of more common occur-rence than the noun forms.

mezzo. As mentioned under *metà*, this is the adjective meaning 'half', e.g. *mezzo chilo*, 'half a kilo'; *mezzo libro*, 'half a book'. Adjectivally, it also means 'middle', as in *di mezza età*, 'middle aged'. It is also an adverb, again meaning 'half', as in *mezzo matto*, 'half crazy' and *mezzo chiuso*, 'half closed'. You some-times have to be on the lookout for side meanings, as for example in *mezzo guanto*, which means 'mitten', *mezza stagione*, meaning spring or autumn, and *mezza cartuccia*, which you might think means 'half a cartridge', but which in actual fact means 'person of little importance' (as does *una persona di mezza tacca*).

Mezzo as a noun is not (usually) used in the same way as *metà*. Primarily it means 'middle' (of place or time), as in *nel mezzo della stanza*, 'in the middle of the room'; *nel bel mezzo della festa*, 'right in the middle of the party'. Note that *una via di mezzo* means 'a middle course', 'compromise'. Another com-mon meaning is 'means', as in *mezzi di produzione*, 'means of production', *mezzi di trasporto*, 'means of transport'. *Mezzi di fortuna* are any vehicles used to substitute others in case of need ('makeshift vehicles', etc.). Colloquially, *un mezzo* is sometimes used to mean 'bus', as an abbreviation of *mezzo di trasporto pubblico*. Note, too, that in the plural, *mezzi* can often refer to 'money'. For example, *lui è un uomo con molti mezzi* means 'he is a very well-off person'. *Non ho i mezzi*, 'I haven't the money' (or 'I can't afford it'). Note, in conclusion, the expression *levare di mezzo qualcuno* (*o qualcosa*), 'to get someone (or something) out of the way' (even to the extent of killing the person!). *Levati di mezzo!* 'Get out of the way!'

mezzogiorno (m). This word has two meanings, 'midday' and 'southern Italy'. With the latter meaning it is written with a capital letter. The *Mezzogiorno* is Italy's 'Deep South', with an appreciably lower general standard of living than in the north of the country. In 1950 the government set up the *Cassa per il Mezzogiorno*, the Southern Italian Development Fund, when the south had 37 per cent of the country's population but less than 22 per cent of the national income. The *Cassa*, as it is often called, simply, was the first large-scale, coordinated attempt to redress the north–south balance. Basically the area includes Sicily, Sardinia, Calabria, Apulia, Basilicata, Campania, Abruzzi, Molise and the southern part of Lazio, with odd pockets elsewhere. An inhabitant of the *Mezzogiorno* is a *meridionale* (q.v.), 'southerner', 'southern Italian'.

mica. This is an extremely common little word, used to give the idea of 'not at all', 'not in the slightest', or perhaps just 'not'. *Mica male*, thinks the man as he eyes the good-looking girl going past, 'not bad at all!' *Mica sò sordo*, 'I'm not deaf', says the poor chap, rubbing his ears, after being shouted at unnecessarily. *Non è mica colpa mia*, 'It's not my fault', sighs the girl as she arrives half an hour late. *No, mica!* retorts her boyfriend ('Oh, no!'). The little boy eyes the cherished toy and, looking imploringly at his father, says *non costa mica tanto*, 'it doesn't cost all that much'.

micio (m). 'Cat'. Naturally, the proper dictionary word is *gatto*, but you will find *micio* being used familiarly.

miele (m). 'Honey'. As you have 'honey' in English 'honeymoon', and '*miel*' in French '*lune de miel*', so also in Italian you have *luna di miele*.

miliardo (m). One thousand million. This, we know, is the equivalent of the American 'billion'; and we know, too, that there is some confusion in England as to what a 'billion' means. Of course, traditionally it means 'a million million', which is the meaning of the Italian *bilione*; but in economics, etc., it is these days often used in the American sense, i.e. a thousand million.

militare (m and adj). As a noun, 'soldier'. As an adjective, 'military'. *Fare il militare* is 'to do one's military service' (see also under **naia**). There is nothing so very special about this, but you should remember that the English 'salute' corresponds to the Italian *saluto militare* (because just *saluto* is 'greeting' or 'salutation').

minestra (f). 'Soup', containing rice, spaghetti and/or vegetables. *Minestrone* (m) is also commonly used. Remember that the Italians have several words for 'soup'. There is also *brodo*, which corresponds not to our 'broth', but to our consommé, and there is *zuppa*, the word usually used when the soup is qualified, as, for instance, in 'pea soup', *zuppa di piselli*, or 'fish soup', *zuppa di pesce* (note, however, *zuppa inglese*, 'trifle'). The unfortunate choice *o mangiare questa minestra o saltare questa finestra*, 'either eat this soup or hop out of the window' corresponds to the English 'sink or swim'.

missino (m). A member of the MSI (Movimento Sociale Italiano-Destra Nazionale), referred to in the British press as the 'neofascist party'.

mitomane (m and f). The accent is on the o. The exactly corresponding English word is 'mythomaniac', but the Italian word is used, whereas the English one isn't. In English we tend to say instead 'compulsive liar'. What the person concerned is suffering from is *mitomania*, accented on the next-to-last syllable, 'mythomania'.

mò. Either a shortened form of *modo*, in the combination *a mò di* (e.g. *a mò d'esempio*, 'by way of example'), or a colloquial adverb meaning 'now'. *Mò vediamo* means 'Let's see now', and *mò arriva* 'he's (she's, it's) just coming'.

mobile (m). 'Article of furniture'. The Italian word is an ordinary one with regular singular and plural, *un mobile*, *due mobili* ('one article of furniture, two articles of furniture'). 'Sectional furniture' is *mobili componibili*. The generic word 'furniture' is usually *mobilia* (f). *Mobile* is also an adjective, sometimes meaning 'mobile', sometimes other things (e.g. *la squadra mobile* is 'the Flying Squad', *beni mobili* are 'personal property' or 'personal assets' [as opposed to *beni immobili*, 'real estate'], and 'fickle': all opera-goers know that *La donna è mobile* does NOT mean 'Woman is a piece of furniture'!).

modo (m). 'Way', 'manner'. *Il suo modo di camminare* is 'his (her) way of walking'. *Per modo di dire* means 'in a manner of speaking'. *In questo modo*, *in qualche modo*, *in nessun modo*, mean 'in this way', 'in some way' and 'in no way', respectively. Note especially *in ogni modo*, 'at any rate', 'in any case', 'anyway'. For example: *vengo dopo pranzo, e in ogni modo prima delle cinque*, 'I'll be along after lunch, and at any rate before five'.

modulo (m). In these bureaucratic times, this word (accented on the first syllable) is in very common use, meaning 'form' (the sort you fill in). *Riempire* (or *compilare*) *il modulo* means 'to fill in the form'.

momentaneamente. This may mean either 'at the moment' or, more commonly, 'temporarily'.

mondano. This adjective has nothing to do with prostitution, although *una mondana* does mean 'a prostitute'. It may in fact mean 'worldly', although it is usually connected with fashionable society; *vita mondana* is 'social life' and *una riunione mondana* is 'a fashionable (or society) gathering'.

monocolore. This adjective means 'of one colour, plain-coloured', but it frequently qualifies *governo*, 'government', in which case it means 'one-party'. If there are two parties in coalition, on the other hand, it is called a *governo bicolore*, 'two-party cabinet'.

Montecitorio (m). A building in central Rome originally designed about three centuries ago by Bernini. Since 1870 it has been used as the Chamber of Deputies. Thus in political language *Montecitorio* is used to indicate the Lower House (Parliament), and the members composing it. E.g. *Montecitorio ha approvato il disegno di legge* means 'Parliament has approved the bill'.

montgomery (m). 'Duffel-coat'.

morbido. A false friend. This adjective means 'soft' (and the corresponding noun is *morbidezza*). The English 'morbid' is *morboso* (and likewise 'morbidity' is *morbosità*).

morboso. 'Morbid'. See under **morbido**.

morire (da). If a film, for example, is funny (*divertente*) *da morire*, it is 'terribly funny'. Again: *fa freddo?* ('Is it cold?')—*Sì, da morire!* 'Yes, tremendously cold!'

morte (f). 'Death'. *Morte bianca* is 'fatal accident at work'. According to statistics, there are 45 workers killed in Italy in this way for every 100,000 workers in industry, against 9 in the USA, 13 in France, etc.

morto (adj or m). Note that this is the past participle of *morire*, and that as a noun it means 'dead person'. *Più morto che vivo* means 'more dead than alive'. *Un morto di fame* refers to 'a down-and-out'. *Fare il morto* may be simply 'to pretend to be dead', but it may also be 'to float (on one's back)'. In playing cards, the *morto* is the 'dummy'. *Il giorno dei Morti* is 'All Souls' Day'.

motivo (m). 'Reason'. *Adesso lui ha un motivo di più per fare così* means 'Now he has yet another reason to do that'. *Per quale motivo?* is 'for what reason, on what grounds?' *Dar motivo da credere* means 'to give reason to believe'. Note that the English 'motive' is *movente* (m).

moto (f). Abbreviated form of *motocicletta*, 'motorcycle'. Another word for the same thing is *motociclo*.

motocross (m). A sports term coined from the English 'motorcycle cross-country race'.

motoretta (f). 'Motor scooter'. Also *motorino*.

motorista (m). Beware, this means 'motor mechanic' and not 'motorist', who is *automobilista*. *Motorista di bordo* is 'flight engineer'.

mozzarella (f). A sort of cheese, made in rather shiny white (or whitish) rounded shapes, sometimes (and traditionally) made from buffalo's milk (*mozzarella di bufala*). It is eaten fresh or used in cooking, on pizzas or in rice-balls, for example. It can be drawn out to great lengths, like chewing gum (some people would say that it can't help being drawn out!).

mucchio (m). A physical 'heap', also used figuratively a great deal meaning 'a lot'. *Un mucchio di gente* is 'a whole lot of people'.

municipio (m). This may mean 'municipality', although this is usually *comune*, in the sense of the 'commune' or 'municipal area' and of 'municipal authorities'; and it may—and more usually does—mean 'town hall'.

mutua (f). 'Health insurance scheme'. Also known as *cassa mutua*. A contributor to such a scheme is a *mutuato*. *Il medico della mutua* is 'panel doctor'.

mutuo (m). 'Loan', specifically 'secured loan'. *Mutuo ipotecario* is 'mortgage loan'. *Mutuare* means 'to lend', 'to loan' or 'to borrow'. *Mutuante* is 'lender' and *mutuatario* is 'borrower'.

N

nafta (f). This does not often correspond to the English 'naphtha', but usually means what is burnt in the central heating system (i.e. 'fuel oil') or in a vehicle that runs on 'diesel oil'. A system that is *a nafta* is 'oil-fired'.

naia (f). The commonness of this piece of army slang persuades me to include it. It means 'military service', 'national service'. *Essere sotto la naia* means 'to be doing one's national service'. Strictly speaking, *naia* refers to 'army discipline', but the idea that comes first to mind is the extended meaning of the period of service spent *sotto le armi* ('in the forces').

nascere. 'To be born'. I mention this to remind you that while in English we say 'I was born', in Italian they say *sono nato* (i.e. 'I am born'). For example, *lei è nata il 6 giugno 1932*, 'she was born on 6th June 1932'. 'Date of birth' is *data di nascita*, while 'birthday' is *compleanno* (m).

nascita (f). As stated above, *data di nascita* is 'date of birth', just as *luogo di nascita* is 'birthplace' and, for example, *controllo* *delle nascite* is 'birth control'. When, however, we come to 'birth-rate', the word to use is *natalità* (q.v.). The law says that births have to be registered in Italy within ten days of the event, the requisite 'declaration' being called *la denuncia della nascita* (no, it does not mean 'denouncing' it, just 'reporting' it). The parents will then be issued with a *certificato (atto) di nascita*, 'birth certificate'.

nascondino (m). The game of 'hide-and-seek'. 'To play hide-and-seek' is *giocare a nascondino*. An ordinary 'hiding place' (or 'hideout') is *nascondiglio*.

naso (m). 'Nose'. Small, turned-up and snub noses are called *nasi all'insù*. Quite straightforward, *ficcare il naso in qualcosa* means 'to stick one's nose into something'. I am very fond of the expression *a lume di naso*, meaning 'by instinct', 'by guesswork'. *Giudicare (andare) a lume di naso* (or simply *a naso*) means 'to judge (go) by instinct'. *Rimanere con un palmo* (or *un tanto*) *di naso* means 'to feel one has been done'. See also under **menare**.

natalità (f). 'Birth-rate'. Officially, the full term is *quoziente* (f) *di natalità*, while one usually finds *indice* (m) *di natalità* used in books and papers, or just *natalità*. The opposite is *quoziente* (or *indice) di mortalità*, or just *mortalità*, 'death-rate'.

nazionale. *La nazionale* is the 'national team' (feminine because 'team', *squadra*, is feminine), while each of the players in it is *un nazionale*, i.e. international player. *Un nazionale di calcio* is 'an international footballer'. You note that while we refer to 'internationals' (since membership of a country's national team implies playing internationally), Italians use 'nationals', *nazionali* (or more frequently *azzurri* [see under **azzurro**]).

ndr. These letters (in brackets) are often to be read in newspaper articles, and may mystify us. They mean *nota della redazione* and are the equivalent of 'editor's note'.

ne. You should get it quite straight that while *ci* gives the basic idea of 'there' (place you are going to), as in *Ci vado domani*, 'I'm going there tomorrow', *ne* gives the idea of 'from here' or 'from there'. *Me ne vado* is 'I'm going' (from here, of course). You say *Vattene via* to order someone to 'Go away'. Note the use of both *ci* and *ne* in the following: *Ci sono stato l'anno scorso, per un mese. Ne sono partito solo quando non avevo più soldi* ('I was there last year for a month. I didn't leave until I had run out of money')

Naturally, this is just one of the uses of *ne*. It is very important to practise its use meaning 'of' (or 'about') him (or her, or them, or it, or this, or that), or again as the partitive ('some', or 'any' or 'none' in negative expressions). Just a few examples: *Non ne voglio sapere*, 'I don't want to know about it'; *ne ho letto le prime cinque pagine*, 'I've read the first five pages of it'; *ne ho sentito parlare*, 'I've heard about him' (or 'her', etc.); *ne sono certo*, 'I'm sure of it'; *ne ho tre*, 'I have three of them'; *non ne ho*, 'I haven't any of them' (or 'of it'), or 'I have none of them' (or 'of it').

Remember also that the same word with a written accent, *nè*, means 'neither' or 'nor'. The construction *nè . . . nè . . .* means 'neither . . . nor . . .'.

neanche. 'Neither', 'nor', or 'not . . . either'. *Non ho una lira—Neanche io*, 'I haven't a penny'—'Neither have I'. *Non lo farò, e lei neanche*, 'I won't do it, and she won't either'. *Neanche per sogno*, means 'not on your life'. *Neanche* may also mean 'even' to strengthen a negative, as in: *non ho neanche una lira*, 'I haven't even a penny'; *lui non sa neanche leggere*, 'he doesn't even know how to read'. Instead of *neanche*, *nemmeno* may be used in every sense, while *neppure* is used with the meaning of 'neither, nor' or to mean 'not even', but not usually with *sogno*.

negozio (m). Most dictionaries tell you that this means 'business', first and foremost, but the fact of the matter is that it is the usual word for 'shop'. 'Shopkeepers' are *negozianti*. 'Business' that is carried on is usually *affari* (m pl), or *commercio* (m), and it is *azienda* (f) when 'firm' or 'concern' is meant. A 'bargain' is usually *affare* (q.v.).

nero. 'Black', but not always. The Englishman tends to understate, the Italian to overstate, so when the Italian says *occhi neri*, for example, they are probably less than black, whereas our 'brown eyes' are very likely deep brown, and the same colour as the Italian has in mind. Again, *pane nero* is 'brown bread'. Both languages agree however over *borsa nera*, 'black market' and *pecora nera*, 'black sheep'. *Bestia nera* is 'bugbear' or the French '*bête noire*'. Note that the English 'black eye' is also *occhio nero* in Italian (or *occhio pesto*).

neroazzurri (m pl). *I neroazzurri* are the Juventus F.C., the Inter of Milan. These players are otherwise called *i juventini*.

netturbino (m). One who works for the municipal street cleaning and rubbish collection department. Aha! someone will say, you mean *spazzino*. Well, opinions vary somewhat as to the difference, if any, between *netturbino* and *spazzino*. Those who do make a difference, as I do, point out that *netturbino* is the equivalent of our 'dustman' and *spazzino* of our 'street sweeper'. The *spazzino* has his little *carrello* ('handcart') and the dustman goes round on the *camione* (m) *della Nettezza Urbana* (the *Nettezza Urbana* being the relevant department). The 'rubbish' collected is called *immondizia* (or the plural form, *le immondizie*) (q.v.). *Spazzatura* is another word for 'rubbish'.

neuro (f). This word is feminine because it refers to *clinica* (*di malattie nervose e mentali*), i.e. 'hospital for nervous and mental diseases'. In point of fact, *neuro* is an abbreviation of the old name of *clinica di neurologia e di psichiatria* ('hospital of neurology and psychiatry'). One section is called *la neurodeliri*, where those in the last stages of alcoholism or those liable to be a danger to themselves and others are placed. You will not find *la neuro* in any dictionary, but you will quite commonly come across it in newspapers.

niente. There are a few expressions to be emphasized here. *Non c'è niente da fare* means 'There's nothing that can be done'. (More about this later.) *Di niente* is the polite answer to give when someone thanks you (or even more commonly just *Niente*). *Grazie mille.—Di niente* ('Thank you very much'.— 'Don't mention it'). Or: *Grazie.—Niente!* ('Thanks'—'You're welcome'). Instead you could of course use *prego* (q.v.). *Non fa niente* means 'It doesn't matter', 'It's quite all right'. *Non sa nuotare per niente* shows the use of *per niente* to stress the negative. In this case the meaning is: 'He can't swim for toffee', 'He hasn't got the first idea of how to swim'. *Lei non è intelligente per niente* means 'She isn't at all intelligent'.

Niente da fare, as indicated, means 'There's nothing you can do', 'There's nothing that can be done' and so on. Said perhaps with a shrug of the shoulders. If you ask a taxi-driver to get you somewhere quickly in the rush hour, avoiding the traffic, he'll probably do his best, but he'll not be able to avoid all the jams, and apart from his curses he'll tell you *Non c'è niente da fare*. This is one of the two vocabulary indications of acceptance of things as they are. The other one, the more submissive one, is the often-used *pazienza* (q.v.). Both expressions give an idea of one's being unable to change things, however wrong they may be. After a long wait in the queue at the registry office (*anagrafe*), for example, a man might be told that he had all his documents in order except for one signature on the last birth certificate, perhaps ten years old. And without this, the clerk will explain, *Non c'è niente da fare. Ci vuole assolutamente la firma* ('It's indispensable to have the signature'). And the poor chap, not being able to claim family allowances yet, may well collect up his papers and make off, muttering *Pazienza!*

An expression in common use is *non serve a niente*, 'it's no use'. Another one is *fare finta di niente*, which means 'to pretend not to know' (or not to have seen, not to have heard, not to be put out, or that nothing is up, that one is not doing anything in particular, etc.). The idea of pretence is also sometimes conveyed in the words *come se niente fosse accaduto*, 'as though nothing had happened'; on the other hand, without the last word, i.e. just *come se niente fosse*, it means 'with the greatest of ease' (often used jokingly or ironically). For example: *Ho una fame! Potrei mangiare un abbacchio intero, come se niente fosse!* ('I'm mighty hungry! I could eat a whole lamb, as easy as anything!'); or: *lui è capace di correre cinque chilometri in un quarto d'ora, come se niente fosse*, 'He's able to run five kilometres in a quarter of an hour, as easy as pie'). You could also use *come niente* in the same sense. You often hear the encouraging advice, *niente paura!* 'never fear!', 'don't worry', and so on. And another combination you frequently hear is *un bel niente*, 'nothing at all'. For example, *è qui da sei mesi, ma non ha ancora imparato un bel niente!*, 'he's been here six months, but he hasn't learnt a single thing yet!'

night (m).   Another English word used in everyday Italian, albeit incorrectly. It means 'night club', but the 'club' part is omitted. *Il proprietario di un night* is 'the owner of a night club'.

nipote (m and f).   The article will of course tell you whether 'nephew' or 'niece' is possibly intended, and it is all the easier if the diminutive is used, too, i.e. *il nipotino, la nipotina*. But whether the reference is to a nephew or niece, on the one hand, or to a grandchild, on the other, you just cannot tell from the word. You can only find out from the context, or by directly asking. Thus, for example, *la mia nipotina* might be either 'my niece' or 'my granddaughter'.

noia (f).   Usually, *la noia* is 'boredom'. *Che noia!* is 'What a bore!' or 'What a nuisance!' Likewise, *noioso* is 'boring'. *È una persona molto noiosa* is 'he's a very boring person'. However, there is no hard and fast dividing line between 'bore' and 'annoy', and we could also add 'bother', 'trouble', for good measure. I would say that the English words have a clearer distinction one from another than the corresponding Italian words, which are *scocciare, seccare* and *infastidire (dare fastidio a)*, apart from *annoiare*. As stated, *annoiare* generally conjures up the idea of boredom, and *mi annoio*, for example, means 'I feel bored'. *Seccare* and *scocciare* vary according to the context, tone of voice, etc., from 'bore' and 'bother' to 'annoy' (but tending more towards 'bother' and 'annoy'). *Infastidire* is certainly 'to annoy' more than anything else, and *dare fastidio* is 'to be a nuisance', 'to annoy'. *È molto fastidioso* means 'it's very annoying' or 'he's a great nuisance' (see also **fastidio, scocciare, seccare** and **stufo**).

non so.   As you know, this means 'I don't know'. Rather elementary, you'll no doubt be thinking. Are you one of those people who are always putting in 'I don't know' in English sentences? Many speakers of all languages do this, you know, usually not realizing it and certainly hardly ever willing to recognize the fact. Well, in Italian you'll often hear *non so* said. Sometimes at the beginning of, sometimes inside and sometimes at the end of sentences. It's one of those 'prop' expressions, to support an unbalanced sentence, to put an end to an unfinished one, to let you out of finding the *mot juste*, or even a fairly suitable word or expression. In Italian, the users of *non so* are usually those who use also *come si chiama?* and *coso* (q.v.). 'I don't know—what d'you call it?—what's its name?' and so on.

norma (f).   Italian has the words *norma, regola* and *regolazione*, and in English we have 'norm', 'rule' and 'regulation', but they do not correspond exactly, by a long chalk. The Italian *norma* is certainly far more common than is 'norm'. Technical standards or specifications, for example, are *norme*, as are instructions or directions for use (*norme per l'uso*); 'currency regulations' are *norme valutarie*, and international flight rules are *norme per il volo* (*a vista*, i.e. 'visual' and *strumentali*, 'instrumental'), while *le norme vigenti* are 'the regulations in force'. *Seguire le norme* (or *attenersi alle norme*) is 'to act according to the rules' (the opposite of *trasgredire le norme*, 'to break the rules').

normativo. 'Normative' in the sense of prescribing rules and regulations, as in *grammatica normativa* (as opposed to 'descriptive grammar', *grammatica descrittiva*), and in the sense of containing specific regulations, which are legally binding, as in *accordi normativi*, which are agreements on conditions and qualifications for engagement, holidays, shifts, working hours, promotion, etc., in a 'collective agreement' (*contratto collettivo di lavoro*). That is, 'general conditions'.

notabile (m). A 'prominent person', but not *any* prominent person. A *notabile* is one with sufficient personal authority, influence, patronage, etc., to warrant special consideration and treatment. You can't go pushing him around. He is a *pezzo grosso*, a 'VIP'. Probably a politician.

notorio. The English adjective 'notorious', we know, has come to be used in a bad sense, corresponding to the Italian *famigerato* or *tristemente noto*. The Italian word *notorio*, however, retains its original meaning of *noto*, i.e. 'well-known'. 'Famous' is *famoso* or *celebre* (stress on first syllable). *Notorietà* (f) may therefore be either 'fame' or 'notoriety', according to the case.

novecento. As an adjective, this means 'nine hundred'; but as a noun (capitalized) it means 'the twentieth century'. Mind you, if you use the word *secolo*, 'century', with a number, the same pattern as in English applies, i.e. in this case *il ventesimo secolo*. The other system is used, and is the normal system, for the thirteenth century onwards, e.g. *il Duecento, il Trecento*, etc. When turning the Italian century to the English one, add eleven to the first digit, e.g. *il Quattrocento*, 4 plus 11 equals 15, hence 'fifteenth century'. The corresponding adjective to *il Novecento* is *novecentesco*, 'twentieth-century', 'relating to the twentieth century'. The same form exists for the other centuries, too. For example, the compound adjective 'fifteenth-century' is *quattrocentesco*.

novella (f). Not a 'novel' (which is *romanzo*), but a 'short story'.

numero (m). 'Number'. But also 'size' for clothing and shoes. *Il mio numero di scarpe* is 'my size in shoes'. The colloquial *dare i numeri* means 'to be off one's head', 'to be round the bend'.

O

occasione (f). Sometimes 'occasion', but quite as often 'opportunity' or 'chance'; for instance, *dare occasione a qualcuno di fare qualcosa* means 'to give someone the opportunity to do something'. *D'occasione* may be 'secondhand' or 'bargain' (and 'a real bargain' may be *un'occasione*, *una vera occasione*, just as it may also be *un buon affare*). The adjective *occasionale* may be 'chance' in the sense of 'fortuitous' or 'occasional', and in like manner *occasionalmente* may be either 'by chance' or else 'occasionally', 'now and then'.

occorrere. Surprisingly, this verb means 'to be necessary', 'to be required', while the verb 'to occur' is *succedere* or *accadere*. If you say enough to make your point, you might well comment *non occorre aggiungere altro* (as you could equally well say *non c'è bisogno di aggiungere altro*), 'there's no need to add any more'. *Occorre farlo* is 'it has to be done'. *Occorre un bel po' di tempo* means 'quite a long time is necessary'. *Mi occorrono mille lire* is 'I need a thousand lire'. Notice also *all'occorrenza*, 'in case of need', 'if need be'.

odg (m). 'Agenda', in the sense of the list of subjects for discussion. The abbreviation is for *ordine del giorno*.

o dio! A very commonly heard exclamation. *O dio, che cosa ho fatto?* 'Good Lord, what have I done?' It corresponds to 'Good heavens', 'My goodness', and so on. Sometimes you hear quite a string of them, *o dio, o dio*, etc. Then, in another sense it can be used in quite unexcited tones with more or less the meaning of 'I mean to say', as in *Sicuramente lui non ha fatto questo. O dio, non voglio dire che sia un santo, ma . . .*, 'It's quite certain he didn't do this. I mean to say, one can't claim he's a saint, but . . .'.

offendere. Most commonly, this means 'to insult', 'to be offensive to', 'to give offence', etc. *Non voglio offendervi, ma . . .* means 'No offence meant, but . . .'. Reflexively, *offendersi*, is 'to take offence', 'to take umbrage'. The noun, *offesa* (f), means 'insult', 'affront', 'offence'. The past participle of *offendere* is *offeso*, 'insulted', etc. In some parts of Italy, in particular, certain words and actions may (intentionally or even unwittingly) give offence to the extent of causing the one who feels *offeso* to harbour thoughts of vendetta.

officina (f). Not 'office' (which is *ufficio*) but 'workshop'.

oggigiorno. You know that *oggi* means 'today', and that 'giorno' means 'day'. Together as a single word the meaning is 'nowadays' (more common than the synonym *oggidì*).

olio (m). 'Oil', but not 'crude oil', which is *petrolio* or *grezzo* (literally, 'petroleum' and 'crude oil'). The basis of Italian cooking, of course, is olive oil, and this is *olio d'oliva* (and those who know will use *olio d'oliva vergine*, or even better, *olio d'oliva extravergine*, instead of the ordinary common or garden *olio d'oliva*). The word *vergine*, 'virgin', is stressed on the first syllable.

oliva (f). 'Olive' (the fruit). For 'olive oil', see above. An 'olive tree' is *olivo*—it is the rule, of course, that the tree in Italian has the same name as the fruit, apart from the fact that the fruit normally ends in *a*, while the tree ends in *o*. For example, *mela* is 'apple' while *melo* is 'apple tree'.

oltranza. Used only in the expression *ad* (or *a*) *oltranza*, properly meaning 'to the bitter end'. However, I have known strikes, for example, claimed to be *ad oltranza*, which have lasted only an hour or two, without necessarily gaining their objectives. This is something like when the busy waiter, passing your table, calls out *subito* in answer to your request to place your order. Your dictionary might tell you this means 'immediately', 'at once', but experience will tell you that it is a word bandied about to stem people's impatience, and may actually mean half an hour, or even more. On this subject, I must also mention *andare fino in fondo*, 'to get to the very bottom of things'. Scandals might break out, and politicians might (and will) thunder *andremo fino in fondo* ('we'll leave no stone unturned!' . . . etc.); but we know very well that this *fondo* is not very deep and that the question will soon be forgotten about (or rather 'shelved').

oltre. You will know that as an adverb of place this means 'further' and of time it means 'longer', while as a preposition it may mean *al di là di*, i.e. 'beyond', *più di*, i.e. 'more than', or—followed by *a*—'besides' or 'apart from'. I want to mention a number of words combined with *oltre*, which forms the first element in them. We have *oltremanica*, for instance. Where is France from the English point-of-view (and England from the French point-of-view)? *Oltremanica*, 'the other side of the Channel' ('the Channel' being 'la Manica'—with the accent on the first syllable). *Oltremare* likewise is 'overseas'. *L'oltre-tomba* (m) means 'the hereafter', 'the beyond'. Other geographical names tacked on to *oltre*, are seen in *oltralpe* (dropping the e), 'the other side of the Alps', *oltrarno* (m), 'the part of Florence the other side of the Arno', *oltrepò*, 'the land immediately beyond the Po'. In Rome, the word meaning 'the part the other side of the Tiber' is *Trastevere*, where the *Trasteverini* live (and remember to stress *il Tevere*, 'the Tiber', on the first syllable). What, then, can *oltretevere* mean? Now, what else is there on 'the other side of the Tiber'? Oh, yes, the Vatican, of course! So, instructions from *oltretevere* denote orders from that source.

omaggio (m). The definition of 'homage' doesn't go very far towards helping us here. You will see the word quite often, for example, on a weekly magazine cover. *Omaggio* is in fact used to mean 'free gift', and on the magazine cover it corresponds to our 'free gift inside'. A book presented to someone by the author will have the words *omaggio dell'autore* written inside, 'with the author's compliments'. *Copia in omaggio* is 'complimentary copy'. The plural form of the word is very common, meaning 'respects' or 'compliments'. *I miei omaggi a sua signora*, for example, means '(please give) my respects to your wife' (you could also use *ossequi* or *rispetti*).

opportunità (f). This means 1) the opportune nature of something, i.e. its 'advisability', 'appropriateness', 'expediency', or 2) a favourable occasion, namely 'opportunity'. The adjective *opportuno* may well be 'opportune', or 'advisable', 'suitable', perhaps 'best'.

oppure. An alternative to just saying *o*, 'or', 'or else' (and sometimes 'otherwise'). At times such a short word as *o* seems inadequate, as we also feel in English with the word 'or' in some circumstances, because we often tack on the word 'else' to help out. So in Italian we have *oppure* instead of *o*, as in *Vengo alle cinque; oppure se non vengo allora, vengo alle nove, dopo cena*, 'I'll come at five. Or if I don't come then, I'll come at nine, after supper'. *Vuole del vino oppure della birra?* 'Would you like some wine or some beer?' Remember the difference from *eppure* (q.v.), which means '(and) yet'.

ora (f and adverb). This is the word to use, for example, in 'it's time to go now' (*è ora di andare adesso*). With emphasis, it can also mean 'and about time, too!' as in *era ora!* If you wish to say 'about an hour' instead of 'one hour', why not use *un'oretta*, rather than *circa un'ora*? *Le ore piccole* are 'the small hours', as you would expect them to be. *Fare le ore piccole* means 'to stay up half the night'. *Non vedere l'ora di . . .* is 'to be itching (etc.) to . . .'; e.g. *non vedo l'ora di partire*, 'I just can't wait to start'. *Di buon'ora* means 'early'. (But *alla buon'ora!* means 'at last!') *Ora legale* is the common way of saying what could otherwise be called *ora estiva*, 'summer time' (and perhaps also 'daylight saving time').

In the adverbial sense, notice first the difference between *fino ad ora*, meaning 'so far', and *fin d'ora*, meaning 'already', 'in advance' (as in the commercial expression *ringraziandovi fin d'ora*, 'thanking you in advance'). *D'ora in poi* is 'from now on'. Doubled, but dropping one *a*, i.e. *or ora*, it may mean 'just a moment ago' or 'in just a moment', according to the sense. For example, *l'ho visto or ora* is obviously 'I've only just seen him' or 'I saw him just a moment ago', while *te lo faccio vedere or ora* is 'I'll let you see it in half a moment'.

orario (m and adj). As an adjective, note its use in *fuso orario*, *segnale orario* and (*in*) *senso orario* ('time-zone', 'time-signal' and 'clockwise', respectively); otherwise its meaning is 'hourly' as in *velocità oraria*, 'speed per hour', far more commonly rendered by *velocità all'ora*. Regarding the noun, many people seem to learn that it means 'time-table', which is true enough, and then try to apply this meaning in every circumstance, which cannot always be done. *Orario d'ufficio*, for instance, means 'office hours'. *Essere* (*arrivare*) *in orario* is 'to be (to arrive) on time (or punctually)'.

orbita (f). 'Orbit', naturally. *Mettere in orbita* is the modern verb 'to put in orbit'. But when a friend of mine used to say of someone that *è in orbita*, he meant that he was 'well away', i.e. 'tight'.

ordinario (adj and m). Be a little careful in using this adjective, as it may mean 'common', even 'cheap', as in *un tessuto ordinario*, 'a cheap sort of cloth' (not cheap in price but in quality). Otherwise it corresponds to the English 'ordinary', 'normal' or 'average'. As a noun it usually refers to *professore ordinario*, 'university professor'.

ordine (m). About this word, I want just to point out its use meaning 'nature' as in *problemi d'ordine morale*, 'problems of a moral nature' (viz. 'moral problems'); in the expression *di prim'ordine*, 'first-rate'; and with the meaning of 'with regard to' in *in ordine a*.

orecchio (m). 'Ear', used in many expressions in which we use 'ear' in English, too; e.g. *sono tutto orecchi*, 'I'm all ears'; *entrare da un orecchio e uscire dall'altro*, 'to go in one ear and out the other'. Notice the expression *fare orecchi da mercante*, 'to pretend not to hear', 'to turn a deaf ear'.

orecchioni (m pl). The popular name for the scientific *parotite* (f), 'mumps'.

orfano (m). 'Orphan', female *orfana* (accent on first syllable). *Lei rimase orfana a sette anni* means 'she was orphaned at the age of seven'. I include this word only to point out its usage in Italian, meaning only half an orphan in the English sense, i.e. *orfano di madre, di padre* (where in English we say 'motherless' and 'fatherless', respectively). 'Orphanage' is *orfanotrofio* (accented on the next-to-last syllable).

organico (m). This noun means 'staff', 'personnel'. As an adjective it is quite regular, 'organic'.

oriundo (adj and m). The adjective, referring to Italy, means 'of Italian extraction'. *Essere oriundo di Sicilia* is 'to be of Sicilian extraction'. In sport, *un oriundo* is a foreign player (especially footballer) of Italian extraction, therefore eligible to play in league games.

ormai   (Sometimes *oramai*).   Years ago, a lady of my acquaintance, who knew very passable Italian, frequently asked me to explain to her the meaning of this word. I would tell her that it usually means 'now' or 'by now', as in *è troppo tarde ormai*, 'it's too late now', or *saranno arrivati ormai*, 'they'll have arrived by now'; but that it can also mean 'then', 'by then', when reference is made to the past, as in *era troppo tarde ormai*, 'it was too late by then'. I would add that it might also give the idea of 'almost', as in *ormai è finito*, 'it's nearly over now'. But she would not have it. 'There's something more to it,' she would say. 'You're holding out on me.' And she was right, there *is* more to it. This very common little Italian word is often used as a whole sentence, and an expressive one, in itself. To quote a few circumstances: the boy has been waiting for the girl to turn up for over an hour. The film they had decided to see has already started. Eventually she arrives. 'I'm dreadfully sorry I'm late,' she apologizes, 'but please just wait another minute or two. I have to make a quick phone call.' With a grimace, the boy says: *Va bene. Ormai!* (perhaps *Tanto, ormai*). Meaning, of course, 'oh, go ahead! After all, just another minute or two after all this time, what's the difference?' (need I stress the ironic tone?). Again: the husband arrives home and smells burnt food. With trepidation, he enters the kitchen. His wife smiles sheepishly, holding a charred piece of meat in her hand. 'I've . . .' she starts to explain, only to cut her words short as she drops the meat on the floor. 'Oh, dear,' she exclaims, 'I'm so sorry! . . .'. *Non fa niente*, her husband answers quietly, *ormai* . . . (insinuating 'it's ruined already, what does it matter at this stage?'). 'Yes,' the lady mentioned at the beginning (by now, let us say, an extremely proficient speaker—and understander—of Italian) might well say, 'very interesting, but *ormai!* . . .' ('And *now* he tells me! I found that out years ago!').

oscuro (adj and m).   'Dark', indicating lack of light. This might also be *scuro* or *buio* (q.v.). If you wish to say 'dark' referring to a colour, use *scuro*. *Oscuro* is also used figuratively, in the sense of 'obscure', 'unknown'. *Camera oscura* is 'darkroom', although it is also 'camera obscura'. The noun is used in the combination *all'oscuro*, 'in the dark' (likewise *al buio*). *Sono completamente all'oscuro di questa faccenda* means 'I'm absolutely in the dark about this business'.

ossequio (m).   Usually in the plural, *ossequi*, meaning 'regards', 'respects'. See under **omaggio**. *I miei ossequi*, 'my respects'. *Ossequioso* is 'respectful' more than 'obsequious', although it can mean this, too. However, to bring out the full English idea of 'obsequious', i.e. 'servile', 'fawning', I would advise the use of *servile*.

ossia.   This normally means 'namely', 'viz.', 'that is'. For example: *endemico, ossia diffuso in un determinato territorio*, 'endemic, viz. widespread in a given area'. *Ovvero* may also be used.

ottavino (m). You would have expected the Italian for the musical instrument the 'piccolo', to be the same, wouldn't you? Well, it so happens that it is not, but is instead *ottavino*.

ottobrata (f). Strictly, a country outing or picnic in October. By extension, because outings are enjoyed on lovely days, 'a lovely October day'. Local fame attaches to *le belle ottobrate romane*, formerly 'the beautiful outings into the Roman countryside in October' (and now generally, by extension, 'beautiful October days in Rome').

ottocento (adj and m). The number 'eight hundred', or (capitalized, *l'Ottocento*) 'the nineteenth century'. *Ottocentesco* means 'nineteenth-century', as in *un palazzo ottocentesco*, 'a nineteenth-century palace'. See also **novecento**.

P

paese (m). This means 'country' in the sense of 'nation', but not only this. It very often means 'village' or '(small) town'. The place you come from is your *paese natio*, i.e. 'birthplace' or 'native village', etc. Note the expressions *mandare qualcuno a quel paese*, 'to tell someone to go to hell', *paese che vai, usanza che trovi*, 'when in Rome, do as the Romans do', and *tutto il mondo è paese*, 'things are the same the whole world over'. It is common practice to write *Paese* with a capital P when the meaning is 'country' (e.g. Italy), to distinguish it from its other meanings.

pagella (f). 'School report'. When a child brings his report home, the *genitore* ('parent') has to sign it before it is returned to the school. It shows the marks (*voti*) received in the various subjects (*materie*).

palazzo (m). Sometimes 'palace', sometimes rather like 'mansion' and very often 'building', as in *Palazzo di Vetro*, i.e. 'the United Nations Building'. That is to say, a *palazzo* is a building distinguished from ordinary houses by its larger size or greater grandeur and due to its monumental character. It can be used for private dwellings, or—more frequently—for public offices, to house museums, etc. Note that, because some of these *palazzi* are used by well-known institutions, etc., the name of the building stands commonly for the body using it, as is the case, for example, with 10 Downing Street. Palazzo Chigi in Rome, for instance, is the address of the prime minister's office, and Palazzo Madama is the Italian Senate. Note that *palazzo* *municipale* means 'town hall'. It should also be noted that *palazzina* indicates a block of flats, usually not very large, although larger than a *villino*, which is definitely of limited height and general size.

palestra (f). 'Gymnasium'. The Italian *ginnasio* denotes certain grades of the secondary school, namely the first two years, i.e. prior to the *liceo*, in what is called the *linea classica*. The upper grades of the secondary education system are divided into five 'lines', *classica* (emphasizing, naturally, classical studies), *scientifica*, *artistica*, *musicale* and *magistrale* (teacher training).

palo (m). Usually a 'pole' or a 'post'. For example, *palo della luce*, 'lamp-post', *palo telegrafico*, 'telegraph pole', *palo della porta*, 'goal-post'. Among criminals, the *palo* is the 'lookout', the one left to keep watch when a robbery is being attempted. *Fare il palo* in this sense means 'to keep watch'. In the building trade, *palo* means 'pile', not to be confused with *pila*, which—apart from being 'battery' or 'pile' (i.e. 'heap')—means 'pier' (in the sense of *pilastro*, 'column' or 'foundation pile'); but 'pier' such as the typical English seaside resort structures would be *molo*; as the outer works sheltering a harbour—e.g. Tynemouth pier —it is *diga foranea* or *frangiflutti*; and as a landing-stage—e.g. Admiralty Pier and Prince of Wales Pier in Dover—it is *banchina*.

panettone (m). The Italian counterpart of Christmas cake, but not at all similar to the English one. Originally a Milanese speciality, but now popular all over Italy. It is normally light in texture and in colour, with large air spaces and little addition of fruit.

panna (f). 'Cream'. *Panna montata* is 'whipped cream'. *Crema* can also be 'cream', and in fact *latte scremato* is 'skimmed milk'. *Crema* also refers to the mixture of egg yolk, milk and sugar used as a cake filling, sometimes referred to as 'custard', but not the same as the English custard.

panno (m). 'Cloth' (the sort that takes the plural 'cloths'). In the plural, *panni*, it means 'clothes', and we note the expressions *mettersi nei panni di qualcuno*, 'to put oneself in someone else's shoes', and *lavare i panni sporchi in pubblico*, 'to wash one's dirty linen in public'. *Pannolino* may be 'baby's napkin' or 'sanitary towel'.

pantera (f). One of those animals always in the feminine, 'panther'. And a word often used in newspapers. For example, I see in today's paper *entro 10 minuti erano arrivate sul luogo sette fra pantere e gazzelle*. Naturally, this does not refer to wild animals. In fact, police cars are called *pantere*, while the patrol cars of the Carabinieri are called *gazzelle*. Thus the newspaper excerpt means '7 police and Carabinieri cars had arrived on the scene within the space of 10 minutes'.

papa (m). Remember, the stress determines the meaning of this word. *Papà* (stressed where the written accent falls) means 'daddy', 'dad', while with no written accent and stressed on the first syllable it means 'pope'. I am fond of the expression *ad ogni morte di papa*, literally 'at every death of a pope', which is the equivalent of 'once in a blue moon'. Note that *babbo* means the same as *papà*, and that 'Father Christmas' is *Babbo Natale*.

papera (f). The dictionary may well tell you this means 'duckling' or 'female gosling', but in actual use it means a 'blunder', a 'slip of the tongue'. *Prendere una papera* means 'to make a slip of the tongue' (as also *prendere un granchio*). Remember that this is the *lapsus linguae* type of mistake, whereas otherwise 'to put one's foot in it' would be *fare una gaffe*. *Paperino* means 'Donald Duck'.

paradiso fiscale (m). Also *rifugio fiscale*, 'tax haven'.

paraffina (f). Without going into all the intricacies of paraffin, petrolatum, kerosene, and the like, I would just point out that although your dictionary may tell you that this word means 'paraffin', the Italian has a solid in mind, i.e. 'paraffin wax', and that the English use of 'paraffin' is usually *petrolio* (*da illuminazione*) or *cherosene*.

paragone (m). 'Comparison'. *Fare un paragone*, 'to make a comparison'. *Paragonare una cosa con un'altra* is 'to compare one thing with another'. *Senza paragone* is 'beyond compare'. The English 'paragon' is *modello* (*di perfezione, di eccellenza*).

parente (m and f). 'Relative' or 'relation'. *Un parente stretto* is 'a close relation' (the opposite is *parente lontano*). *Parenti acquisiti* are 'in-laws'. 'Parents' are *genitori*.

parentesi (f). 'Parenthesis' or 'bracket'. Sometimes used to mean 'lull'. *Tra parentesi*, in addition to meaning 'in parentheses', also means 'by the way'. *Tra parentesi, arriveranno alle 10 stasera* means 'By the way, they will be arriving at 10 this evening'.

partecipazione (f). 'Participation' in the sense of 'presence', and 'share' in the sense of 'participation'. *Partecipazione agli utili* is 'profit sharing'. An important Italian ministry is the *Ministero di partecipazioni statali*, which you could call the Ministry of State Participation, or of State Holdings, or of State Control. *Partecipazione* also means 'announcement' or 'notification'. For example, *partecipazione di nozze* is 'wedding announcement' (and it is common practice, when sending round these announcements, to give small, prettily packed bags of what are called *confetti*, namely 'sugared almonds' (notice that the English 'confetti' are *coriandoli* (m pl)).

partita (f). Three distinct meanings, according to context. Ordinarily, 'game', as in *partita di calcio*, 'football match', 'game of football'. In commerce, it means 'consignment', 'batch' or 'lot', while in bookkeeping it is an 'entry'. Notice that *partito* (m) means 'party' as in *partito socialista*, 'Socialist party'.

passaggio (m).   'Passage', in its various usages, and so forth. The meaning I wish to bring out here is that of 'lift' or 'ride', in *dare un passaggio a qualcuno*, 'give someone a lift'. *Vietato il passaggio* naturally means 'no thoroughfare'. *Passaggio pedonale* is 'pedestrian crossing' (the 'stripes' are called *le strisce*). *Passaggio a livello* is, as you would think, 'level crossing'.

passamontagna (m).   A word frequently read in newspapers, but infrequently found in dictionaries. Bank robbers intent upon avoiding identification when in action cover their faces with a *passamontagna*, i.e. 'balaclava helmet'. It is another word like *tema*, *delta*, etc., which ends in –a but is nevertheless masculine.

passeggiata (f).   'Walk' or 'stroll', on foot, or 'ride' (in a car, on horseback [i.e. *passeggiata a cavallo*], etc.). *Fare una passeggiata* is 'to go for a walk'. A public place where one walks is sometimes referred to, also, as a *passeggiata*. Note that *passeggino* means 'pushchair', 'stroller' (whereas the child's pram is *carrozzina*). Note also that *passeggiatrice* is one of the most common ways of referring to a prostitute, i.e. literally 'streetwalker'.

pasta (f).   As a mixture of flour and water, this is 'dough', or it may be 'pastry' (*pasta frolla* is 'sweet pastry' and *pasta sfoglia* is 'puff or flaky pastry'). Again, it may mean 'paste' or 'pulp', as in *pasta dentifricia*, 'toothpaste' and *pasta di legno*, 'wood pulp'. Or it may refer to a small cake. But far and away the most important meaning of the word is 'pasta', 'spaghetti', 'macaroni' or 'noodles'.

Pasta, the staple Italian food, comes in dozens of different shapes, sizes, thicknesses and patterns. Various sizes and shapes call for different cooking procedures and sets of sauces. Homemade pasta (*pasta casareccia* or *pasta fatta in casa*) is usually made of wheat flour and eggs, rolled out into a thin, flat sheet and cut into different shapes, lengths and widths, depending on whether it is to be used for noodles, *lasagne* or stuffed specialities, such as *ravioli*. Pasta bought in shops is made from hard durum wheat and water. Its range of shapes is spectacular: long and narrow or short and broad, flat or tubular, solid or hollow, smooth or ridged. Among the plethora of names attached to the various types I have selected the most common which I give here with a summary description: a) *agnolotti*, crescent-shaped, ravioli type, containing meat. In many regions they are the traditional prelude to the Christmas dinner (also traditional at Christmas time are *cappelletti*, small boat-shaped dumplings containing a mixture of chopped meat, ricotta and Parmesan cheese and nutmeg); b) *bucatini*, which are thicker than ordinary spaghetti, and hollow; often associated with the little town of Amatrice, in Abruzzi, hence *bucatini all'Amatriciana* (or, popularly but incorrectly, *bucatini alla Matriciana*), served with a sauce (*sugo*) of *pancetta* (bacon), tomato, red pepper and *pecorino* cheese (of strong, pungent taste). Note that *bucatini* are difficult to fork up; many a person has been bespattered with *sugo* as the springy *bucatini* fling and flay about, completely out of control!; c) *cannelloni*, broad tubes of pasta about 15 cm long filled with minced meat (or spinach) and often served with melted cheese on top; d) *conchiglie*, 'sea-shells', which they obviously resemble in shape. Usually served with a meat sauce; e) *fettuccine*, the Rome counterpart of the slightly broader and thinner *tagliatelle* and of the Genoese *trenette*. They resemble long, flat ribbons; f) *fusilli*, spiral-shaped pasta, good at trapping peas and other vegetables and bits of meat in their coils. Easy to eat; g) *pappardelle*, very broad strips of pasta, usually served with a rich game sauce (especially *lepre*, 'hare'); h) *pastina*, a range of tiny shapes (e.g. *stelline* or 'little stars'), usually served in broth, *pastina in brodo*; i) *penne*, 'quills', sliced diagonally, smooth or fluted. Very commonly served with a hot (i.e. piquant) sauce, as *penne arrabbiate* (literally 'angry quills'); j) *ravioli*; k) *rigatoni*: these are squat and hollow, slightly curved and fluted; l) *spaghetti,* the king of them all. The thinner variety are called *spaghettini* (in Naples and the south of Italy, *vermicelli* and *vermicellini* are often used instead of the words *spaghetti* and *spaghettini*). This most widespread and popular of all types of pasta is eaten with a great variety of sauces. Two very popular sauces are 'garlic and oil' (with the frequent addition of hot pepper), i.e. *spaghetti all'ajo, ojo e peperoncino* (note that these dialect spellings of *aglio* and *olio* are used on menus); and *alle vongole* (with baby clams); m) *tortellini*, small, ring-shaped ravioli-type pieces with a filling of ricotta cheese and spinach.

Note that pasta, particularly of the spaghetti type, should be cooked just the right amount, so that it is tender but not sloppy, and firm to the bite. This is called *al dente*. If it is undercooked, it is too stiff and unyielding to the bite, and if overcooked, soft and mushy. It's a question of vital seconds.

A child once visiting Italy, and presented with a plate of spaghetti, asked why it was served 'all tangled up'! He had eaten it (or 'them', as one says in Italian: *gli spaghetti*) on other occasions, but always in short pieces, which is all right for a spoon but not for a fork, which of course is the proper implement to use (occasionally a dessert spoon is used to act as a foil for the fork, to twirl the spaghetti against, but the usual thing in this case is to use the *edge* of the plate for *rolling* purposes).

One last thing: the pasta not used in a broth is often referred to as *pasta asciutta* or *pastasciutta*, i.e. 'dry pasta'.

pasticcio (m). 'Pie'. But people using this word are not usually referring to pies. The main connotation of this word is of something in confusion, all messed up. *Che pasticcio!* means 'What a mess!' A *pasticcione* is a person who messes things up. If you say: *Tu sei un grande pasticcione* to someone, you are as good as saying. 'Trust you to muck things up'. The sense of the word *pasticcio* corresponds to that of *guaio* (q.v.). You can say *essere nei pasticci* and *essere nei guai*, the former expression meaning rather that the person in question is 'in a bit of a mess, in trouble', while the latter expression means that there is perhaps 'real trouble', a really embarrassing or unfortunate predicament. However, I shouldn't like to make too much of this difference, as the force of the meaning depends more on the tone of the voice and on the exact form of the sentence, and even more on the personal choice of the speaker. Still, perhaps we could say that *pasticcio* is relatively light-hearted compared to *guaio*. *Pasticceria* can be the 'pastrycook's shop' (i.e. 'cake-shop') or the goods themselves (*una pasta* is used to denote a small cake, and *torta* a larger one that has to be cut up). The 'pastrycook' is the *pasticciere*. A newspaper once reported the case of the illegal business carried on by a pastrycook in a southern Italian city: the report ended by saying that *Il pasticciere si trova, adesso, nei pasticci*. He got four years.

pasto (m). 'Meal'. *Tre pasti al giorno* is 'three meals a day'. *Antipasto* is 'hors d'oeuvre'. *Vino da pasto* is 'ordinary table wine'.

patente (f). This is a licence, normally referring to the 'driving licence' (*patente di guida*). Other sorts of licence are usually *permessi* (m pl), 'permits'. The English 'patent' as a noun is *brevetto* ('The Patent Office' is *l'Ufficio Brevetti*). A 'patent medicine' is *una specialità farmaceutica*.

paternità (f). Often in the old days, but much less so today, one of the items required when filling up a form was *paternità*. Of course, nothing to do with a paternity order pending, but simply 'father's name' (just as *maternità* refers to 'mother's name').

patrimonio (m). Everything owned by a person, i.e. his 'estate', 'property', 'assets' or 'fortune'. *Patrimonio pubblico* is 'public property'. *Accumulare un patrimonio* is 'to make a fortune', and *ereditare un bel patrimonio* is 'to inherit (come into) a nice fortune'. Strictly speaking, the *stato patrimoniale* is the 'balance sheet' part of the annual accounts, which are properly *il bilancio*. *Tassa patrimoniale* is 'property tax'. Note the expression *costare un patrimonio* (or *un occhio della testa*), 'to cost the earth'. Note also that *patrimonio* is used of assets of a cultural and spiritual nature, which corresponds to our 'heritage'.

pavimento (m). A common false friend. This word refers to the 'floor', while 'pavement' (American 'sidewalk') is *marciapiede* (m).

pazienza (f). 'Patience'. As mentioned under *niente da fare* (see **niente**), this word often gives the submissive idea of 'It's no good complaining', 'can't be helped, I suppose', etc. In dealing with officialdom it is frequently a necessary attribute. In such sentences as the following there is the idea (enforced acceptance or disappointment) of 'Oh well!' or 'Too bad!': *Stamane ho fatto tarde; pazienza*, 'I came late this morning; oh, well'; *Mi hanno bocciato all'esame; pazienza*, 'I failed my examination; too bad'. At times, mingled with one's acceptance or disappointment there might be an overtone or undertone of reproach, as when, speaking of someone's actions (against one's own ideas of what ought to be done), one comments: *Se a lui va bene così, pazienza*, 'If that's the way he wants it (if it suits him like that), that's his own lookout!' (too bad for him!).

pazzo. This adjective means 'mad' or 'crazy'. *Un'idea pazza* (or *pazzesca*) is 'a crazy idea'. *Far diventar pazzo* (*qualcuno*) means 'to make (someone) go mad'. *Vado pazzo per il luccio* means 'I'm mad on pike'. The exclamation *cose da pazzi!* means 'sheer madness!' or 'absolutely incredible!' *Pazzia* is 'madness'.

pelo (m). 'Hair' in the sense of 'one strand of hair'. Do not use the word in the Spanish sense of 'your hair is black', for instance. The hair of your head is *i capelli*, definitely plural. And notice the other pitfall, that of spelling and pronunciation, which is caused by the existence of the word *cappello*, 'hat'. So *capelli* means 'hair/s', and *cappelli* 'hats'.

There are a few things to notice about the use of *pelo*. *Il pelo dell'acqua* is 'the surface of the water'. *Non aver peli sulla lingua* means 'to be outspoken, blunt'. *Cercare il pelo nell'uovo* is 'to split hairs'. *Si è salvato per un pelo* is 'he saved himself (his life) by a hair's-breadth'. *Se l'è cavata per un pelo*, similarly, is 'he had a very narrow escape'. *Essere a un pelo dal . . .* means 'to be within an ace of . . .', 'on the point of . . .'.

pendolare (m). This neologism means 'commuter', in the travel sense.

perchè. I mention this simple and fundamental word to remind you that it is used not only for 'why?' and for 'because', but also in the following way: *La ragazza implorava la madre perchè le desse una bambola*, 'The girl begged her mother to give her a doll'. Here the word *perchè* is the equivalent of *affinchè*. Note the subjunctive afterwards. *Il perchè e il siccome* is 'the why's and the wherefores'.

permesso (m). You should know all about this word meaning 'permission', 'leave', and so forth. The important thing to remember is that this is the word to say when you wish someone to move aside to let you go past: 'Excuse me, please'. Also, when leaving someone's company, you would politely say *Con permesso*.

pernacchia (f). 'Raspberry', but the sort that are blown, not the sort you can eat (which is *lampone* (q.v.)).

però. Spanish speakers should note the accent at the end of the word, and also the fact that 'but' ('pero' in Spanish) is *ma* ('mas' is the Spanish cognate), while *però* means 'however', 'yet'. *Però* is quite a common exclamation, in the sense of 'My!', 'Just imagine that!', etc., in which case there is sometimes additional stress on the first syllable. The unaccented *pero* means 'pear tree'.

persona (f). Remember that 'person' is a feminine word, whatever the actual sex of the person concerned. Thus 'he is a wonderful person' is (*lui*) *è una persona meravigliosa*. 'In person' is *in* (or *di*) *persona*. *Una persona per bene* is 'a decent sort of person'. *Persona non grata* is 'an undesirable'. *Persona fisica* is 'individual', as opposed in law to *persona giuridica*, 'corporate entity', 'body corporate' or 'legal person'.

personale. As an adjective, this means 'personal'. As a masculine noun, it may mean 'personnel' (e.g. *personale amministrativo*, 'administrative staff'), or 'figure' (referring to a person's body). *Lei ha un bel personale!* means 'She has a lovely figure!' Again, as a feminine noun, it means 'one-man show' (which could be *una mostra personale*).

pesca (f). This is the correct word for 'peach' and also for 'fishing', in the sense of both 'going fishing' and 'the fishing is good'. It also refers to what is caught, i.e. the 'catch'. An individual 'fish', remember, is *pesce* (m).

peso (m). Weight. In athletics, 'shot'. *Un inglese ha migliorato oggi il proprio primato europeo di lancio del peso* means' An Englishman has today improved his own European record for putting the shot'. The various boxing weights are as follows: *gallo*, 'bantam'; *leggero*, 'light'; *medio*, 'middle'; *mediomassimo*, 'light-heavyweight'; *massimo*, 'heavy'; *mosca*, 'fly'; *piuma*, 'feather'; *welter*, 'welter'. *Peso specifico* is 'specific gravity' or 'density'.

petroliera (f). 'Oil tanker'. *Petroliera gigante* is 'jumbo tanker'. Do not confuse with *petroliere* (m), 'oilman', 'oil magnate'.

petrolio (m). Generally, 'oil', 'petroleum', but sometimes (*petrolio da illuminazione*) 'paraffin oil'. 'Crude oil' is *grezzo*. 'To strike oil' is *trovare il petrolio*. An 'oil stove' is *forno a petrolio*, while *lampada a petrolio* is 'paraffin lamp'. Remember that English 'petrol' (American 'gasoline') is *benzina*, and is bought from the *distributore* ('petrol pump' or 'filling station'). The adjectival form is *petrolifero* (accented on the *if* part), as in 'oil well', *pozzo petrolifero*, or 'oil policy', *politica petrolifera*.

pezzo (m). This is the usual word for 'piece' or 'bit'. *Un pezzo di carta* is 'a piece of paper' (otherwise, 'a sheet of paper' is *un* *foglio*). There are, however, two common usages of the word which deserve to be mentioned. *Un pezzo grosso* is 'an important person', 'a V.I.P.'. The other meaning refers to time. *Da un pezzo non la vedevo così allegra* means 'I had not seen her looking so cheerful for quite a long time'. *Già da un pezzo era giorno* is 'It had already been light for some time'.

piacere (m). Quite apart from the idea of pleasure, of which you are well aware, *piacere* is the word to use for 'a favour'. *Mi fa un piacere?* is 'Would you do me a favour?' *Per piacere* is 'please', and is used quite frequently. And remember that *piacere* is the word which corresponds to 'How do you do?' when being introduced (*presentato*) to someone. You say *piacere*, and he says *piacere*, and then, when you take your leave, you say *piacere* again.

piantagrane (m and f). 'Nuisance' or 'troublemaker' (see **piantare**).

piantare. Quite apart from meaning 'to plant', etc., the familiar uses of this verb may be seen in *piantare una grana*, 'to make trouble', in *piantare in asso* (*qualcuno*), 'to leave (someone) in the lurch', and in *piantala!*, 'quit it!', 'cut it out!' *Piantala di fare domande* is 'stop asking so many questions!'

piazza (f). Note the expression *fare piazza pulita*, 'to make a clean sweep', as in *i ladri fecero piazza pulita*, 'the thieves took just about everything'. In commercial parlance, *piazza* means 'market', e.g. *la piazza di Milano*, 'the Milan market' (I repeat, commercially speaking; a market for the sale of fruit and vegetables and suchlike is of course *mercato*). Thus *piazzista* is 'commercial traveller' or 'salesman'. If you read of the populace 'taking to the square', i.e. *scendere in piazza*, you know that a 'demonstration' is in the offing, but *andare in piazza* means 'to be getting a bit thin on top'. *Un letto a una piazza, a due piazze* means 'a single, double bed' (*posto* is also used).

piazzale (m). Your dictionary will tell you that this, too, as *piazza*, means 'square'. But the two are not interchangeable. A *piazzale*, in my experience, is more secluded than a *piazza* in the sense that traffic (if allowed) can go round a *piazza*, while one part at least of a *piazzale* is blocked to traffic. Then *piazzale* also has the technical meaning of a large, open space fronting a station, airport, etc., where vehicles can park, turn round, etc. That is to say, '(parking) apron' in an airport, 'forecourt' of a petrol station, etc. *Piazzale di carico* in an airport is '(loading) ramp'.

piede (m). 'Foot', of course. I mention this particularly to point out that *a piedi* is 'on foot', as in *andare a piedi* ('to walk'), whereas *in piedi* means 'on your feet' (e.g. *bisogna essere in piedi prima delle 7*, 'you have to be up before 7'). *Andare coi piedi di piombo* is 'to proceed with extreme caution, or very slowly'. If someone is *tra i piedi*, he is 'in the way', and may well be exhorted as follows: *togliti dai piedi!* i.e. 'get out of the way!', 'scram!', etc. If you miss a train, bus, etc., then you may well use the expression *perdere il treno, l'auto*, etc., but you may also say *rimanere a piedi*. *Non reggersi in piedi* may be used in a physical sense when, for example, someone is too tired, weak, etc., to stand up, or it may be used figuratively, when speaking of someone's argument, for instance: *il tuo ragionamento non si regge in piedi per niente*, 'your reasoning is absolutely without any foundation' (i.e. wrong). Lastly, we have the legal expression *a piede libero*, which dictionaries inform us means 'on bail'; but 'on bail' means that the person concerned is temporarily at liberty (*in libertà provvisoria*) against security (*su cauzione*), while if someone is *imputato a piede libero* he has just received a notification of a charge against him but is not under arrest.

pieno (adj and m). 'Full'. *Pieno zeppo* is 'full right up' or 'packed', 'chock-a-block'. Motorists should note that *fare il pieno* means 'to fill (her) up'.

pigione (f). Nothing to do with birds (the 'pigeon' is *il piccione*), but what you have to pay monthly for your room, flat, etc., namely 'the rent'. The more formal word is *l'affitto*.

pigliare. This is a popular synonym of *prendere*, as far as meaning is concerned. In tone, it is much more familiar, even slangy. Children are taught at school not to use it, but it comes out in the spoken language all the same. I have personally found it used most in two senses, one when inviting someone to have a drink (e.g. *Che pigli?*, 'What are you having?'), and the other in the expression *Che ti piglia?*, 'What's the matter?', 'Whatever's come over you?' *Pigliare fuoco* is 'to catch fire'. *Chi dorme non piglia pesci*, literally 'he who sleeps catches no fish', is the same as saying that 'the early bird catches the worm'. In general, my advice is not to use the word, but to stick to *prendere*. Language-wise, *prendere un raffreddore* is better than *pigliare un raffreddore* ('to catch a cold').

pignolo. 'Fussy', in the sense of being over-careful, a hair-splitter. About the same as 'pedantic'. *Lui è troppo pignolo* means 'He's much too fussy' (or 'finicky'). The noun, 'fussiness', is *pignoleria*.

pila (f). This has a variety of meanings. First, 'heap' or 'pile', quite straightforwardly. Second, 'battery', such as you have in a torch (but the car battery is *batteria*). Next, 'reactor' as in *pila atomica*, 'nuclear reactor' or 'atomic pile'. Again, 'pier' (as of a bridge). See also under **palo**.

pilota (m). Note that this is a masculine word, and also that it refers in Italian not only to the ship's pilot, and the pilot of an aircraft, but also to the driver of a racing car, i.e. 'racing driver', or of a motorcycle, i.e. 'motorcyclist'.

pirata (m). Another masculine noun ending in –a. It corresponds to 'pirate', in the sense of 'buccaneer', but has other common applications. *Un pirata della strada* is 'a hit-and-run driver', while *un pirata dell'aria* is 'hijacker' or 'skyjacker' (also called *dirottatore* (m); 'to hijack a plane' is *dirottare un aereo*). 'Hijacking' may therefore be *pirateria* or *dirottamento*.

pisolino (m). 'Forty winks'. *Fare un pisolino* is 'to have forty winks', 'to have a nap'. A common alternative for this in Rome, particularly, is *pennichella* (f).

più (adj, adv and m). I have made a selection of the main uses of this word, apart from its ordinary use in forming the comparative (*più caldo* = 'warmer' or 'hotter') or the superlative (*il più grosso* = 'the biggest'). *Mai più!* is 'never again!' *Più che mai* is 'more than ever'. *Al più* or *tutt'al più* is 'at most'. *Di più* is 'more' as in *voglio di più*, 'I want (some) more'. *Niente di più* is likewise 'no more'. *Per di più* is 'what's more' or 'moreover'. *Più che altro* is 'more than anything else', 'mainly', 'chiefly'. *Il più delle volte* is 'most times' or 'mostly'. *Il più è già fatto* means 'most of it has already been done'. I should also remind you of the basic construction 'the more ... the more ...'. This is *quanto più ... tanto più ...*, very often shortened to just *più ... e più ...*, as in *più lo vedo e più mi piace*, 'the more I see him the more I like him'. *Quanto più studio, tanto più imparo*, 'the more I study, the more I learn'. (*Speriamo!* i.e. 'let's hope so!').

piuttosto. This adverb means 'quite' in the sense of 'fairly' or 'rather'. *Era piuttosto grassa*, 'She was rather plump'. *Fa piuttosto caldo*, 'it's quite hot'. It is also commonly used to denote the choice of one thing rather than another, as in *piuttosto morire che tradire*, 'rather die than be a traitor'. Sometimes the alternative is not specified, as in *piuttosto vado a casa*, 'I'd rather go back home' (i.e. rather than whatever the alternative happens to be).

pizza (f). In its culinary meaning, it is best not translated, but left as 'pizza' in English. It comes in a variety of guises. One distinction to be drawn is between the type bought in the breadshop, etc., usually in the morning, and the sort served in the restaurant. The shop sort is baked in a large pan and cut into lengths at the customer's order (usually asked for in terms of weight (*un etto*, etc.) or of price (e.g. *da cento lire*)). It comes basically in two sorts of topping, white and red (*pizza bianca* and *pizza rossa*), the white being with oil and salt and the red with tomato. There are many other types, however, with mushrooms, onion, anchovy, and so forth on top. If it has risen quite well it is called *pizza alta* and if not then *pizza bassa*. The restaurant sort is round, sometimes too large for the plate, and again comes in a variety of toppings, with tomato, hard-boiled egg, anchovy, mozzarella cheese, and so on. Restaurants that serve pizza usually advertise this fact by adding the word *pizzeria* with their name, together with *trattoria*, etc. Note that you do not buy pizza in a *pizzicheria*, which is a grocer's shop (also *salumeria, salsamenteria*). The *pizzicagnolo* (with the accent on the a) is therefore a 'grocer'.

In cinema parlance, *pizza* refers to a 'reel' or 'reel box'. Then we have the common colloquial expression *Che pizza!*, 'What a mess!' *È una vera pizza!* 'It's a proper mix-up!' Note that the word *pizzo* means 'lace', often used in the plural *pizzi* (*pizzo* also means a beard coming to a point).

poco, po'. As an adjective, this means 'little'. In the plural, 'few'. *Conosco poche persone*, 'I know very few people'. *Poco fa* means 'a short time ago', while *fra poco* means 'in a short while'. The reason for including this simple word here is that it is so often used, in its shortened form *po'*, in colloquial Italian, to signify 'just' in the sense of 'just look' or 'just listen'. *Senta un po'* would be '(just) listen', and *dimmi un po'* 'tell me'. The exclamation *Ma guarda un po'!* means 'Just take a look at that now!' (or perhaps 'the cheek of it!', 'how dare you?', etc., according to the particular circumstances).

poi. As you know, this is the word for 'then' in the sense of 'after that'. 'Then', the past of 'now', is of course *allora*. *Poi* is the word to shoot in when recounting a story and so on, '. . . and then . . .'. When someone else is telling a story, and breaks off part way through, you may say *E poi?* where you might also say 'And then?' in English. Notice: *d'ora in poi*, 'from now on'; *da domani in poi*, 'from tomorrow onwards; *prima o poi*, 'sooner or later'.

polemica (f). A far more common word in Italian than 'polemic' or 'polemics' in English. It is far more often 'controversy'. *Essere in polemica con qualcuno* is 'to be in disagreement with someone'. The corresponding adjective *polemico* is often more like our 'argumentative'. *Polemizzare* is anything from 'to argue' to 'to disagree strongly with'.

politica (f). This may be 'politics' or 'policy' (i.e. *linea di condotta*). *Politica estera* is 'foreign policy' and *politica commerciale* is 'trade policy'. Notice the difference between *economia politica* and *politica economica*. The former is 'economics' or 'political economy' while the latter is 'economic policy'. *Un uomo politico* is 'a politician', while *un politicante* is 'a petty (or would-be) politician'.

politicizzare. One could quite simply state that this means 'to politicize', and be done with it. But the term is far more widely used in Italian than is the English word. The meaning is to give a political imprint to an artistic, social, etc. activity (i.e. one that is not normally associated with politics). 'To give a political tone or character to', 'to make politically minded or aware'. *È solo da qualche anno che la scuola magistrale sforna ragazze politicizzate* means 'Teacher Training Colleges have been turning out politically-minded girls only in the last few years'.

polizia (f). English people are used to the idea of a single police
force with a single uniform, engaged on all-purpose police
work. I mean, they are the ones who try to prevent and to re-
press crime, who direct the traffic, who see children and old
people across roads, who break up riotous assemblies, who
prevent smuggling, enforce the food regulations, who try doors
especially at night to see they are properly locked, and so forth.
In Italy, however, these various duties are not assigned to
just a single body; on the other hand, the distribution is not
absolutely clear. The men who most resemble the British
policeman in appearance are the Municipal Police (*Metro-
politani*), with their blue uniforms and helmets in the cooler
months. They are responsible for enforcing traffic, health and
sanitary regulations, for seeing that shop closing times are
respected, and so on. Naturally the aspect of their work which
hits the eye is directing the traffic. With the advent of traffic
lights they have far less point duty to perform than formerly,
but when they do take over control in the middle of the street
they are a sight for sore eyes, with their complete control of the
situation in a highly efficient manner.

Otherwise, more general police duties are the task of the
Corpo della Pubblica Sicurezza (in slang, *la madama*). The
members of this body are called *agenti*, and wear light blue
trousers and dark blue tunics, with a gilt eagle and a small red
shield on their caps (with the letters 'R.I.', i.e. *Repubblica
Italiana*). Their municipal headquarters is called the *questura*,
wherein resides the *questore*, or police chief, whose immediate
inferiors are called *vicequestori*, or Deputy Police Chiefs. A
city will be divided up into various police zones in each of
which there is a *commissariato*, the chief of which is the *commissario*. Police patrol cars are called *pantere*. As their headquarters is the *questura*, the men are often called *questurini*.
Naturally one of the slang expressions to describe them, as in
so many languages, is *piedi piatti* ('flatfeet'). Since the higher
officers in the police have university degrees, they are called
dottori, i.e. 'doctors', as they have passed their doctorate.
Whereas an ordinary British policeman would say 'sir' to an
inspector, for example, his Italian counterpart in the *Pubblica
Sicurezza* would call his *commissario*, for instance, *dottore*.

The *Pubblica Sicurezza* are military. But the *Carabinieri* are
more military. They are very proud of their reputation for
smartness and efficiency. I am well aware that certain persons
cast aspersions on their I.Q., but I will not go into that. Their
duties largely overlap those of the ordinary police, and in many
respects they are more wide-ranging. Their dress uniform is very
picturesque and well known to almost everybody: black in
colour with tail coats, red-striped trousers and three-cornered
hats. Whereas the *Pubblica Sicurezza* will very rarely take over
traffic control duties, for example, the *Carabinieri* will readily
do so. They will in fact readily step in anywhere, in all sectors of

policing. There is without doubt some degree of rivalry between the *Carabinieri* and the *P.S.* According to some people, this rivalry makes for efficiency. There is also the possibility of certain tasks being done twice, lacking general coordination. Three times, perhaps, because we also have the *Guardia di Finanza*, the customs' police. They patrol the Italian frontier, both land and sea, but oddly enough they are also found doing certain ordinary police duties not even distantly concerned with customs duties. If there is a riot to be quelled in Rome, Milan, Reggio Calabria, or elsewhere in Italy, the club (*manganello*) that strikes the rioter may equally well be wielded by a *poliziotto*, a *carabiniere* or a *finanziere* (so you see that an Italian *finanziere* may be either a financier, banker, etc., or a guard in the customs' police!).

These various forces are referred to in Italian as *corpi separati*, i.e. 'separate bodies', each with its own uniform and separate command. There are other *corpi*, too. But a full list and description is out of place here. I will just mention in conclusion some of the commonest terms met with in this context. The *Polizia Giudiziaria* is the counterpart of the British C.I.D. A *vigile urbano* is a municipal policeman engaged largely on traffic duty; his female counterpart (since a few years ago) is sometimes called a *vigilessa* (I know that purists will wrinkle their noses, but people *do* use the word, and there has been a film of this title). I have not seen a *vigilessa* on point duty, but they are often busy with their little pads writing out *contravvenzioni* ('fines'). The 'Flying Squad' is the *squadra mobile*. The *scientifica* is the equivalent of 'Scotland Yard', more or less. The police surgeon is called the *medico legale*. The *polizia stradale* or just *la stradale* is the 'traffic police'. And lastly, not police at all, strictly speaking, we have the *vigili notturni*, night watchmen in near black or black uniforms, on their bicycles (without lights, in most cases), sometimes vespas or in cars. Slightly sinister looking, they are a private force and do night rounds guarding the property of those who have subscribed for their services. They have certain powers, one of them being that of arrest during hours of darkness (rarely exercised).

poltrona (f).   The dictionary will tell you, quite correctly, that *poltrona* means 'armchair', 'easychair', or, in the theatre, an 'orchestra stall'. But there are two other points to notice. First, it often corresponds to ordinary 'chair' or 'seat' in English, when it is a question of none too large a *poltrona*, and second, it may refer to the position occupied by the one entitled to sit on it, namely that of a company director, etc. I quote from a recent magazine (from a column actually entitled '*Poltrone*': '*In realtà, avrebbe preferito servire lo Stato da un'altra poltrona, sicuramente più prestigiosa: quella di governatore della banca*'. ('In actual fact, he would have preferred to serve the country from another and undoubtedly more prestigious position: that of governor of the bank'.) The diminutive is *poltroncina*, meaning either a small armchair or, in the theatre, a 'pit-stall'.

ponte (m). In general, 'bridge'. I will not detail the various sorts of bridges, but will instead mention a very particular sort of Italian *ponte*, namely the one commonly built between a national holiday and the weekend. Let us say that Thursday is a national holiday. Well, it is not much fun going back to work just on Friday, of course, and then having the weekend off as usual. Far better to 'build a bridge' and have the Friday off, too. Those who are particularly expert in constructing themselves these long weekends are sometimes called *pontisti* (some of them manage to take the Monday, Tuesday and Wednesday off as well, somehow or other, and include two weekends; but these are the 'deck' as well as the 'bridge'.

At a more mundane level, I will just mention two *ponti* that are not called bridges in English, viz. *ponte aereo* and *ponte radio*, 'air lift' and 'radio link', respectively. On a boat the *ponte* is the 'deck' as well as the 'bridge'.

portato. This means 'inclined' or 'gifted', i.e. to have leanings towards something either momentarily or more permanently. For example, *sono portato a credere che* . . . 'I'm inclined to believe that . . .' or *mio figlio è portato alle lingue*, 'my son has a flair for languages'.

portiere (m). Porter, caretaker, janitor, etc. The man who looks after a block of flats, etc., also known as the *portinaio* (with the stress on the a). His female counterpart is the *portinaia*. The little room where he sits and keeps watch when not on other duties is called the *portineria*. These are all important words due to the widespread use of this concierge system in Italy. Note, too, that the goalkeeper in football is the *portiere*.

possibilmente. This means 'if possible', while 'possibly' is usually *forse* ('perhaps') or *può darsi*.

posto (m). Place, or 'room' in the sense of 'place'. *Non c'è posto* means 'There isn't any room'. The word is used in a very general sense. A police-station may be *un posto di polizia*, and a fire-station *posto di pompieri*. 'On the spot' is *sul posto*. *Mettere tutto a posto* means 'to put everything in order' or 'to put things straight'. It may also mean 'post' in the sense of 'employment'. *Ho trovato un posto magnifico*, 'I've found a wonderful job'.

povero (adj and m). Remember to stress this word, meaning generally 'poor', on the first syllable. Note the expression *in parole povere*, 'in plain words', 'to put it plainly'. The noun of course means 'poor man'. You will probably know that *povero* may come before or after the noun it qualifies, but with a difference. In the usual position for an Italian adjective, i.e. after the noun, it means 'needy', 'without means', etc., while when placed before the noun it indicates affection, compassion, pity, commiseration, and so on. For instance, *povero me!* 'poor me!'; *povera donna,* 'poor woman!'; *la mia povera madre*, 'my poor mother'. It might also indicate scorn, irony or a threat. The diminutive of the noun is *poverino*, very commonly heard in terms of commiseration; and *poveraccio* is also heard quite a lot, referring to one who has had a hard time of it.

pratica (f).   Apart from 'practice', this means 'experience', as in *lui ha molta pratica di queste cose*, 'he has a great deal of experience in these things'. The other meaning I wish to stress is the bureaucratic one, 'file', 'dossier' or 'papers'. *Fare le pratiche per qualcosa* means 'to attend to the formalities for something' ('get the papers ready', etc.).

praticamente.   This adverb corresponds to the English 'practically' or 'in practice'. You will hear it used very often—not in the sense of the English 'I've practically finished', where the meaning is 'very nearly' and the Italian is *quasi*, but more with the idea of 'in actual fact'.

pratico.   This is the ordinary adjective for 'practical', and there is nothing particularly difficult about it. I wish just to point out its very widespread use meaning 'experienced' or 'skilled' in something. *Sono molto pratico della città* means 'I know the city very well' (i.e. 'I'm very experienced . . .').

prefetto (m).   Nothing to do with boys' schools. He is in actual fact the representative of the government in every province. He is legally at the head of the provincial police force (i.e. the *Pubblica Sicurezza*). The building where he has his office is called the *Prefettura*.

pregiudicato (m).   As a noun, this designates a person who has a previous conviction, i.e. 'previous offender'. It is a much used word in Italian newspapers. In speaking of someone roped in by the police, they will report whether he is a *pregiudicato* or someone *incensurato* (q.v.), i.e. a previous offender or with a clean record. Our 'prejudiced' is usually *prevenuto*. *Lei è prevenuta contra di me* is 'she is prejudiced against me'.

prego.   You absolutely must get into the *prego* habit. You say it to someone who thanks you—'Don't mention it', 'not at all'. You say it when you let someone go past you, when giving up your seat to someone, when handing someone something, in short, when doing a service with a smile (or without one). *Ve ne prego* is 'I beg you'. TV announcers, in a live telecast, use *Ve ne prego* or *Vi prego* in an attempt to calm noisy audiences. 'Ladies and gentlemen, please . . .'.

prendersela.   To take something the wrong way, to get all hot and bothered, to lose one's temper or become angry with someone. *Non prendertela* is 'don't worry about it'. *Se l'è presa con il mio amico* (notice the feminine form of the participle) is 'he got angry with my friend'. The question *che ti prende?* inquires 'what's up?', 'what's eating you?'

preoccupare. Most often used reflexively, *preoccuparsi*, meaning 'to worry, be anxious, be worried'. *Non ti preoccupare* means 'Don't worry', 'Don't let it trouble you' and so on. The corresponding noun is *preoccupazione*, 'anxiety', 'worry'. The adjective *preoccupato*, 'worried' (sometimes 'apprehensive') is very common.

prepotente. This adjective is of much more frequent use than the dictionary equivalent, 'overbearing'. The noun *prepotenza*, 'overbearingness', as it were, is also common. *Fare il prepotente* is roughly 'to be too big for one's boots'. *È molto prepotente* therefore often means 'He's got too big an opinion of himself', 'he throws his weight around'.

presalario (m). Pre-salary, i.e. a salary granted by the state for certain university students, considering their studies to be the premise for future working and earning activity.

presente. 'Present'. Note the expression *avere presente qualcosa*, 'to know about something', 'to be aware of it'; *ha presente Paolo Rossi?* is 'Can you call Paolo Rossi to mind?' *Ha presente il Colosseo?* is 'Do you know where the Colosseum is?' *Far presente qualcosa* means 'To point something out'. Lastly, although as a masculine noun it is possible to use this word to mean 'present, gift', the usual word for this is *regalo*.

pressappoco, press'a poco. 'About'. *Ci sono due strade, e la loro lunghezza è press'a poco la stessa*, 'there are two roads of about equal length'. Another way to indicate 'approximately' is *circa*, usually used with a number and often following it: *ho vinto due cento mila lire circa*, 'I've won about two hundred thousand lire'.

presuntuoso. 'Presumptuous', 'conceited', 'big-headed'. The corresponding noun is *presunzione* (f), 'conceit'. A common adjective, *presuntuoso*.

pretendere. This common transitive verb means 'to claim' or 'to demand', *not* 'to pretend'. *Lei pretende d'aver ragione* is 'she claims she is right'. *Pretendo di essere rispettato* is 'I demand to be respected'. The usual verb for 'to pretend' is *fingere* or *fare finta di*.

preventivo (adj and m). As an adjective, 'preventive, precautionary'. As a noun, 'estimate'. *Il bilancio preventivo* is the estimated expenditure, etc., viz. 'the budget'. After the event, when the various totals have been totted up, we have the *bilancio consuntivo* (see under **bilancio**).

primario (m). A very important person in a hospital, being the head physician of a department.

primato (m). Record, of the sort which is broken in sport. *Giorgio Rossi ha migliorato il primato mondiale di lancio del giavellotto* means 'George Rossi has improved on the world record for the javelin throw'. The person with the record, male or female, is the *primatista*. The record played by the disc jockey is, of course, *un disco*.

prima visione (f). Literally, of course, 'first vision'. Italian newspapers listing films to be seen classify them as *prima*, *seconda* and *terza visione*. By and large, newly issued films are *prima visione*, and when they have finished their run they go down to the *seconda* and *terza visione* cinemas. Reissues of old films are also classified under *prima visione*, although more accurately they could be called 'tenth vision', etc. Generally, the 'better' and more expensive cinemas always have *prima visione* films, the next-best places have *seconda visione*, etc. Therefore the classification of the film tends to become the classification of the cinema itself—seats get harder and the volume of sound increases the further down the scale you go.

problematica (f). This is generally the ensemble or complex of problems concerning a specific discipline. Some people, disliking the simple and the ordinary, use it when they really mean just *problema* (and remember that *problema* is one of the masculine words ending in –a). Thus *problematica* may be 'problem complex', 'ensemble of problems', 'problems' or 'problem', according to the case.

processo (m). This may be 'process', as in *processo chimico*, 'chemical process', or 'trial', 'action', 'lawsuit' or 'proceedings'. *Processo penale* is 'criminal trial' and *processo civile* is 'civil proceedings'. *Sotto processo* is 'on trial'.
   Processo verbale is 'minutes' (of a meeting, etc.).

procurare. An example of an Italian verb which sounds stilted, or even immoral, to the English ear, but which is a common enough Italian equivalent of another English verb, in this case 'to get', in the sense of 'to obtain', 'to secure'. *Procuratemi dell'acqua* would be 'Get me some water'. *Procurarsi* is quite common, meaning 'to get for oneself'. *Mi sono procurato . . .* is 'I have got hold of . . .'.

prodotto (m). 'Product', just as *produzione* (f) is 'production', and *produttività* (f) is 'productivity'. But not always. For where we would say 'products', as in 'the full range of our products', Italians tend to use *produzione*, while speaking of 'output' (i.e. 'production') in ordinary statistical terms, there is a tendency in Italian to use instead *produttività*. So be on your guard for these variations.

professionista (m and f). In sport, a 'professional'. An 'amateur' is *dilettante*. In business, *libero professionista* refers to someone who carries on a professional occupation on an independent basis; what we would call a 'professional man or woman', perhaps. Or more likely we would specify exactly what he is, e.g. accountant, tax consultant, etc. This is a case where Italian uses a general-purpose word that has no exact equivalent in English.

professore (m). Usually 'teacher'. Also used as a title, as in *Buon giorno, professore* (which translates of course as just plain 'Good morning'). An English-type professor is *professore universitario*. Note also that it is common to refer to a senior doctor as *professore*. *Il professore ha visitato mia figlia* has nothing to do with the teacher visiting the daughter, but states that 'the doctor has examined my daughter'.

promiscuo. This adjective is accented on the i. I always find it a somewhat comical word. Its meaning is 'mixed', as in 'mixed school' (*scuola promiscua*) or 'mixed marriage' (*matrimonio promiscuo*). To give the idea of a 'promiscuous person', you would have to say something like *libertino*, or *una persona sregolata*.

pronto. 'Ready'. *Lei è sempre pronta ad aiutare* means 'She is always ready to help'. *Pronto soccorso* is 'first aid'. 'Ready, steady, go!' is *Pronti . . . via!* The Spanish word, one of the several taken into English via American from Central America, means 'at once', which is *subito* in Italian. The strange thing, perhaps, is the universal use of *Pronto* on the telephone, meaning 'Hello'. Don't take this any further, however, as I have heard some unknowing people do, and use it as the general word corresponding to 'hello'. It would be ludicrous to call out *pronto* to someone you knew in the street, unless you happened to be telling him that you were ready.

proposito (m). The special reference here is to the much-used phrase, *a proposito*, which is what you often say if struck by an afterthought, 'Oh, by the way . . .'. *A proposito di . . .* means 'Speaking about . . .', 'And, on the subject of . . .'. Notice also the expression *fare una cosa di proposito*, which means 'to do something on purpose'. 'On purpose' may also be *apposta*.

proprio. As an adjective this word corresponds to the French 'propre', and Spanish 'propio' (note the additional *r* in the Italian word), meaning 'own'. *Amor proprio* is *amour propre* or 'self-esteem'. However, it is the use of *proprio* as an adverb that is so common and so important in Italian. The fundamental meanings are 'precisely' and 'really'. *Lui è proprio matto* means 'He is really round the bend'. *Proprio quello che immaginavo!* is 'Just what I thought!' *È proprio una cosa spiacevole* means 'It's something really unpleasant'. *È proprio suo cugino che l'ha fatto* is 'It's (none other than) your cousin who did it'. *Ho ricevuto la lettera proprio stamane* means 'I received the letter this (very) morning'. *Lei giura che è proprio vero* is 'She swears that it is really true'. *Sì, è proprio quello che volevo dire*, 'Yes, that's exactly what I meant'. *No, non conosco proprio nessuno di quelli* means 'No, I don't know a single one of those'. *Penso che per te sarebbe proprio meglio tornare a casa*, 'I think the best thing for you to do would be to go home'.

Non riesco a farlo, non riesco proprio, 'I can't manage to do it, I really can't'.

provare. Do not automatically think this means 'to prove'. It may, but there are many more things it may also mean. For example 'to try', as in *proviamo di entrare,* 'let's try to get in', or in the other sense as in *è stato duramente provato,* 'he was sorely tried'. Speaking of clothes, it may be 'to try on'. *Provare una sensazione di* . . . would be 'to have (experience) a feeling of . . .'. Note also the half-threat *provaci!* i.e. 'just you dare!'

provocare. This may perhaps mean 'to provoke', but in actual fact it nearly always means 'to cause'. *Lui provocò un incidente* means 'he caused an accident'. *La pioggia provocò il crollo della casa,* 'the rain caused the house to collapse'.

provvedere. A much used Italian verb. It indicates doing whatever is necessary to achieve the desired result. 'To take steps', 'take measures', 'see to it that', 'arrange', 'make provisions', etc. It sometimes means doing whatever is necessary to resolve a particular situation, often taking restrictive or disciplinary measures. In this sense the undertaking *provvederò* ('I will see to it!', 'Measures will be taken!') might be a veiled threat. *Sarò costretto a provvedere molto severamente nei confronti dei colpevoli,* 'I shall be forced to take very severe action against the guilty parties'. The measures taken are *provvedimenti.*

pull (m). Abbreviation of *pullover* (m).

pullman (m). Quite sensibly, you would expect this to mean a pullman railway coach. In fact, it is a comfortably upholstered coach, but not on the railway. So if you hear someone say that he's been somewhere by *pullman,* he's travelled by road and not by rail.

punto (m). Italians very often say *a un certo punto.* When telling a story, for example, they rarely fail to say it. We could translate it literally into English, 'at a certain point', but in Italian it is much more frequent than in English. 'Up to a point' is *fino a un certo punto.* Note that when we say in English 'The point is that . . .', Italians say *si dà il caso che . . . .* Another very common Italian expression is *fare il punto della situazione,* 'to see how things stand', 'to sum things up', 'to take stock'. For *punto di contingenza,* see under **contingenza.**

pure. An extremely useful little word to put in in several contexts, to make a sentence which would otherwise perhaps be a little stilted sound Italian. *Andate* means 'go', while *andate pure* (concedingly) is 'you may go'. If someone asks your permission to do something, you may, of course, answer *sì* or *certo,* and so on; but a very common and polite answer is *fate pure,* which is 'just go ahead', and a very Italian way of putting it.

Then, *pure* can have the meaning of *anche. Anch'io* means 'So do I', etc., as does *e io pure,* too. *Lui vuole andare via e tu pure* means 'He wants to go and so do you'. *È stato trovato pure il suo amico* means 'his friend has been found, too'. *Pure allora* gives the idea of 'even then', just as *pure adesso* means 'even now'.

We must not forget, of course, that *pure* sometimes translates as 'but' or 'yet'. For example: *quella donna è molto povera, pure non si lamenta mai*, 'that woman is very poor, yet she never ever complains'.

purtroppo.   This exclamation, etc., is quite straightforward, meaning 'unfortunately', but is mentioned here in an attempt to persuade learners actually *to use it*, and to dissuade people from over-using the otherwise quite acceptable *sfortunatamente*.

Q

quaderno (m).   Exercise book.

quadri (m pl).   Quite apart from being the plural of *quadro*, 'pictures', 'tables', 'squares' (*a quadri* is 'check', of patterned cloth), and so on, *quadri* refers to all those who hold positions of responsibility and guidance at any level, especially in business and in the civil service. They are usually the middle managers or lower executive grades.

qualche.   This adjective, remember, cannot be declined, and is followed by a singular noun in Italian, meaning 'a few . . .', which corresponds to a plural noun in English. *Qualche esempio* would thus be 'a few examples'. Remember this in *qualche volta*, 'sometimes'.

qualunquismo (m).   In 1944 Guglielmo Giannini founded the satirical political weekly called *L'uomo qualunque*. This became quite popular, to the extent that in 1946 he decided to start a political movement based on the systematic criticism of all democratic systems and violent opposition to the post-war antifascist movement, and some of its rather exaggerated manifestations. By extension *qualunquismo* has come to mean an attitude of indifference towards political and social questions. One with such ideas is called a *qualunquista*. This is nowadays used to describe someone who feels and shows himself to be quite indifferent to, or who scorns or disdains political and social ideologies, activities or problems (for no deep or well motivated reasons). It is quite a common term of political abuse.

quartino (m).   One quarter of a litre. If you are not too thirsty, and unaccompanied, or accompanied by someone not wishing to drink wine, your table order in the *trattoria* may well include *un quartino di bianco* (or *rosso*), i.e. a quarter of a litre of white (or red) wine.

quattrini (mpl). One way of referring to 'money'. *Essere a corto di quattrini* is 'to be short of cash'.

Quattrocento (m). *Il Quattrocento* is 'the fifteenth century'. The adjective *quattrocentesco* is 'fifteenth-century'.

questione (f). This is the appropriate word to use in 'it's a question of', whereas the question you ask someone is *una domanda*.

questura (f). The provincial police headquarters. In a city, such as Rome, the central HQ is the *questura*, while each city district has its *commissariato*. The man in charge is the *questore*, the provincial chief of police, or 'city police chief'.

questurino (m). One who works at the *questura* (q.v.), and therefore a member of the police force (*Pubblica Sicurezza*), or policeman, patrolman. I would say that the word is rather more pejorative than *poliziotto*.

quindi. One of the most-used words in colloquial Italian. It means 'so', 'therefore', 'consequently'. *Fa caldo oggi, quindi vado alla spiaggia* means 'It's hot today, so I'm going to the beach'. *Lui mi ha detto che non poteva venire, quindi non so che cosa fare*, 'He told me that he couldn't come, and so I don't know what to do'. *Ha cominciato a strillare, e quindi è stato messo fuori*, 'He started to shout, and so he was put outside'. You will quite often hear the word used by itself, as a complete idea, as, indeed, many people use the English 'So'. Someone may explain something, and the implications are clear, and you say just *Quindi*, meaning that you realize what the consequences are, or you appreciate his state of mind, or something else. Again, in interviews, *Quindi* is a common word. The person being interviewed has just answered one question, and this leads the questioner on to another question, which he will begin with *Quindi* .... For example, *Quindi è contento, sul serio?* 'So you're really happy?'

quinquennio (m). A 'period of five years'. From it comes the adjective *quinquennale*, often seen in *piano di sviluppo quinquennale* ('five-year plan').

quintale (m). Your dictionary may glibly tell you this is 'quintal', but you mustn't forget that although it is a common measure in Italy (production and export statistics frequently quote amounts in *quintali*), it is not so in English-speaking countries. So you have to convert the relevant figure to kilos (by adding two noughts) or to tonnes (by taking away one nought), one quintal being 100 kilos or 0.1 tonne.

R

raccomandare. 'To recommend'. Note the double *c* and single *m* of the Italian word, as against the single *c* and the double *m* of the English one. And speaking of letters (the sort you post), this verb means 'to register'.

The important point to note, however, is that *raccomandare* or *raccomandarsi* are used when you wish to stress a point to someone. *Vi raccomando* is approximately 'Pay special attention to', 'Don't forget', 'Be sure to do it', and so on. *Mi raccomando, non chiudere mai quella porta* means 'Be sure never to close that door'. It's very usual to add *Mi raccomando!* at the end of a conversation, in which an order has been given, to make sure that the order really will be carried out. To render the English 'recommend' it is best to use the verb *consigliare*.

raccomandazione (f). As stated under *clientelismo*, the practice of 'recommendations' is one of the most widespread and traditional applications of the system. Given that *clientelismo* means 'patronage' or 'jobs for the boys', the system of recommendations refers to the obtaining of the jobs in question. There may well have been a competitive examination (*esame di concorso*), but that is not to say that the winners will be those who get the jobs, unless they also happen to have been given 'recommendations' from on high. Obviously, the higher the source the stronger the recommendation. The recommendations which are so strong that they cannot be denied are called *raccomandazioni di ferro* and the one who receives such a recommendation is a *raccomandato di ferro*. The source may be political, ecclesiastical, a *barone* (q.v.) of the university, etc. There is a strong movement against this system, but its roots go deep and it is a difficult matter to eradicate them.

raffreddore (m). This is the word for the common cold, so don't go catching a *freddo* ('cold' as an adjective). *Temo che stia per venirmi un bel raffreddore* means 'I'm afraid I'm in for a heavy cold'. *Lei è molto raffreddata* is 'she has a nasty cold'.

ragione (f). You will very often hear *ha ragione*, 'you're right', *lui non ha ragione*, 'he's wrong', etc. If you are in agreement with something that someone is saying, you can slip in the odd *sì, ha ragione* together with *giusto* or *d'accordo*, to denote your agreement. There is another thing: you may well hear someone say *sì, ha ragione* to you, although you haven't even said a word! This has happened to me on more than one occasion. It is said to forestall your criticism when you have perhaps unwittingly been wronged. For instance, you are really first in the queue, but because you are turning the other way you do not see Pinco Pallino as he slips in before you; then you turn round and see him, and before you can say anything, or even before you have noticed anything, he says *si, ha ragione . . .*— meaning that you are or would be quite right to protest, but . . .

'Rightly or wrongly' is *a ragione o a torto*. 'To be in the right' is *essere dalla parte della ragione. Lui non voleva darmi ragione* is 'he wouldn't admit I was right'.

ragioniere (m).   'Accountant'. A fairly prestigious occupation in Italy. 'Accountancy' is *ragioneria*. I include this item to point out that the letters *rag.* before a person's name mean *ragioniere*, just as *avv.* is *avvocato* ('lawyer', 'attorney') and *dott.* is *dottore*.

rapido (m).   As a noun, this word means 'express train'. See also under **espresso**.

rapire.   'To kidnap'. 'Kidnapping' is *rapimento*, the 'kidnapper' is *il rapitore*, and the one kidnapped is *il rapito*. Changing the word slightly we have *rapinare*, which is 'to rob', *rapina* (f), 'robbery' (*rapina a mano armata* is 'armed robbery' or 'a stick-up') and *rapinatore*, 'robber'. 'To rape', on the other hand, is *violentare*. The crime of 'rape' is *stupro* or *violenza carnale*.

razza (f).   This word, meaning 'race', 'breed', etc., is extremely common in the exclamation *che razza di .. .!* 'what a (adjective) . . .!' Whether or not to add an adjective and if so, which one, depends on the circumstances. *Ma che razza di discorsi sono questi?* 'What way of talking is that?' could sometimes perhaps do with a 'stupid' or 'ridiculous', etc., between 'what' and 'way'.

realizzare.   Not usually 'to realize' (which is rather *rendersi conto*), but 'to carry out'. In English it means 'realize' only when speaking of dreams (*realizzare i propri sogni*, 'to realize one's dreams') or of converting something into cash.

recapito (m).   The stress is on the a. 'Address', not necessarily where you live, but where things may be delivered to you. *Recapitare* is, in fact, 'to deliver'.

recarsi.   'To go to a place'. *Ieri mi sono recato alla palestra . . .* means 'Yesterday I went to the gymnasium . . .'.

reggere.   'To bear, support, carry, hold'. *Reggere un peso* is 'to bear a weight'. There are various other meanings, too. The ones I wish to stress are 'to take' in the liquid sense, e.g. *Giovanni non regge il vino*, 'Giovanni can't take (much) wine', 'not to make sense' as in *il suo discorso non regge*, 'his words don't make sense', and *non reggere più*, 'not to (be able to) go on any longer'. *Reggersi a qualcosa* is 'to hold on to something'. *Reggersi in piedi* is 'to stay on one's feet', 'to be able to remain standing'. *Alla fine della quinta ripresa il pugile non si reggeva più*, 'at the end of the fifth round, the boxer was unable to stay on his feet'.

regione (f).   'Region'. Italy is divided into twenty regions, five of them 'special' (Sicily, Sardinia, Valle d'Aosta, Trentino-Alto Adige and Friuli-Venezia Giulia) and 15 'ordinary' (Piemonte, Liguria, Lombardia, Veneto, Emilia-Romagna, Toscana, Marche, Umbria, Lazio, Abruzzo, Molise, Campania, Puglia, Basilicata and Calabria). Each region has certain administrative and legislative powers. Each one is divided into a number of provinces, and each one of these has a capital (*capoluogo*). Umbria, for example, is divided into two provinces, Perugia and Terni. These provincial capitals have code letters (PG for Perugia and TE for Terni, for example) which are seen on car number plates.

relax (m). The correct Italian word for 'relaxation' is *rilassimento*, but Italians use this English verb as a noun, and speak of *un po' di relax*, 'a bit of relaxation'.

rendersi conto. 'To realize'. Remember that the past participle is *reso*. *Mi sono reso conto che . . .* means 'I realized that . . .'. See also **realizzare**.

residence (f). Block of service flats.

responsabile. 'Responsible'. Remember that the Italian word is spelt with an a before the b. 'To be responsible for something' is *essere responsabile di qualcosa*. It sometimes translates into English as 'liable', when money is concerned (*danni* are damages). *Il responsabile* is 'the person in charge', and *il direttore responsabile* (of a newspaper, etc.) is simply 'the editor'.

resto (m). Two things here. Firstly, it means 'change' such as you hope to get back from 5,000 lire when the bill is 4,500 lire, and secondly, in the expression *del resto* it is much used, this meaning 'anyway', 'at any rate', 'besides', 'after all'. *Non capisci proprio niente—del resto sei troppo giovane*, 'You don't understand anything at all—after all, you're too young.'

retta (f). This may be 'straight line', in geometry, or 'fee' as paid for boarding, but the usage I wish to point out here is in the expression *dare retta a qualcuno*, 'to take notice of someone', 'to take someone's advice'. *Da' retta a tuo padre!* is 'do as your father says!'

ricovero (m). This may be 'shelter' or 'refuge', or it may be 'home' as in poor people's home, but it is usually seen meaning 'admission to hospital', i.e. 'hospitalization'. The person so hospitalized, i.e. the 'patient', is called *il ricoverato* (he may also be an inmate in an institution). Likewise the verb *ricoverare* is 'to hospitalize', 'to admit to hospital'. To recover, on the other hand, is *riprendere conoscenza* when it means 'to come round again', 'regain consciousness', *ricuperare* or *ritrovare* when it means 'to get something back', and *riprendersi* or *guarire* when it means recovering after an illness, a setback, etc.

rimanere. One meaning of this verb is quite straightforward, 'to remain'. *Rimanere a casa* means 'to stay at home'. However, the verb is used in a good many ways where we could not use 'to remain', 'to stay', 'to be left' or anything similar in English. In several expressions *rimanere* gives the idea of 'to become', although I do not mean to say that it would be possible to use the English word in rendering the meaning. For instance, *Cinque persone sono rimaste uccise ieri in un tragico scontro*, 'Five people were killed yesterday in a tragic accident'. But, *Fortunatamente lui è rimasto illeso*, which is 'Luckily he was uninjured'.

One of the commonest expressions using *rimanere* is *rimanere male*, 'to be disappointed'. *Sono rimasto molto male* is 'I was very disappointed'. *Rimanere male*, according to the sense, may also be 'to be put out' or 'to be hurt' (offended). *Sono rimasto!* (without specifying what) means 'to be flabbergasted'; 'you could have knocked me over with a feather!' If you say that someone *è rimasto lì*, you understand that he is dead. *Rimanere in asso* is 'to be left in the lurch'. *Rimasto soddisfatto* is 'satisfied'. *Rimanere* may also be 'to be situated', as in *dove rimane il Senato?* 'where is the Senate?'

In reporting that certain people were in agreement on some point, Italians may well state that *Loro sono rimasti d'accordo circa* or *su* . . .—that is, 'They were in agreement about . . .'.

In short, *rimanere* is a verb you will do well to cultivate, and especially bearing in mind that as likely as not the meaning will deviate from the seeming one of 'to remain'.

risiamo (ci).   *Ci risiamo* is 'here we go again', 'the same old story once again', and so on.

rispondere.   I put this in to remind you that it is the correct word for 'to reply', 'to answer'. The answer itself is *la risposta*. At the same time, remember that 'to ask a question' is *domandare* or, more frequently, *chiedere*.

risultare.   *Dalla conversazione risulta che* . . ., 'from the conversation it appears that . . .'. It would be stretching the point somewhat to say 'result' in this context in English. As with *rimanere* (q.v.), for example, almost the exact counterpart of the word exists in English, and is used, but for just one of the meanings of the Italian verb, while in fact other meanings are more typical and common. 'To ensue', for instance. *Da ciò risultò molta confusione*, 'great confusion ensued'. *Risulta chiaro che* . . . is 'it is clear that . . .'. *I nostri sforzi sono risultati soddisfacenti*, 'our efforts turned out to be (proved to be) satisfactory'. *Non mi risulta* means 'I know nothing about it' or 'that is not so'.

ritardo (m).   'Delay'. This word is included here because of the common expression *arrivare con* . . . *di ritardo*, which is 'to arrive . . . late'. *Beppe è arrivato con due ore di ritardo* is 'Beppe arrived two hours late'.

riunione (f).   A 'meeting', and not usually a 'reunion'.

rivendicazione (f).   A much-used word in trade union language. It means 'claim'. *Rivendicazioni salariali* are 'wage claims'.

rivista (f).   A 'magazine', of the sort you buy at bookstalls. The Italian *magazzino* is 'store'. *Grandi magazzini* are 'department stores'. *Rivista* is also 'parade' ('review') and 'variety show'.

roba (f).   'Stuff', 'things'. Here are a few examples of its usage: *roba da mangiare* ('things to eat'); *cos'è quella roba?* ('what's that stuff?'); *di che roba è fatto?* ('what's it made of?'); *non è roba per te* ('this is something beyond your scope'). The common expression *roba da matti!* (also *roba da pazzi!*) denotes criticism or else great surprise, e.g. 'He's (she's, they're, etc.) crazy!' Then we have two other exclamations, *che roba!* meaning 'it's terrible' or 'what a mess!' and *bella roba!* which is uttered ironically, 'a fine thing!'

romanesco (m).   This is the dialect of Rome, sometimes called *romano* and at times, pejoratively, *romanaccio*. Now a dialect is not just a different accent, comprising as it does not only this different pronunciation, but also changed grammatical forms and in particular a special vocabulary of its own. *Romanesco* refers more to this passed-on old dialect, while people are thinking more of the slangy words in the dialect when they refer to it as *romanaccio*. This is not to be a treatise on the Roman dialect, but it is worth while mentioning a few general points about it. The pronunciation tends to be more voiced than ordinary Italian, and endings of words are cut off, often missing the last syllable altogether. This is especially noticeable in the case of infinitives, *capire* becoming *capi*, for example, and *andare* becoming *annà*. In this last example there is an indication of another point, the substitution of the combination *nd* by *nn*. Where Italian has the combination *gl*, as in *moglie*, Romanesco has a written *j*, pronounced as an *i*. *Moglie* therefore becomes *moje*. Then you have other occasional letter changes. *Il* is *er*, *del* is *der* and so on, although note that there is no universal substitution of *l* for *r*. The indefinite article loses its vowel, becoming just *n*. 'A friend of mine' for instance, is *'n amico mio*.

I have no intention of including any vocabulary list here; suffice it to point out that the vocabulary is pure Italian, with a number of vogue words and a few, just a few, real dialect words: for example, *Ella è ita* instead of *è andata*. Before making one or two short quotations in Romanesco, I must point out that they often double what are really single consonants (or drop one of what are really double ones!). For example, *subbito* instead of *subito*. Now here are a few quotations:

Roma, infatti, s'è spopolata. Tanti se ne so' iti in montagna, tant'artri ar mare. Pochi so' rimasti. Pe' me, tutti ponno partì; io nun farò artro che accompagnalli a' la stazione, ripetenno a me stesso: Io, da bôn Romano, lontano da Fontan de' Trevi e da Trinità de' Monti nun ce saprebbe vive manco un giorno.

You will immediately see the deviations from Italian—*sono* becomes *so'*, *altri* is *artri*, *possono* becomes *ponno*, *partire* is *partì*, *accompagnarli* is *accompagnalli*, *non* becomes *nun*, *buon* is *bôn*, and so on. Notice especially the use of the third person singular conditional (here *saprebbe*) instead of the first person (should be *saprei* in ordinary Italian). Thus also *io preferirebbe* instead of *preferirei*. This is very common.

Ma fa sempre così caldo la notte a Roma? chiese Romina.— Quarche estate sì, quarche estate no ... rispose Piero ... certo che le staggioni so' cambiate, perchè 'na vorta ce stava er ponentino che mò nun c'è più. Er ponente era un venticello fresco che ... ebbè, che ne so, te dava più voja, nun so si me spiego ... Piero's answer contains these words: *quarche* for *qualche*, *staggioni* for *stagioni*, *so'* for *sono*, *'na vorta* for *una volta*, *ce stava* for *c'era*, *er* for *il*, *mò* for *adesso*, *nun* for *non*, *voja* for *voglia* and *si me* for *se mi*. Note in particular *mò*, very frequently heard, meaning 'now'.

An English version of this is: 'But is it always so hot at night in Rome? asked Romina.—Some summers it is, some summers it isn't ... replied Piero ... it's a fact that the seasons have changed, because once there was the "ponentino" wind, but not any more now. The "ponentino" was a nice cool breeze that ... well, what can I say, that gave you a bit of "go", I don't know if you follow me ...'

romanista (m and f).   A fan of the Rome Football Club. Their immediate adversaries are the *laziali*, fans of the Lazio F.C. (see **biancoazzurri**). Both teams are based in Rome.

romano (m).   A Roman. As an adjective, also Roman. Notice the expression *fare alla romana*, 'to go Dutch'.

rompiscatole (m and f).   This is a slightly vulgar word meaning 'nuisance', 'pest' or 'bore', always referring to a person who has irked, pestered or bored you.

rondine (f).   'Swallow' (*rondine* is stressed on the first syllable). Under *rosso* below I mention the phenomenon of 'modulation'. Another example is *una rondine non fa primavera*, the equivalent of 'one swallow does not make a summer'. Italian says spring, we say summer, but the meaning is the same, an isolated fact does not determine a general situation.

rosicare.   'To nibble, gnaw'. *Chi non risica, non rosica*, 'nothing venture, nothing gain'. Both *risica* and *rosica* are accented on the first syllable.

rosso.   You are well aware that this adjective means 'red'. I would like to mention a linguistic phenomenon known as modulation. This is a slight shift of type, number, colour, etc., from one language to another in more or less the same expression. For instance, for 'to kill two birds with one stone', Swedes say 'to kill two flies with one blow'. The meaning is the same, but the words are a bit different. In Italian, for example, the inside of the egg, which we call the yolk or the yellow, is called *il rosso*; again, what we call a goldfish is called *pesce rosso* in Italian. Quite apart from modulation, and even further away from any form of moderation, there is the expression *bruciare il rosso* or *passare con il rosso*. The *rosso* here refers to the red of the *semaforo* or 'traffic light' (*semaforo* is stressed on the second syllable), and the reckless action concerned is going against the red light. *Bruciare il rosso* gives the idea of accelerating at the last minute and racing to cross before the amber changes to red and the other line of cars starts across (and what if someone there is going to *bruciare il verde*?), while *passare con il rosso*—which may well be the same thing—indicates just going against red. Many hundreds of fines are levied each year in Rome alone for this type of traffic offence.

rossoblu (m pl). *I rossoblu* are the Bologna Football Club, a First Division (*Serie 'A'*) club.

rossoneri (m pl). *I rossoneri* are the Milan Football Club, leading lights in the First Division.

rubare. 'To steal'. 'To pilfer' is *rubacchiare*. *Un rubacuori* is a 'ladykiller'.

ruffiana (f), **ruffiano** (m). The 'procuress' and the 'pimp', respectively. Ruffians, yes, but of a sort. The usual word for 'ruffian' is *mascalzone* or *furfante*. See also under **sfruttare.**

rumore (m). An odd-sounding word to English ears for 'noise'. We have *il rumore del fiume*, *il rumore del treno*, *i rumori della strada*, and so forth ('sound of the river', 'noise of the train', 'street noises'). *Rumore* can also be the English 'rumour', but the usual noun is *diceria* (note *corre voce che*, 'it is rumoured that . . .'). *Rumore* can also mean *scalpore*, in the expression *fare rumore*, 'create quite a stir'.

S

sacco (m). Apart from 'sack' or 'bag', I want to mention the meaning of 'lots'. *Un sacco di soldi* is 'lots of money'. *Lei ha un sacco di amici* is 'she has heaps of friends', etc. Note also the expressions *vuotare il sacco*, 'to spill the beans' or 'to make a clean breast of things', and *essere colto con le mani nel sacco*, 'to be caught red-handed'.

salario (m).   Not 'salary' (which is *stipendio*), but 'wages' or 'pay'. *Salariato* means 'wage-earner' and by extension 'workman', and by further extension 'working class'.

salire.   A bit of a false friend for those who know Spanish. The Italian verb means 'to go up', 'to rise'. *Salire le scale* is 'to go upstairs'. *Salire in autobus* is 'to board a bus'. 'To go out' (the meaning of the Spanish verb 'salir') is *uscire* in Italian.

salsamenteria (f).   The same as *salumeria* (f).   The shop round the corner from me going by this name is quite definitely a grocery store. We also have a *drogheria* (q.v.) nearby, which sells soap, detergents, brooms, cotton wool, combs, toothbrushes, tooth-paste, razor blades, deodorants, and so on. A sort of general store, perhaps, but at any rate not a grocer's, as is sometimes stated. The *pizzicheria* is also a grocery store.

salutare.   Too elementary to be a false friend, no doubt. It can of course be 'to salute', militarily. In common use, however, it is 'to greet (to say hello)' and 'to bid farewell'. *Saluta la signora*, says the mother to the little boy on taking leave of Mrs Smith, 'Say goodbye to Mrs Smith'. Perhaps one might say *Ti saluto* on leaving someone, whereas we should hardly say 'I salute you' in English.

salute (f).   Not 'a salute' (which is *un saluto*), but 'health'. The point to notice is the use of the word when having a drink. *Salute* corresponds to 'Cheers'. *Cin cin* is even more common. Also said after someone has sneezed ('Bless you').

salve.   A fairly common salutation on meeting someone—'hello', 'hi!'

santo (m).   'Saint'. There are two expressions using this word which appeal to me. *Qualche santo ci aiuterà*, literally 'some saint will help us', meaning 'something is bound to turn up', 'let's hope for the best', and *non sapere più a che santo votarsi*, 'to be at one's wits' end'.

sapere.   I do not intend to go into all the intricacies of this verb, but just to mention three things. 1) *non si sa mai* means 'you never know', 'you can never tell'. 2) *saperla lunga* means 'to know more than a thing or two', 'to know what's what'. 3) *Mi sa che . . .* means 'it seems to me that . . .', 'I have a feeling that . . .'.

saporito, saporoso.   These adjectives both mean 'savoury' or 'tasty', but *saporito* is sometimes a bit saltier than *saporoso*.

sbafare.   'To scrounge, sponge'. A second meaning is 'to gobble up', 'to stuff oneself'. The 'scrounger' or 'sponger' is *sbafatore*. *Sbafo* is 'scrounging', and *vivere a sbafo* is 'to scrounge a living'.

sbandata (f).   This colloquial word means a 'crush' (the sort one has on someone). *Prendere una sbandata per qualcuno* is 'to have a crush on someone' (the same as *prendere una cotta*). *Sbandata* may also mean 'skid', from the verb *sbandare*, 'to skid' (in nautical terms, it means 'a list', 'to list').

sbandato (m). 'Drifter', 'drop-out'.

sbarcare il lunario. *Lunario* means 'almanac', and *sbarcare* is 'to land, to unload'. But in combination they mean 'to make ends meet'.

sbornia (f). This word usually occurs in the expression *prendere una bella sbornia*, 'to get blind drunk', 'to be rip-roaring drunk'. *I postumi* (*di una sbornia*) means 'hangover'.

scala mobile (f). If you can stand on it, it's an 'escalator', but otherwise it refers to the 'sliding scale' (of wages).

scalata (f). Ordinarily, this is 'climb'. It is also used in the expression *dare la scalata a*, in two senses. Politically, we say *dare la scalata al potere*, meaning 'to climb to power', while in the business world it refers to a 'takeover bid'.

scappatella (f). A common word in describing a spouse's temporary deviation from the straight and narrow. We could call it 'flirtation' or 'escapade'.

scaramanzia (f). A gesture, an object, etc., to ward off bad luck. The commonest such gesture is to point the hand downwards with the two outside fingers outstretched and the two inside ones curled up. It is considered even more effective if you use both hands. Asked why he does this, an Italian might answer: *per scaramanzia*. If he's really convinced, he might mean by this: 'to ward off the evil eye', etc., but if he just does it out of habit, he might smile sheepishly and mean 'it's mere superstition'.

scarogna (f). Alternatively *scalogna*. 'Bad luck'. *Che scarogna!* 'What bad luck!' If someone is *scarognato* (*scalognato*), he is 'dogged by bad luck', 'plain unlucky', etc.

scemo (adj and m). Adjective, 'stupid', 'idiotic'. As a noun, 'fool', 'dope', 'lunatic'. *È mezzo scemo* is 'he's not all there'.

scheda (f). 'Card' (but not of the 'postcard' variety, which is *cartolina postale*). *Schedare* is the verb, meaning 'to card-index'. The 'card-index' itself (or the 'filing cabinet') is called the *schedario*. In a rather ominous sense, *essere schedato* normally means 'to have a (police) record', and *uno schedato* is 'someone with a (police) record'.

schedina (f). The poor man's hope of riches, the 'football-pool coupon'. The Italian coupon, which should be handed in at an official *ricevitoria* (receiving office, always a *bar*) by midnight on the Saturday night before the Sunday games, is far less complex than the English pools. There are thirteen games only, and you have only to guess the results of all thirteen. See also **tredici**.

scherzo (m). 'Joke'. The verb is *scherzare. Uno scherzo di cattivo gusto* is 'a joke in bad taste'. *Stare allo scherzo* is 'to take a joke'. *Tu scherzi!* is 'are you joking?' or 'are you kidding?' *Per scherzo* is 'for fun'. *Non scherzare col fuoco* is 'don't play with fire'.

schifo (m). 'Disgust'. *Mi fa schifo*, 'it makes me sick'. This word is to be avoided in the best Italian, but it is of very common usage in everyday conversation. Football fans, disappointed with their team's prowess, make liberal use of the word. *La nostra squadra ha fatto schifo!* 'our team was absolutely lousy!' The corresponding adjective is *schifoso*, 'disgusting' or 'lousy'. *Schifezza* means 'filth', 'filthiness', etc. *Che schifezza!* is 'how revolting!', 'how utterly disgusting!'

scientifica (f). The department of the police using scientific methods to combat crime. *La scientifica* is called in when there is a murder, for example, to take photographs, look for fingerprints, seek out clues, etc. Corresponds to Scotland Yard.

sciocco. A false friend. It does not refer to something shocking but means 'silly', 'stupid', 'foolish', etc. *È sciocco da parte mia* means 'it's stupid of me'. The corresponding noun is *sciocchezza* (f), which means 'something foolish', 'foolishness', 'nonsense', and so on. *Dire sciocchezze* is 'to talk nonsense'. *È una sciocchezza* means 'it's a mere trifle'.
  'A shock' is usually *una scossa*, 'an electric shock' being *una scossa elettrica*. 'To shock' is usually *scandalizzare*, sometimes also *disgustare* or *colpire* (which is literally 'to strike, hit'). 'Shocking' is *disgustoso, scandaloso, orribile*, and so on according to the context.

sciolto. According to the thing referred to, this may be 'melted', 'loose', 'unfastened' or 'untied'. *Vino sciolto* is unbottled wine, i.e. 'wine from the barrel'. *Aver la lingua sciolta* means 'to be a good, fluent speaker', 'to have the gift of the gab'.

scioperare. 'To strike', in the sense of refusing to work. 'A strike' is *uno sciopero*. I am well aware that these days it is normal to define the type of strike, so I will give a list of the main types of Italian strikes and their English equivalents. *Sciopero a braccia incrociate* is 'sit-down strike'; *sciopero a gatto selvaggio*, 'wildcat strike'; *sciopero a scacchiera*, 'staggered strike'; *sciopero bianco*, 'go-slow' (also *sciopero pignolo*) or 'work-to-rule' (also *sciopero di regolamento*); *sciopero a singhiozzo*, 'intermittent strike'; *sciopero lampo*, 'lightning strike'; *sciopero di protesta*, 'protest or token strike'; *sciopero di solidarietà*, 'sympathy strike'; *sciopero generale*, 'general strike'; *sciopero della fame*, 'hunger strike'. 'To be on strike' is *essere in sciopero*. A 'blackleg' or 'scab' is *un crumiro*.

scippo (m). This is unfortunately a common word in big Italian cities, particularly Naples and Rome, being the universal word for the all-too-common practice of bag-snatching. I say 'universal', although strictly speaking the police call it *strappo*. The *scippatore* ('bag-snatcher') usually works with an accomplice, and they more often than not cruise along on a Vespa until they have singled out a victim. While the accomplice waits with the Vespa ready for a lightning getaway, the *scippatore* comes up behind the lady concerned (sometimes a man, but usually a lady), gives her a sharp push and then grabs her bag as she thrusts her arms out to steady herself. And he grabs it hard, so that resistance usually lands the victim with a crash on the ground, and often in hospital. This applies even more so when the *scippo* is performed without the *scippatore* dismounting. The obvious advice is to keep one's handbag not on the side nearer the road, and even better advice is not to carry a handbag at all, or at most to carry only the barest essentials in it, and not to resist too hard if you wish to prevent your shoulder, etc., from being dislocated. The verb is *scippare*, and the most common form of the word is the past participle, *scippato*, as in *la sua amica è stata scippata ieri*, 'his friend had her bag snatched (i.e. she was bag-snatched) yesterday'.

scirocco (m).   The *scirocco* or *sirocco* is the Italian name for the simoom wind blowing from the Sahara over to Italy. Originally a dry wind, it picks up moisture over the Mediterranean, and especially in the winter it is sultry and rain-laden as well as being warm. It makes the atmosphere particularly oppressive. When there is a *scirocco* blowing there will be thick layers of sand on the cars in the streets of Rome, for example.

scocciare.   The dictionary may mention that this means 'to shell eggs' and so on, but this is of little consequence. The important thing is that *scocciare* is another of the verbs meaning 'to bore', 'to bother' or 'to annoy'. A *scocciatore* is a 'pain in the neck'. *Che scocciatura!* is 'what a bore!' or 'what a nuisance!' See also **noia**.

scogliera (f).   A *scogliera* is a series of *scogli* ('rocks') emerging from the water (usually the sea). It all depends how far they emerge. If they are barely above the surface, they are 'reefs', if they are a bit further above the surface they are just 'rocks', while if they tower above it they form a 'cliff'. A *scoglio*, as noted, is a 'rock', or a 'reef' if at about sea level. It is also used figuratively, meaning 'obstacle'. For example, *la matematica è uno scoglio per lei*, 'maths is her bugbear' or 'maths is a stumbling-block for her'.

sconosciuto (adj and m).   'Unknown' or a 'stranger'. I include this word as people do tend to forget, or rather not to call to mind at the right moment, such words as this, beginning with s and meaning the opposite of the word without the s. *Scomposto*, for example, means 'ruffled, disconcerted', while *composto* is 'unruffled, composed'.

sconto (m). This means 'discount', and is perfectly straightforward, the reason for mentioning it here being that it is of quite widespread use in Italy, although it is decreasing. Some people make a point of asking for *uno sconto* whatever they buy and wherever they may buy it. 'Couldn't you possibly make a little reduction for me?' The practice of haggling over prices is fairly regional, strong in the south and taboo in much of the north of the country. In Rome it is definitely less extensively used than, say, ten or fifteen years ago. It is the rule in Porta Portese, Rome's Sunday morning flea market, but this is of course a question of straight bargaining, and you would not ask for a mere *sconto*. Note that the *tasso ufficiale di sconto* is the 'official bank rate'. Note also the word *scontato*, meaning 'discounted' in commercial language, but otherwise 'expected'. *Dare per scontato che . . .* means 'to take it for granted that . . .'.

scoperta (f). 'Discovery'. I mention this word because of the expression *bella scoperta!* spoken in ironic tones, meaning more or less the same as 'Yes, Queen Anne's dead!'

scoprire. 'To discover, find'. This is quite straightforward. You can find, for example, an unknown island (*una isola ignota*) or the truth (*scoprire la verità*). Ironically, *hai scoperto l'America!* means 'you're too smart for words!' etc. The verb may also mean 'to reveal or disclose', 'to expose', 'to uncover' or—and this is the reason for my including this word—'to unveil', when speaking of a statue, monument, etc. I have on several occasions seen it mistranslated that a statue has been 'discovered' when it has obviously really been 'unveiled'.

Scotch (m). This is not the whisky distilled in Scotland, by any means. It is in fact 'scotch-tape'.

scudetto (m). *Lo scudetto* is the soccer championship shield for the First Division (*Serie 'A'*).

scusare. 'To excuse' or 'to forgive'. *Scusate il mio ritardo* is 'excuse me for being so late'. The forms *scusa, scusi* and *scusate* are all extremely common, more so than their English counterpart, 'excuse me'. For example, a man had been arguing with someone and another person had taken the adversary's part, whereupon the first man turned angrily to the intruder and said: *Ma lei perchè non s'impiccia degli affari suoi, scusi?* We might say 'why don't you mind your own (. . .) business?', but we would hardly end up with an 'excuse me!' And it is not just a question of being angry. Other feelings come into it, indignation, for example. *E perchè lo devo fare proprio io, scusa?*, 'and why should I be the one to do it?' Of course, there are many things we could add, such as 'eh?', 'for the love of Mike!', 'for crying out loud', and so on, but not 'excuse me'. Often *scusi* is said when you have missed someone's words and want them to be repeated, in which case we would probably say 'I beg your pardon' or 'What did you say?'

The corresponding noun is *scusa*, 'excuse', 'apology'. *Chiedo scusa* is a very common form of saying 'excuse me'.

seccare. Apart from meaning 'to dry (up)', this commonly means 'to annoy', 'to bother', 'to bore'. *Essere seccato* is 'to be annoyed or bored'. Something that annoys (bores) you is *seccante*, and the person concerned is a *seccatore* ('nuisance', 'bore'). See also **noia**.

sede (f). This is usually 'head office' or 'registered office', but may be 'headquarters'. Although normally referring to a place, it is sometimes used with reference to time, as in *in sede d'esami*, 'during the examinations', or *in sede della esecuzione dei lavori*, 'during the performance of the works'. Likewise, *la Santa Sede* is 'the Holy See' while *Sede vacante* is the period between the death or resignation of the Pope or a bishop and the election of his successor. If someone is *fuori sede* he is 'away from the office' and probably 'out of town'. *In separata sede*, in law, means 'in a special session', but by extension it usually means 'privately'.

seicento. 'Six hundred'. *Il Seicento* is 'the seventeenth century'.

semmai. This is the combined form of *se mai*, very commonly used with the adverbial meaning of *caso mai* (see under **mai**).

sensazione (f). This may be the 'sensation' that comes to you, and also the type of 'sensation' that is created (another word is *scalpore* (m)), but more often than not *sensazione* corresponds to the English 'feeling'. For example: *ho la sensazione che . . .*, 'I have a feeling that . . .', *lui ha la sensazione di non riuscire*, 'he feels he is not going to succeed'.

sensibile. A famous false friend, meaning 'sensitive'. *Sono molto sensibile ai cattivi odori* means 'I'm very sensitive to bad smells'. *Sensibilmente* usually refers to another meaning of *sensibile*, namely 'noticeable' (i.e. 'that can be measured'). *Ha diminuito sensibilmente* means 'It has decreased noticeably'. 'Sensible' is often *sensato* or *intelligente*.

sensibilizzare. 'To sensitize'. Technically quite an old word, but a neologism in the sense of 'causing to be aware of', 'making known to', as in *sensibilizzare l'opinione pubblica*, 'to bring to the notice of (or sensitize) public opinion'.

sentenza (f). 'Judgment' (and 'sentence' in this sense). A sentence in the grammatical sense is *una frase* or *proposizione* (f).

sentire. I am well aware that there is a long list of possible meanings in the dictionary, but in almost every case there is another verb possible, and it is nearly always this other verb which is used. For example, the dictionary says that *sentire* means 'to touch', but we mostly use the other verb given, *toccare*. There is no question that, to most people, *sentire* is the accepted way of saying *udire* 'to hear'. Of course, if you use it reflexively, you automatically think of how you are feeling. *Mi sento male*, for example. But, I repeat, 'to hear' is the meaning which springs to mind. You will so often hear *Senti* and *Senta*. Some house-wives say, or rather shout, this word as they enter a shop, in order to attract attention and to try to avoid waiting their turn. You could say it was the same as the English 'I say!' but used much more frequently. If you go up to someone to ask some-thing, you should begin, politely, *Per cortesia* . . . or *Scusi* . . ., but very often people do say *Senta* . . ..

senza. This means 'without', as you must know. *Senza fallo* is 'without fail', and *senza dubbio* is 'without doubt'. These are common enough dictionary expressions. *Senza complimenti*, on the other hand, you will look hard to find under *senza*, yet you will hear it used very often. You may offer someone a cigarette, for example, and seeing him hesitant about taking one, you may say *Prego, senza complimenti*, meaning 'Go on, please take one', that is to say, 'it's a genuine offer'. Accompany-ing a friend to visit another of his friends, you may well be invited to come in and sit down *senza complimenti*, 'Do come in and sit down' ('We're not formal, come in and feel at home'). *Non faccia complimenti*, by the way, often means 'Do just as you wish', 'Say no if you want to', 'Say yes if you want to', etc.

Senz'altro is one of the common ways of saying 'of course', 'surely'. *Non posso venire domani, ma vengo senz'altro dopo-domani* means 'I can't come tomorrow, but I'll come the next day for sure'. *Posso usare il telefono?—Senz'altro* ('May I use the telephone?' 'Of course'.)

A rather tricky series of words is *senza soluzione di continuità*. The puzzle lies in the meaning of *soluzione* in this context. It in fact means 'interruption', and therefore the whole expression means 'without interruption', 'uninterruptedly'.

sequela (f). This refers to a string of several usually unpleasant things, coming one after the other, as in *una sequela di guai*, 'one trouble after the other', 'a succession of troubles'. Not to be confused with the English cognate word 'sequel', which in Italian is nearly always *il seguito* or *la continuazione*. The Italian *sequela* is just about the same as *sequenza*, 'sequence'.

sequestro (m). 'Sequestration', 'distraint', 'confiscation' or 'seiz-ure', according to the context. The usual meaning in the newspapers these days, however, is *sequestro di persona* in the sense of *rapimento*, 'kidnapping'. Similarly with the verb *sequestrare*: 'to seize, confiscate', etc., or 'to imprison a person unlawfully' or (usually) 'to kidnap'.

Serenissima (La). This refers to the Republic of Venice. Speaking of Venice, it is worth pointing out some of the common local words used in place names. *Calle* (or *salizzada*) is 'street', *campo* is 'square', *rio* is 'canal', and *fondamenta* or *riva* is 'quay'.

servizi (m pl). Speaking of the gas, electricity, water and other services of a town, these are the 'public utilities'. Advertisements for flats tell you what floor it is on (the *attico* or 'penthouse' being at a premium), how many rooms there are, and how many *servizi* there are (*doppii*, *tripli* and so on). This refers to the bathrooms and like rooms. Commonly a flat will have 'double services', the main bathroom and another one where there is a tub to do the washing, or a smaller room with washbasin and W.C.

settecento. 'Seven hundred'. *Il Settecento* is 'the eighteenth century'. *Settecentesco* is 'eighteenth-century'.

sfottere. A very common colloquial verb meaning 'to poke fun at', 'to take the mickey out of'. *Un tono sfottente* is 'a mocking tone'.

sfruttare. This is usually 'to exploit', in the sense of using resources or of causing to overwork. *Sfruttare una situazione* is 'to take advantage of a situation'. In a lower key, it is the action of a 'sfruttatore', one who sends prostitutes out on the streets (otherwise known legally as a *lenone*, and in slang as *magnaccia* or *pappone*; *ruffiano* has become rather a term of abuse).

sfumatura (f). A 'nuance' or 'shade' of meaning. If something has *sfumato*, it has 'come to nothing' or 'vanished'. *Le sue speranze sono sfumate dall'oggi al domani*, 'his hopes were dashed overnight'.

SG. These mysterious-looking letters on a menu mean *secondo grandezza*, 'according to size', i.e. the price depends on how big the item (meat, fish, etc.) is.

sì o no? Obviously, this means 'yes or no?' But you will find it in very frequent use, where we would say 'or not?', as in *vieni domani, sì o no?*, 'are you coming tomorrow or not?' *Capisci, si o no?*, 'do you understand or don't you?'

SID. The former Italian secret service. The letters stand for *Servizio Informazioni Difesa*, i.e. 'Information Service (of the) Defence (Ministry)'. Now replaced by the *Digos*.

signore (m or f pl). Remember, and avoid, the easily understandable error of those who know no Italian, or very little, that *signore* can be either the masculine singular, meaning 'sir' (not the title, of course), or the feminine plural, meaning 'ladies'. Confusion often leads to embarrassment, and in fact many public conveniences use *uomini* and *donne*, and increasingly schematic pictures instead of the words.

simpatico. This adjective means 'pleasant', as you are probably already aware, or 'nice' or some such thing, but not 'sympathetic', which is *compassionevole* or *comprensivo*, as likely as not. *Simpatico* is very much used, of people in particular but also of things. The opposite is also common, *antipatico*, 'unpleasant', 'nasty'. A *simpaticone* is a 'very likeable person'.

sindacato (m). 'Trade Union', 'Labour Union'. The main Italian unions are *CGIL* (*Confederazione Generale Italiana del Lavoro*), *CISL* (*Confederazione Italiana Sindacati Lavoratori*) and *UIL* (*Unione Italiana dei Lavoratori*). An industrial *sindacato* may be 'syndicate', 'trust', etc. A 'trade unionist' is *sindacalista*, and 'trade unionism' is *sindacalismo*. 'Claims' are *rivendicazioni*, which are put forward when there is a *vertenza*, 'dispute, controversy'.

sindaco (m). Quite simply, and perhaps surprisingly, this is the 'mayor'. The accent is on the first syllable. *Sindaco* also means 'auditor'. It is Italian practice not to call in outside auditing firms, but for a company to have its own *sindaci* or *collegio sindacale* ('Board of Auditors').

sistemare. A very common verb. The main meaning is 'put in order, fix, clear up, arrange'. *Senz'altro potremo sistemare qualcosa per loro*, 'Of course we'll be able to fix something up for them'; *non so come si può sistemare la faccenda*, 'I don't know how we can arrange this business'; *proviamo la nuova macchina. Ci sistemiamo tutti i quattro, e via*, 'Let's try out the new car. All four of us get in, and off we go'. Next it means 'to' find work, a job, for someone', 'to fix someone up (with a job)'. *Ha sistemato suo figlio in una banca*, 'he's got a job for his son in a bank'. It may also mean to 'marry off' a daughter. In all instances, therefore, the basic idea is to 'fix' things. Sometimes there might be a threat involved, as in *Lo sistemerò io!* 'I'll fix him!'

Remember that the noun *sistema* is masculine—*il sistema*.

sistemazione (f). 'Arrangement', 'arranging', 'fixing-up', sometimes 'installing'. Very often 'job'. *Ha trovato una buona sistemazione a Milano*, 'he's found himself a good job in Milan'. It is also used in a sense that is very difficult to translate in technical jargon. *Sistemazione del fiume Po*, for example, or *sistemazione della strada*. It really means 'doing what is necessary to the river', and the only general-purpose word we have in English is 'works'. In the case of a river, the works may well be bank protection, or straightening, or deepening, or a combination of these, and for a road they may include levelling, straightening, repairing, etc. Unless you know precisely what is involved, you will have to make do with 'works'.

smarrire. This transitive verb basically means 'to lose' or 'to mislay' (but remember the common verb meaning 'to lose' is *perdere*). As side meanings we have 'to bewilder', 'to confuse' and 'to mislead'; in this sense the reflexive form is common, and so *smarrirsi* may mean 'to lose your way', 'to get lost', 'to go astray'; 'to be bewildered'; 'to get confused'. These meanings come out in the adjective *smarrito*, which can be 'lost', 'mislaid', 'bewildered' or 'confused'. *Lei ha l'aria smarrita* means 'she looks lost'. The 'Lost Property Office' is *l'ufficio di oggetti smarriti*. The corresponding noun is *smarrimento*, usually meaning the feeling of being lost, or 'bewilderment': *ho avuto un attimo di smarrimento* is 'for a moment I was at a loss'. It also means the same as *svenimento*, i.e. a 'fainting fit' or a 'faint', of short duration.

sociale. Not only 'social', as in *assistenza sociale*, 'social work', but also 'company', as in *gita sociale*, 'company outing'. The *statuto sociale* is the 'articles of association'.

sofisticato. It is a neologism in Italian for this to mean 'sophisticated' as in the ordinary English use of the word. Its prime meaning is 'adulterated', especially of food products. The first meaning of the verb *sofisticare* is thus 'to adulterate (food)', while its learned meaning is 'to quibble', 'to split hairs'.

soggezione (f). This may mean 'subjection' (as also *sottomissione*), but more frequently means a feeling of respect and awe, or else uneasiness and embarrassment. *Mettere (incutere, ispirare) soggezione a qualcuno* is 'to make someone feel uneasy, to overawe someone', while from the other person's point of view, *avere soggezione di qualcuno* is 'to feel uneasy with someone'.

sogni d'oro (m pl). 'Sweet dreams' or 'sleep tight'. From the noun *sogno*, meaning 'dream'.

soldi (m pl). 'Money'. This is far and away the most-used Italian word for money. Remember that it is used in the plural. *Denaro* is also possible, of course, but *soldi* is the universal word. If you are unlucky enough to be completely broke, then you are *senza un soldo*, 'without a bean'. Otherwise you could use *essere al verde*, 'to be broke'.

solito. *Al solito* is 'as usual'. Remember the accent on the first syllable. *Alla solita ora* means 'at the usual time'. *Come al solito* is 'just as usual'. *Siamo alle solite!* is 'here we go again!', 'it's the same old story (all over again)!'

sonare. See **suonare.**

sono io. In English, on the telephone, we say 'this is . . . (speaking)'. In Italian, you say '*sono* . . .' or '*sono io*', i.e. not 'it's', but 'I'm'. The same construction when in English we say 'It is I who said that', for example, *Sono stato io che l'ho detto*. You cannot start with *È io* . . . . The same thing applies in the case of other persons. *Sei tu?* for instance, is 'Is that you?' Again, *sono loro* is 'it's them'.

sottogoverno (m). This is a pervasive Italian phenomenon, yet the dictionaries turn a blind eye to it. It consists fundamentally of the manipulation of patronage on a really vast scale to provide cash, jobs and votes for political parties and their allies. It refers to the complex of powers, especially of an economic nature, available to the parties in government, in the main posts of the civil service, public corporations, etc., to benefit their supporters (see also **clientelismo**). It includes the systematic assignation of directorships, etc., of institutes, corporations and agencies (forming what is sometimes called the *sottopotere*, q.v.) to the various parties and factions, each according to its political 'weight'.

sottopotere (m).   See also **sottogoverno** above. It is both the ensemble of organs (public agencies, RAI/TV, etc.) which are *under* the government, and the system of distributing posts and benefits on the basis of criteria of patronage, never of efficiency.

spegnere. 'To switch off', 'to put out'. *Spegnere la luce* is 'to switch the light off'. The past participle is *spento*. *Non ho ancora spento il motore*, 'I haven't switched the engine off yet'. The opposite is *accendere* (past participle *acceso*). *Spegnere* is accented on the first syllable, and *accendere* on the second.

spettacolo (m). This is the usual word for 'show', 'performance'. *Il più grande spettacolo del mondo* is 'the greatest show on earth'. *È uno spettacolo magnifico* is 'It's a wonderful show'.

spiccioli (m pl). Sometimes shortened to *spicci*. A word often heard in a country where 10, 50 and 100 lire coins always seem to be in short supply. It means 'change', usually in the sense of 'coins' (although, unless otherwise specified, if you asked for *spiccioli* for, say, a 10,000 lire note in a bank, you would be given 10 one-thousand notes in exchange). *Non ho spiccioli* is 'I have no change'. The word for 'change' in the sense of the money you receive back when you have paid, say, ten thousand lire for something that costs seven thousand, is *il resto* (in this case, of course, three thousand lire).

spiritoso. 'Clever' or 'witty'. *Non fare lo spiritoso* is 'Aren't you clever?'

sportello (m). This may be 'door', especially of a car, but in a post office, bank, etc., it is the position, window or counter where the teller or the clerk sits. Where tickets are sold, it is the 'ticket office' or 'ticket window'. In banking parlance, it also refers to the number of branches, when we say for example that a bank has *200 sportelli in tutto il paese*.

spumante (adj and m). Some call it 'champagne', but of course the proper denomination is 'sparkling wine'.

squallido. Something of a false friend, because the Italian word means more 'dreary' or 'bleak' than 'squalid', which is rather *sordido*. However, the borderline between these ideas is tenuous.

stabilimento (m). 'Factory', 'plant' or 'works'; but the special meaning of this word is in connection with the seaside (the beach, *la spiaggia*). In many resorts the whole stretch of sand is divided up among private *stabilimenti* or 'beach-stations'. Until recently, if you did not wish to pay to enter one of these, in order to have a swim or even get within hailing distance of the sea, you had to find a *spiaggia libera*, 'free beach'; it has now been ruled that anyone has a right to get down to the sea, so that *stabilimenti* must allow even non-payers through to the final five metres of sand fronting the water. But to enjoy the services of the stations it is still naturally necessary to pay. Some *stabilimenti* are quite luxurious, with swish pools and cabins, restaurants, etc., and others are less so, with rudimentary cabins, showers that work when they feel like it, and so on. Certain amenities have to be provided, including beach guards (*bagnini*).

stanza (f).   'Room'. The particular room I wish to mention is the one called the *Stanza dei Bottoni*. And it is not really a room. It refers to the decision-making centres, the key ministries (*Interno*, *Grazia e Giustizia*, *Difesa*, *Esteri*, *Tesoro*, i.e. 'Home Office', 'Justice', 'Defence', 'Foreign Office', 'Treasury'). Control these and you control the country. Therefore by extension it means 'power' in general. Such is the reasoning.

straccio (m).   The general word for 'rag', 'cloth', 'duster'. You may also hear someone referred to as *uno straccio*, which indicates that he looks 'worn out'.

studio (m).   Remember that as a place this may be 'studio' (for an artist, for making movies), 'study' (in a house, school, etc.), or 'office' (for a lawyer, architect, engineering consultant, etc.).

stufo.   'Fed up', 'sick' (of something). *Sono stufo di aspettare qui senza fare niente*, 'I'm fed up waiting here not doing anything'. *Stufo da morire* is 'bored stiff' or 'fed to the back teeth'. *Stufare* is 'to bore, annoy, make fed up'. It also means 'to stew', because *uno stufato* is 'a stew'. *Mi sono proprio stufato* is 'I'm sick and tired of it'. Notice that *una stufa* is 'a stove'.

stupidaggine (f).   'Stupidity', 'stupid thing', 'stupid action'; 'nonsense', 'rubbish', 'rot'. Also 'a mere trifle'.

su.   The point of mentioning this word is to draw attention to its use as an interjection. You wouldn't perhaps imagine it to be of very frequent use judging by usual dictionary entries such as 'Courage!' 'Bear up!' and so on. However, it *is* much used. In English we should usually say 'Come on', 'Come along' or 'Go on'. *Su* is used to encourage, much in the same way as *dai*, although *su* is somewhat gentler. Parents use it a lot in talking to their children. *Su, cammina, su* means 'Come along, walk, come on'. Animals are encouraged to take offered food from you, for example, by your saying *Su*. You encourage words from a hesitant mouth by saying *Su*. Sometimes you may add another word to vary things. *Su, forza*, for instance. A quiz-master, met with dead silence on asking a question, could use *Su* to try to get an answer. *Forza* would be somewhat stronger (in fact, it is used more to encourage someone who is beginning to wilt). Note the combinations: *su, sbrigati!* ('get a move on!'), *su, coraggio!* ('come on, cheer up'), *su, non piangere* ('come on, don't cry'). Note also the expression *su per giù*, meaning 'approximately'. *Era su per giù la stessa passeggiata che aveva fatta il sabato*, 'It was just about the same walk he'd had on Saturday'.

sub (m).   'Skin diver'.

subito.   This almost always means 'at once', 'immediately', 'right away'. *Subito dopo* means 'directly afterwards'. Remember the emphasis on the first syllable, as opposed to the emphasis on the past participle of *subire* ('to undergo'), which is also written *subito* but accented on the middle syllable. *Vengo subito* should mean 'I'm just coming'. 'I'll be with you directly', and it does mean just this, if you have it from the right person. If you are dubious about it when someone promises to come *subito*, you could repeat it, *subito subito*, to emphasize that it's important.

successo (m).   This can be a masculine noun or the past participle of the verb *succedere* ('to happen', 'to ensue'). The noun means 'success'; *senza successo* is 'without any success'. The main meaning of the verb form *è successo* is 'has happened'. *Cosa è successa?* means 'What's happened?'

succhietto, succhiotto (m).   A child's 'dummy' ('pacifier').

suggestionabile.   'Impressionable', 'easy to influence', 'easily influenced'.

suggestivo.   I do so wish compilers of guide books would realize that *suggestivo* is NOT 'suggestive' (which is rather *allusivo* or *insinuativo*), but—according to the actual context—'picturesque' 'evocative', 'delightful', 'interesting', 'romantic', 'striking' or 'impressive'. *Un paesaggio suggestivo* could be any of the above. But not 'suggestive'. Apart from this, *una domanda suggestiva* is 'a leading question'.

suonare, sonare.   Apart from being 'to sound' (*suona bene* is 'it sounds good', for example), this may be 'to strike' (of a clock), 'to ring' (of a bell), and—*nota bene*—'to play' (of a musical instrument). The verb is both transitive and intransitive, as in *lui suona il pianoforte*, 'he plays the piano', and *le campane suonano*, 'the bells are ringing', or *suona il telefono*, 'the phone is ringing'.
  As a colloquial adjective, *suonato* or *sonato*, the meaning is 'round the bend', 'off his rocker'.

superbo.   Usually 'arrogant', 'haughty'; it might sometimes be (of a building, for example) 'magnificent', 'imposing', 'grandiose', and here we might use 'superb', too. Rather less than 'arrogant', it may occasionally be 'proud'. *La Superba* is Genoa, due to the splendour of her history. Likewise *superbia* is 'arrogance', 'haughtiness'.

svincolo (m).   The full term is *svincolo autostradale*, and means 'interchange'. *Uno svincolo a quadrifoglio* is 'a cloverleaf'.

T

tagliare.   'To cut'. There is nothing particularly difficult about this verb. I am fond of the expression *tagliare la corda*, 'to leave', 'to be off', in very colloquial vein.

tamponamento (m).   Such a common word in newspapers. It is when one car runs into the back of another one, a 'collision'. A 'pile-up' is *tamponamento a catena*. The verb, 'to bump into (the car in front)' is *tamponare*.

tangente (f).   In geometry, this means 'tangent', but in ordinary language it means the percentage going to someone for his part in a transaction, an operation, etc. Therefore 'percentage' or 'commission', when the game is above board, or 'cut' or 'rake-off' when there is something shady going on.

tangenziale (f).   A 'by-pass'.

tanto.   This word can be adverb, adjective and indefinite pronoun, and is of really basic use and importance. The following are just a few pointers about *tanto*. Apart from them, if you spend some time becoming conversant with how to use the word properly, *tanto meglio* ('so much the better'); if not, *tanto peggio* ('so much the worse').

　　Di tanto in tanto means 'from time to time'. *Ogni tanto* is 'now and then'. *Tanto meglio/peggio per lui* means 'All the better/worse for him'. *Tanta gente* is 'so many people'. *Mio fratello mangia tanto* is 'My brother eats such a lot'. *Il signor X è tanto buono* means 'Mr X is such a good man'. When someone takes leave of another person, he often uses the expression *Tante cose*, which is really a short form of *Tante belle cose*, 'So many beautiful things' (which he hopes will come to you). Returning a greeting, *Altrettanto* means 'The same to you'.

　　One more thing about *tanto*. In a bus, for example, you might hear someone say *Si accomodi, signora*, offering a lady his seat (mind you, you'd have to choose your bus route very carefully to have a chance of finding an example of this!). The lady, perhaps hesitant of accepting, may be slow to sit, whereupon the offerer could say *Prego, si accomodi ... tanto io scendo subito*, 'Please sit down, as I'm getting off soon, anyway'. In this way it's a shortened form of *tanto più che*, meaning 'especially as', or 'seeing that'.

tappo (m). 'Stopper' 'plug', 'cork'. This is what the dictionary might or might not, but in any case should, tell us. In fact, there is the other meaning in colloquial Italian of 'a short person', 'shortie'. *È un tappo* means 'He's very short', 'He's undersized'.

targa (f). The 'number plate' ('licence plate') of a car. Italian car number plates start with the two-letter code of the provincial capital, usually the first two letters of the name, as MI for Milan; but when the letters have already been allocated to another town, the initial letter must be accompanied by another letter from further on in the name instead; e.g. CA is for Cagliari, and so Catania has to take its initial C and add its third letter to it, making CT. Note that Rome takes its full name, *Roma*, and that RO stands for Rovigo. 'A car with the number PG 16653' would be *un'automobile targata PG 16653*.

tassì (m). Also *taxi* (m). With the s sound you should accent the i, but with the x sound you should accent the a. The 'taxi-driver' is the *tassista* (m). The meter showing the price to be paid is the *tassametro*. The 'run' is called the *corsa*. The 'fare' is the *prezzo della corsa*.

tasso (m). Apart from meaning 'badger' and 'yew tree', this word is much used commercially and economically with the meaning of 'rate', as in *tasso di sviluppo* (or *di crescita*), 'growth rate'; *tasso di sconto*, 'discount rate'.

tavola (f), **tavolo** (m). 'Table', as we see, may be either feminine or masculine. More often than not it is feminine, although a small one takes the masculine diminutive form, *tavolino*. The feminine word has other meanings, too, such as 'plank' or 'board', or a 'table' in a book. To call everyone to the table, the cry would be *tutti a tavola!* A *tavola calda* is a cross between a delicatessen and a snack bar.

teleselezione (f). 'STD', i.e. 'subscriber trunk dialling'.

tendenza (f). This may sometimes be 'tendency', but it is mostly 'trend'. The verb *tendere*, apart from 'to stretch or pull out' and 'to tend', often means 'to aim'; e.g. *la nostra politica tende ad addestrare . . .*, 'the aim of our policy is to train . . .'.

teppista (m). 'Hooligan' or 'hoodlum'. What they indulge in is *teppismo*, 'hooliganism'.

tessera (f). Assiduous visitors to places of architectural interest will know that this word is the same in English, 'tessera', plural 'tesserae', meaning a small block used in a mosaic. But the everyday meaning of *tessera* to most Italians is 'season ticket'. It is also 'membership card' (*tessera di iscrizione*) or 'identity card' (*tessera di riconoscimento*).

testa (f). 'Head'. If you are 'in the lead', you are *in testa*. If you do things your own way without being advised by others, you are said to *fare a propria testa*; e.g. *lei fa sempre a testa sua*, 'she always does things her own way'. *Perdere la testa* is 'to lose one's head'. *Non sapere dove battere la testa* is 'not to know which way to turn'. *Tenere testa a qualcuno* is 'to keep up with someone', 'not to be left behind'. *Fare a testa e croce* is 'to toss up', and in fact you call either *testa o croce* ('heads or tails'). If your car spins round after a sudden braking and finds itself facing the wrong way, it has made a *testa coda*.

tifo (m). Not unknown in Italy with the meaning of 'typhus', but far better known in the expression *fare il tifo per . . .*, 'to be a . . . fan'; e.g. *mio fratello fa il tifo per i biancoazzurri*, 'my brother is a Lazio fan'. The fan himself is called the *tifoso*, this, too, a very common word, especially in the plural, *i tifosi*, 'the fans (supporters)'. The corresponding verb is *tifare*, which is either 'to support (be a fan of)' or 'to cheer', 'to root for'.

tight (m). Yet another English word used in Italian, but nothing to do with being drunk, nor with our 'tights' (these are singular in Italian, *calzamaglia* (f)). *Un tight* is in fact 'a morning coat'.

tintarella (f). 'Suntan'. *Prendere la tintarella* is 'to get suntanned'.

tizio (m). 'Individual', 'guy', 'fellow', 'chap'. *Lei stava parlando con un tizio all'ingresso* means 'She was talking to some chap at the door'. The word sometimes has a slightly pejorative sound about it, but nothing to be alarmed about, and it is widely used. One could also say *tipo*.

toccare. The transitive verb is 'to touch', but the intransitive verb means primarily 'to fall to', 'to concern' or 'to be the turn of'. *Tutti i guadagni toccano a lui*, 'all the winnings go (fall) to him'; *il premio tocca a lei*, 'the prize goes to her'; *questo non tocca a te*, 'this does not concern you'; *a chi tocca?—tocca a lui*, 'whose turn is it?'—'it's his turn'. Note the expression *a chi tocca, tocca*, 'that's just (your, his, etc.) bad luck!' As *tocco* means a 'touch', *dare l'ultimo tocco a qualcosa* means 'to give the finishing touch to something'. If things you handle turn out well, perhaps you have *il tocco magico*, 'the magic touch'. The adjective *toccato* means 'touched' in Italian, too (i.e. *un po' matto*, 'a bit crazy').

togliere una curiosità. Literally, 'to remove a curiosity', but in actual fact 'to satisfy someone's curiosity'. For example, if someone says to you *mi toglie una curiosità?* it means 'would you satisfy my curiosity?' or 'do you mind if I ask you something?' It is a preliminary question to the real question. The verb *togliere* once meant 'to prevent', but today this meaning lingers on in only one expression: *ciò non toglie che . . .* (followed by the subjunctive), as in *ciò non toglie che il tuo amico lo faccia*, 'that does not prevent your friend from doing it'.

torcere. 'To wring' or 'to twist' (e.g. 'to wring out wet clothes' is *torcere i panni bagnati*). 'To wring someone's neck' is *torcere il collo a qualcuno*. 'To wring one's hands' is *torcersi le mani*. If something or someone is giving you 'thread to twist', i.e. *ti dà del filo da torcere*, then he or it 'is a hard nut to crack'.

totocalcio (m). The system of public betting on the results of the Sunday's football matches, i.e. 'the football pools'. The coupon to fill in is called *la schedina* (q.v.).

traduzione (f). This means ordinarily 'translation', but also the rather odd-looking 'escorting of persons under arrest to prison or from one prison to another'. The corresponding verb *tradurre* ordinarily means 'to translate' (e.g. 'to translate from Italian into English' is *tradurre dall'italiano in inglese* (or *all'inglese*)), but may also mean 'to take (escort) to prison (or from one prison to another)'.

tramezzino (m). 'Sandwich'. *Un panino* is also a sandwich, but made with a roll.

tramontana (f). A cold, dry wind that blows from the north or the north-east. Rome occasionally receives this wind, which at least brings clear skies with it. The local people often say that it will last one day, three or five days, always an odd number. Don't you believe it. *Perdere la tramontana* means 'to lose your bearings'.

tramonto (m). This word is included, as it looks rather improbable for 'sunset', and usually eludes learners when they want to use it in a sentence. 'At sunset' is *al tramonto*. 'From sunrise to sunset' is *dall'alba al tramonto*. Figuratively, *essere al tramonto* means 'to be in decline'.

trampolino (m). 'Diving-board', where there's water around, but in the snow it is 'ski-jump'.

trasferta (f). In sports terminology, *in trasferta* means 'away from home'. An 'away match' is *una partita in trasferta*. *Trasferta* may also mean 'travelling expenses'.

trattabile. This adjective, referring to a person, means that the one concerned is 'reasonable' (i.e. you are able to talk to him in reasonable terms). But referring to a price, it means that it is open to discussion. If the rent (*fitto* or *affitto*) is quoted as *150,000 lire al mese, trattabile,* for instance, you know that you will be able to knock it down to 130,000—with a bit of luck.

trattamento (m). Generally, this means 'treatment', but in speaking of the *trattamento* you receive in a hotel, you mean the 'service', while a person speaking of the *trattamento* for his job will mean his 'pay', or perhaps the 'general working conditions'.

trattare. Generally 'to treat'. But the usage I wish to talk about here is that of saying *si tratta di* . . ., 'it's a question of . . .'. This corresponds to the French use of *il s'agit de* . . ., by which I mean that although the English meaning is, as stated, 'it is a question of', we do not always say this. *Non si tratta di parlare, ma di agire* is 'this is not a time for words, but for action', or something like that. *Si tratta di una vita umana* could be 'someone's life is at stake'. *Si tratta di deciderci* might be 'we have to make up our minds'. *Di che si tratta?* is 'what is it about?'

trattenuta (f). 'Deduction' (from something). My reason for adding this word here is to point out that if you are paid in Italy for some work performed, 15 per cent of the total will be deducted if you are a resident there, and twenty per cent if you are a non-resident, by way of *trattenuta di acconto* or 'withholding tax'.

trattoria (f). Remember to stress the next-to-last syllable. Some people, I know, claim there is a clear difference between a *ristorante* and a *trattoria*, but the difference is largely illusory. I know many *trattorie* that are better in all ways than many a place calling itself a *ristorante*. The English for them all is 'restaurant', anyway. The man who owns the *trattoria* is, odd as it may seem, *il trattore*, which is exactly the same word as that for 'tractor' (*trattore cingolato* is 'crawler tractor'). The 'tractor driver', by the way, is *trattorista*.

tredicesima (f). This means 'the thirteenth', and the missing word is *mensilità* (q.v.), i.e. 'month's pay'. So *la tredicesima* is the extra month's pay received each year (by law) just before Christmas. Accented on the *-ces-* part.

tredici. Thirteen. The Italian football-pool coupon (*schedina*, q.v.) has thirteen games and *fare un tredici* means to have got all thirteen right. Which may mean that your fortune is made, or again it may not, depending on how many others you have to share the winnings with.

tremendo. This means 'tremendous' in the sense of 'very large'. But the common colloquial meaning of the word may trip you up, as it's a false friend. If, for instance, you are waiting by the water's edge wondering whether or not to take the plunge, as you are afraid the temperature of the water may be rather on the low side, and you ask a person coming out of the water what it's like, he may well say to you *È tremendo!* In this case it would be wiser to stay dry, as the Italian idea is 'tremendously bad', rather than the usual English idea of 'tremendously good'. *Una cosa tremenda* is therefore 'a terrible thing'. (See also under **disastro**.)

U

ubriaco. The usual word for 'drunk'. As in other languages, Italian has a multiplicity of adjectives for this state, ranging from the formal *ebbro* through *allegro* and *alticcio* to *brillo*, *sbronzo* and *bevuto*, not forgetting such expressions as *ha bevuto un bicchiere di più* and *ha alzato il gomito* ('he's been raising his elbow'). *Ubriaco fradicio* (accented on -*aco* and *fra*-) is 'dead drunk'. 'Drunkard' is *ubriacone*.

udire. 'To hear'. As you will know, this verb is full of irregular forms, but this should not trouble you unduly, particularly as the verb for 'to hear' in almost universal use is *sentire* (q.v.).

uffa. This is a very common interjection expressing annoyance, boredom, impatience, etc. More than anything else, it corresponds to an energetic sigh in English. *Uffa! come sei noioso!* is 'My, how boring you are!' *Uffa, che caldo!* 'Phew! What a heat!' It is frequently used by itself, with no accompanying words, which makes it difficult to translate. A child being called in for tea when he is playing happily might well express himself thus: *Uffa!* (perhaps corresponding here to 'Oh, blow it!'). Or as the poor lady misses her aim for the tenth time when trying to thread a needle, she might also exclaim *Uffa!* The circumstances when it is used are manifold, and I leave it to you to supply the corresponding English expression, if any.

ufficioso. Properly this means 'unofficial', but is often used in the sense of 'semi-official'. *Ufficiosamente*, 'semi-officially'.

ultimamente. This does not mean 'ultimately', which is *alla fine*, *finalmente*, but 'recently', 'of late', 'lately'. A very useful word, sometimes also meaning 'lastly'. The accent is on the *ult*- and on the -*ment*-.

umore (m). 'Humour' in the sense of 'mood'. 'To be in a good mood (in good humour)' is *essere di buon umore*. 'Humour' in the sense of perceiving the funny side of things is *umorismo*, while in the sense of the funny side of things itself, it is *comicità*. *Essere di ottimo umore* is 'to be in excellent spirits'.

una tantum (adj and m). This means 'once only'. It is applied to payments, prizes, rewards, etc., which are not of a periodic or continual nature, but are made or given just once. Italian motorists now associate the words with the special tax payable in 1974 by car owners and motorcycle owners (the smallest cars including the famous 500 and the smaller motorbikes were exempt).

unico. 'One and only, single, sole'. *Figlio unico* is 'only child'. *L'unica cosa da fare* is 'the only thing to do', and *è l'unico modo* is 'it's the only way'. If you see a road sign reading *senso unico*, you know it is a 'one-way street'. If it means that there is none other like it, it is 'unique'. *Questo posto è unico nel suo genere* is 'this place is unique (of its kind)'. *Testo unico* corresponds to the English 'Consolidated Act', collecting together all the legal provisions on a given subject.

unificazione (f). To Italians this usually brings to mind the idea of 'standardization', while what they generally call *l'unità d'Italia* is what we call 'the unification of Italy'.

uovo (m). 'Egg'. Remember the plural *le uova*. *Un uovo sodo* is 'a hard-boiled egg'. 'Scrambled eggs' are *uova strapazzate*. 'New-laid eggs' are *uova da bere*. 'Easter egg' is *uovo di Pasqua*. The common expression *è l'uovo di Colombo* means 'it's as plain as a pikestaff'. And always remember, *meglio un uovo oggi che una gallina domani*, 'a bird in the hand is worth two in the bush'.

urbanesimo (m). 'Urbanization' in the sense of 'drift to the towns'.

urbanista (m and f). 'Town planner', 'city planner', 'urban planner'.

urbanistica (f). 'Town planning', 'city planning', 'urban planning'.

urbanizzazione (f). 'Urbanization'. *Urbanizzare* is 'to urbanize', both in the sense of providing urban facilities for a place, and that of fostering city growth by building new houses in the outskirts.

urbe (f). A literary word for 'city'. With the article, and capitalized, *L'Urbe* is Rome. *Urbi et orbi* is not Italian, of course, but Latin. These are the words (meaning 'to the city and to the world') used by the Pope in blessing the Catholics of Rome and of the whole world.

urna (f). Apart from meaning 'urn', this refers to the 'ballot box'. Thus *andare alle urne* means 'to go to the polls', 'to vote'. *Il responso delle urne* is 'the result of the voting'.

uva (f). This singular noun serves for the English 'grape' and the plural 'grapes'. 'Raisin' is *uva secca*. A 'gooseberry' (an unusual fruit in Italy) is an *uva spina*.

V

vaglia (m).   Notice that it is a masculine word. The meaning I am concerned with here is 'money order'. *Un vaglia postale* is 'a postal order'. *Vaglia telegrafico* is 'telegraph money order'. *Un vaglio*, on the other hand, is 'a sieve', and the verb *vagliare* means either 'to sift', 'to screen' or, figuratively, 'to weigh something up'. *Vagliare i pro e i contro* means 'to weigh up the pros and the cons'.

valere.   'To be worth'. *La nostra squadra vale più della loro*, 'our team is worth more than theirs'; *la collana vale cinquecento mila lire*, 'the necklace is worth five hundred thousand lire'. *Non vale la pena* is 'it's not worth while', 'it's not worth the trouble'. *Non vale la pena di imparare questa parola* means 'It's not worth learning this word'. *Valere* also means 'to be of use', 'to serve'. For example, *le nostre proteste non valsero a nulla*, 'our protests were of no use'; *le disposizioni date valgono in ogni caso*, 'the instructions given hold good in all cases'. *Non vale!* is the equivalent of 'that's not fair!', 'that doesn't count!' *Tanto vale* means 'it's all the same', 'it doesn't change anything'. *Se lui lo fai così, tanto vale che non lo faccia*, 'if that's the way he does it, he may as well not do it'. *Vale a dire* is 'that's to say'.

valico (m).   The dictionary tells you that this means 'pass' in the geographical sense, but it is not just that. It is any place where one officially crosses the frontier, i.e. a 'crossing point'. It is accented on the first syllable.

valido.   This is also accented on the first syllable. It means 'valid', basically, but the Italian word is used more than 'valid' is in English. *Un argomento valido* may be 'a valid argument', perhaps, but we are more likely to say 'a sound argument'. Our word for it is sometimes 'effective' or 'efficient': *un valido aiuto* is 'effective help', or even 'great help'.

valuta (f).   'Currency', 'money'. *Valuta legale* (or *valuta a corso legale*) is 'legal tender'. It refers in particular to 'foreign currency', 'foreign exchange'. In banking jargon, it refers to the day from when interest becomes payable: *valuta 20 marzo* is therefore 'interest running from 20th March'.

vediamo.   From *vedere*, 'to see', meaning of course 'Let's see' or 'we'll see'. Very frequently used with *un po*': *vediamo un po*', 'now let's just see'. *Vediamo un po' come stanno le cose*, 'let's just have a good think about things'. *Vediamo domani* would be the same as *vedremo domani*, 'we'll see (e.g. how things are) tomorrow'. Note the very common use with the personal pronoun *ci*: *ci vediamo sabato* is 'be seeing you Saturday', while just *ci vediamo* is 'be seeing you' ('so long', etc.). *Ci vediamo* *abbastanza spesso* is 'we quite often see each other'. *Andiamo* and *speriamo* are the other two members of the trio of common *-iamo*'s, *andiamo* meaning 'come on', 'let's go', etc., and *speriamo* 'let's hope so', 'here's hoping'. *Speriamo bene* is 'let's hope for the best'. If we extend the trio to a quartet, we could add *facciamo*. *Facciamo così* is 'let's do this', 'let's do it this way', and so on.

velleità (f).   How fond Italian politicians are of using this word. And how rare it is to find any mention of it in dictionaries. And, to outdo themselves, these politicians have recourse to the word *velleitarismo*. This is an attitude inspired by vague ambitions that cannot be achieved as they are unfounded or because they are greater than the capacity of the person concerned to achieve them. 'Empty wishes', 'ambitions', 'aspirations', 'vague thoughts' and 'vain hopes' are some of the possibilities. The corresponding adjective is *velleitario*, meaning 'over-ambitious', etc. We hear of *dichiarazioni*, *posizioni*, *pretese*, *proteste* and *scelte* being *velleitarie* ('exaggerated (empty, vain, etc.) statements, positions, claims, protests and choices').

verde.   'Green'. *Verdastro* is 'greenish'. *Essere al verde* is 'to be broke'.

vergogna (f).   'Shame', in the sense of something to be ashamed of. *Avere vergogna* is 'to be ashamed'. Likewise *vergognarsi* is 'to be (feel) ashamed'. The English 'what a shame!' however, is *che peccato!* whereas the Italian *che vergogna!* is more like 'what a disgrace!' 'how disgraceful!' or 'shame on (e.g. you)!' Another complication is that in colloquial Italian *vergogna* is associated with timidity, shyness. *Non aver vergogna* is 'don't be shy!' Correspondingly, *vergognoso* is 'ashamed' or 'shameful' or 'shy, bashful'. *Vergognatevi!* is 'you ought to be ashamed!' Sometimes, perhaps, the best rendering of *è una vergogna* or *è vergognoso!* would be 'there ought to be a law against it!', as in English we almost automatically revert to the law.

verificare.   'To verify', 'to check'. Talking of accounts, it means 'to audit'. The tricky thing is the use of the form *verificarsi*. Properly, this means 'to prove right', 'to turn out to be true', 'to be confirmed', as in *le mie previsioni si sono tutte verificate*, 'my forecasts all proved right' ('all turned out to be true'). Improperly, according to the grammar book, but very commonly, *verificarsi* means 'to take place, happen'. For example, *oggi si sono verificati tre incidenti stradali*, 'there have been three road accidents today', 'three road accidents have occurred today'.

vero.   Here's a refreshing thought. While Italians and others have to struggle with the dozens and dozens of variations (of grammar, form and intonation) of our question-tag system ('Nice day, isn't it?' 'You will come, won't you?' 'You had a lot of trouble, didn't you?' 'I'm here, aren't I?'—just to remind you of the complexity of them) we, on the other hand, have only to learn *Non è vero?* which is sometimes shortened to *Vero? Fa caldo, non è vero?* is 'It's hot, isn't it?' Be careful, and don't overdo this construction. Italians use it quite a lot, but not so freely as we do in English.

Note also that *dire il vero* means 'to tell the truth', just as *dire la verità* does.

vertenza (f). 'Controversy', 'dispute'; frequently used in a trade-union context. *Una vertenza sindacale*, 'a trade-union dispute'.

via (f). 'Street' or 'road'. Also 'way', as in *la via più breve per la piscina*, 'the shortest way to the swimming pool'. *Le vie del Signore* are 'the ways of the Lord'. *Una via di mezzo* is 'a compromise'. 'Air mail' is *per via aerea*, and likewise we have *via mare* and *via terra*, 'by sea' and 'by land'. *Il treno Roma–Milano, via Bologna* is 'The Rome–Milan train via Bologna'.

Via also has great use as an adverb, meaning 'away', 'off'. *Andare via* is 'to go away', like *andarsene*. You may say *Vado via* just as you may say *Me ne vado*. 'To throw something away' is *buttare via qualche cosa*. *Mandare via* is 'to order off'. If you want someone to go away, you say *Via!* (or the longer forms *Andate via!* or *Va' via!*).

Via! is also used with the meaning of 'come on!' (see also *su*). *Via, non dire queste cose* is 'come on now, don't say such things as that!' *Via via* means 'as' in a progressive sense; e.g. *via via che arrivano mandali dal direttore*, 'as they come, send them to the manager'. *In via eccezionale* is 'exceptionally', 'by way of exception'. To start off a race, after saying *uno, due . . .* or *pronti*, the word to set them off is *via!* (As a noun, 'the start' is *il via*.) Another very important point is the use of *e così via*, 'and so on'. And, to bring this entry to a close, I will say *e via dicendo* (or *e via discorrendo*), which also mean 'and so on', 'and so forth'.

viabilità (f). This unlikely looking word has three distinct meanings. First, it is 'road conditions'. Second, it means 'roads' in general (remember, singular in Italian, plural in English). And third, it is the ensemble of standards and regulations governing the upkeep of roads and road traffic.

vigile (m). As a member of the city police (*polizia urbana*), he is a 'policeman' ('patrolman'). *Un vigile del fuoco* is a 'fireman'. *Vigile notturno* is (more or less) 'nightwatchman' (see under **polizia**). *Vigili* ('policemen') may be motorized (in cars or on motorcycles), may direct the traffic at crossings, or be in the vicinity to see that the *Codice Stradale* ('Rule of the Road') is adhered to, or be on the prowl with notebook and pencil, slapping notifications of a fine on cars parked in the wrong place (nearly everywhere). These days he is often aided and abetted by his female counterpart, called *vigilessa*.

vigliacco (adj and m). 'Coward', 'cowardly'. The colour yellow cannot be applied in Italian as it can in English. 'He's yellow!' is *È un vigliacco! Giallo* is applied in Italian to detective stories and films. *Ho letto un buon giallo* is 'I've read a good detective story'.

villa (f). Sometimes 'villa', sometimes 'country house' and sometimes just 'house'. By extension it refers to the grounds or country around the actual house. In Rome, for example, the most popular park open to the public, from the top of the Via Veneto to the Piazza del Popolo and the zoo, is called Villa Borghese.

villino (m). This is a *palazzina*, a fairly good-class house, not more than three storeys in height, usually in town, and surrounded by some sort of garden. If you call it a 'cottage', you will have to have a pretty superior type of cottage in mind.

vincere. 'To win' (a competition, a race, a battle, *e così via*). *La vincita* is the 'win', 'victory' or the 'winnings'. The 'winner' is *vincitore*. *Battere* is 'to beat', although there is not the same clear-cut division between *vincere* and *battere* in Italian, as there is in English between 'to win' and 'to beat'. *Vincere* can, on occasion, be used where we use *battere*, with the meaning of 'overcome'. For example, we 'beat a competitor', while Italians can *vincere un concorrente*.

vino (m). Everybody knows that this is wine. It remains only to specify a few sorts. *Vino amabile*, like *vino abboccato*, is 'sweetish wine', while *vino dolce* is 'sweet wine'. *Vino da tavola* or *vino da pasto* is 'ordinary table wine'. 'Dry wine is *vino secco*. *Vino spumante* (or plain *spumante*) is 'sparkling wine'. You can buy wine everywhere, in cafés, bars, dairies and so on, apart from the shops marked *Vini, olii, liquori*. Note that most Italian wines are supposed to be bad travellers, so that they lose a lot of their special qualities if they are exported. Frascati wines, for example, can hardly do the half-hour journey to Rome without losing something. It is only comparatively recently that Italians have started properly developing and improving their wine-making industry. Wines from an area demarcated carefully and made according to strictly applied regulations qualify for the area DOC (*denominazione d'origine controllata*) certificate (something like the French *appellation contrôlée*). Probably the wines best known abroad are those from the Chianti area (between Siena and Florence). The two best-known trademarks are the cockerel (*gallo*) and the *putto*. The place where the wine is made, and/or where it is stored, is the *cantina*, which may also be used for the shop where the wine is sold. *Annata* is 'vintage'. *Vinello* is any very light but pleasant enough wine.

viola (f). This may be the 'violet' or the 'viola', and the adjective is the colour 'violet'. *I viola* refers to the Fiorentina F.C.

virgola (f). Comma. I include this word for two reasons. First, to stress that the English 'comma' is not *comma* in Italian (the word *comma* is masculine and is used in legal parlance, meaning 'paragraph' or 'sub-section'); and second—and more particularly—to emphasize that in Italian, as in other languages, the comma (i.e. *virgola*) is used in numbers to represent what we call the decimal point (and vice versa, where in English we use the comma to separate thousands, in Italian the point is used). Thus in an Italian context 7.300 is seven thousand three hundred, whereas 7,300 is seven point three. Remember that it is pronounced *virgola*, in this case *sette virgola tre* (and remember also that *virgola* has the accent on the first syllable). Note that a 'semi-colon' is *punto e virgola*.

visione (f). 'Vision'. In connection with cinemas, see under **prima visione**.

visita medica (f). 'Medical examination', 'medical checkup'. The verb *visitare* is also used in this sense, 'to examine' (medically).

voglia (f). 'Desire', 'longing', 'wish'. *Voglia* often corresponds to the English 'feel like doing something', as, for example, in *non avevo voglia di uscire*, 'I didn't feel like going out'. *Ho una voglia matta di un po' di vino* is 'I'm just dying for a drop of wine'. *Muoio dalla voglia di rivederla* is 'I'm dying to see her again'. *Ho una gran voglia di . . .* is another way of expressing 'I'm longing to . . .'.

volentieri. A very useful word to express your willingness to do something. To accept with alacrity (or courtesy) you do it *volentieri*, or else *con piacere*. *Volete accompagnarmi allo studio? —Sì, ben volentieri* or *Grazie, volentieri*. ('Would you like to come with me to the studio?' 'Yes, with pleasure' or 'Thank you, I'd love to.')

volere. The usual verb for 'to want'. Remember the subjunctive after it if you use the construction *volere che . . .*. For example *Voglio che lei faccia così*, 'I want you to do it like this'. Now let's have a look at the expression *ci vuole*. *Ci vuole troppo tempo per fare una cosa simile* means 'too much time is required to do such a thing'. *Ci vuole pazienza* is 'you must be patient'. *Proprio quello che ci voleva* is the expression when just the right thing turns up: 'just the very thing'. *Per imparare bene una lingua ci vuole molta pratica*, 'to learn a language properly, a lot of practice is needed'. Also in expressions of time, *ci vuole* finds a place. *Ci vuole almeno una mezz'ora* is 'it'll be (take) at least half an hour'. *Ci vuole molto?* asks 'will it take (be) long?' And if there is any thought of the local bore turning up just when you're feeling down in the dumps, well . . . *non ci vorrebbe altro!* 'that would really be the last straw!'

volontà (f). 'Will'. 'Good will', *buona volontà*, is something often spoken about in Italy, and often demonstrated. *Di mia spontanea volontà* is 'of my own free will'. *A volontà* is 'at pleasure' or 'at will'. *È un uomo sempre pieno di buona volontà* means 'he's a man always full of good will'. *L'avrei fatto se fosse stato possibile, ma purtroppo non dipendeva dalla mia volontà*, 'I'd have done it if it had been possible, but unfortunately it was beyond my control'.

voto (m). This has several meanings. It is, first of all, the promise made solemnly before God (or the Madonna or a saint, very commonly the case in Italy) to perform an action that will please Him (etc.), or to abstain from actions that would give us pleasure, in return for assistance. That is to say, a 'vow'. *Mantenere, osservare* or *sciogliere un voto* is 'to keep a vow'. *Rompere un voto* is 'to break a vow'. It may also be the actual thing offered, 'votive offering'. Again, and in the plural this is a word very popular with speechifiers in Italy, especially politicians, it means 'wish'; e.g. *i miei più fervidi voti*, 'my most fervent wishes'. But this is not all. It is also the electoral 'vote'; and *un voto di fiducia* is 'a vote of confidence'. And lastly—it is here that mistakes are usually made—in schools it means 'mark'. 'Full marks' are *pieni voti*.

vuotare. 'To empty'. *Vuotare il sacco* is either 'to spill the beans' or 'to make a clean breast of things'.

Z

zampone (m). A speciality of Modena, a sort of sausage stuffed in a pig's trotter and boiled. A Christmas speciality.

zitto. 'Silent'. *Sta' zitto!* is 'be quiet!' or 'shut up!'

zootecnia (f). I have often seen people stumped by this word, which is simply 'animal husbandry'. *Il patrimonio zootecnico* is 'livestock'.

zoppicare. 'To limp', 'to be lame'. There is a saying that *chi va con lo zoppo impara a zoppicare*. The dictionary tells us that this is the same as the English 'birds of a feather . . .', but this is stretching the point somewhat. The sense of the saying is that 'he who is apprenticed to a thief will become a thief himself'—perhaps not always 'thief', but something not quite above board, at any rate. *Zoppo* means 'lame'. *Essere zoppo* is 'to be lame' or 'to limp'.

zuppa (f). 'Soup', used particularly in three contexts: *zuppa di pesce*, 'fish soup'; *zuppa di verdura*, 'vegetable soup'; and *zuppa inglese*, which is not a soup at all, but 'trifle', oddly enough!

False Friends

There are many English words that have counterparts in Italian of similar form—indeed, sometimes the English word itself has been loaned. Remember that we are speaking of the 'form' of the word, and not the meaning. In many cases the meaning, also, is similar, if not exactly the same, but this is certainly not always the case, and it will pay you to be careful and to check the meanings of *all* words when you first meet them, not being content merely to check those of completely different form. For example, suppose you came across the word *villano*. You must not say to yourself, 'ah, this must mean "villain"', and take it for granted. In point of fact, it does *not* mean this, but, as a noun, 'peasant' (the meaning varying according to the context), while 'villain' in Italian is *furfante* or *mascalzone*. Again, even such a recently borrowed word as 'clergyman' is different in meaning. It entered Italian meaning the clothes the clergyman wears informally (black suit and dog-collar), not the man himself. So, take nothing for granted the first time.

Below is a list of words called 'false friends', because their very similarity tends to make us feel already familiar with them, i.e. to treat them as 'friends', whereas in fact they are 'false', because they are misleading. I should mention that this list has no claim to being exhaustive. Against the Italian word is the English translation, or the most usual one, while against the English word of similar form in the second column is the usual Italian word that actually corresponds to it. Sometimes, I know, there could be no mistake because of the logic of things. It would certainly be difficult to confuse a 'convict' and a 'boarding school', for instance! In other cases, however, mistakes could easily occur. If someone were said to be holding a *radicchio*, to be used for the table, you might well confuse it logically with 'radish', which in actual fact is *ravanello*. (For the record, *radicchio* is a type of chicory, chicory otherwise being known as *cicoria*.) If someone were walking to the *ginnasio*, you could be excused for mistaking this for a 'gymnasium', and also for thinking that a handful of *confetti* were made of paper. Then there is another thing I should point out about the following list. It might be thought odd that while *discussione* is given as 'argument', 'discussion' is given as *discussione* (likewise *pilota* as 'racing driver', 'pilot' as *pilota*, and so on). The fact is that the English word against the Italian one in the first column is the typical and differing meaning, although the Italian word has other meanings, too, one at least of which corresponds with the usual English word. It is very often a question of context, and as these words are in a list with no context, the shades of meaning or the circumstances of their use cannot be brought out.

Italian–English

English–Italian

accidenti! damn it!

annoiato, bored

argomento, subject

assistere, attend; witness

attaccare, stick; fasten

attendere, wait

attico, penthouse

attuale, present

attualmente, at present

baracca, hut

barista, barman

bravo, good; clever

camera, room

cantina, cellar

cava, quarry

coincidenza, connection

collegio, boarding school

commedia, play

concussione, extortion

conferenza, lecture

confetti, sugared almonds

confezione, make; wrapping

controllare, check

convitto, boarding school

delusione, disappointment

diplomato, person with diploma

discreto, moderate

discussione, argument

disgrazia, accident

educato, polite, well-mannered

emozione, excitement

esonerare, dismiss

esperienza, experiment; experience

eventualmente, possibly

fabbrica, factory

fattoria, farm

firma, signature

fotografo, photographer

fresco, cool

geniale, of genius

ginnasio, high school

governante, housekeeper

ignorare, not to know

insolazione, sunstroke

accident, incidente

annoyed, seccato, infastidito

argument, discussione

assist, aiutare

attack, attaccare, assalire

attend, assistere

attic, soffitta

actual, reale

actually, realmente

barracks, caserma

barrister, avvocato

brave, coraggioso

camera, macchina fotografica

canteen, mensa

cave, caverna

coincidence, coincidenza

college, scuola superiore

comedy, commedia leggera

concussion, commozione cerebrale

conference, congresso

confetti, coriandoli

confectionery, caramelle

control, controllare; dominare

convict, detenuto

delusion, illusione

diplomat, diplomatico

discreet, discreto

discussion, discussione

disgrace, vergogna

educated, istruito, educato

emotion, emozione; commozione

exonerate, esonerare

experience, esperienza

eventually, alla fine

fabric, tessuto

factory, fabbrica

firm, azienda

photograph, fotografia

fresh, fresco; nuovo

genial, cordiale

gymnasium, palestra

governess, governante

ignore, ignorare; far finta di non vedere

insulation, isolazione

Italian–English

largo, wide
lettura, reading
libreria, bookshop, bookcase
lift, lift-boy
lunatico, moody
lussuria, lust
magazzino, store
marmellata, jam

materia, subject
morbido, soft
night, night club
noioso, boring
notorio, well-known
occorrere, be necessary
paragone, comparison
parente, relation
patente, driving licence
pavimento, floor
petrolio, oil
piccolo, small
pigione, rent
pilota, racing driver
promiscuo, mixed, multipurpose
pronto, hello; ready
pullman, coach
raccomandare, register; recommend
radicchio, chicory
risultare, appear; prove to be
riunione, meeting
ruffiano, pimp
rumore, noise
salario, wage
scalpello, chisel
sciocco, silly
Scotch, scotch-tape
sensibile, sensitive
sentenza, judgment, sentence
sequela, sequence
simpatico, pleasant, likeable

sofisticato, adulterated
squallido, dreary
successo, happened; success
suggestivo, picturesque; impressive
superbo, arrogant, haughty

English–Italian

large, grande, grosso
lecture, conferenza
library, biblioteca
lift, alzare, sollevare
lunatic, pazzo
luxury, lusso
magazine, rivista
marmalade, marmellata d'arance
matter, materia
morbid, morboso
night, notte
noisy, rumoroso
notorious, famigerato
occur, succedere
paragon, modello perfetto
parent, genitore
patent, brevetto
pavement, marciapiede
petrol, benzina
piccolo, ottavino
pigeon, piccione
pilot, pilota
promiscuous, sregolato
pronto, subito
pullman, carrozza di lusso
recommend, consigliare, raccomandare
radish, ravanello
result, risultato
reunion, riunione
ruffian, mascalzone
rumour, diceria
salary, stipendio
scalpel, bisturi
shock, scossa; 'choc', colpo
Scotch, whisky
sensible, sensato
sentence, frase; proposizione
sequel, seguito
sympathetic, comprensivo, compassionevole
sophisticated, sofisticato
squalid, sordido
success, successo
suggestive, allusivo, insinuativo

superb, eccellente

Italian–English	*English–Italian*
tight, morning coat	**tight,** stretto; 'brillo'
	tights, calzamaglia
tremendo, terrible	**tremendous,** enorme

Disconcerting Genders

As you know, most nouns ending in -o are masculine, while most ending in -a are feminine. You will have learned that *mano* and *radio* are the two exceptions to the first rule, while to the second rule there are the following exceptions:

> names of men, professions and titles (e.g. *Luca*, *papa*, *dentista*, *poeta*, *duca*)
> nouns derived from Greek, ending in -ma or -ta: such as *poema*, *clima*, *diploma*, *pianeta*

It's a pretty safe bet that the gender of an Italian word which has the same form, or very nearly the same form, as the French or Spanish word, will correspond. This is, as I say, a very reasonable guide for those approaching Italian from either Spanish or French. However, you should never take things like this for granted whenever you have the opportunity of checking up. Occasionally you will come unstuck: 'blood', for example, *la sangre* in Spanish, is *il sangue* in Italian. And the word for 'tooth' is *la dent* in French, whereas in Italian it is *il dente*.

However, these are not the things that cause overmuch difficulty. The difficult words are those which exist in two forms, with an -a ending and with an -o ending, the two words having completely different meanings. Look at these lists in which I include the more important ones (plus *fine*):

il ballo, dance	**la balla**, bale, bundle
il collo, neck	**la colla**, glue
il colpo, blow	**la colpa**, fault
il costo, cost	**la costa**, coast
il filo, thread	**la fila**, line
il fine, aim	**la fine**, end
il foglio, sheet (paper)	**la foglia**, leaf
il limo, mud	**la lima**, file
il manico, handle	**la manica**, sleeve (**La Manica**, the English Channel)
il mazzo, bunch (flowers)	**la mazza**, sledgehammer
il mento, chin	**la menta**, mint
il modo, manner	**la moda**, fashion
il porto, port	**la porta**, door
il punto, detail, dot	**la punta**, tip
lo spigo, lavender	**la spiga**, ear (corn)
il tasso, rate; badger	**la tassa**, tax
il velo, veil	**la vela**, sail, sailing

Nor is this all. There are also the following, which change gender in the plural (and I include here the nouns which have two different plurals, with different meanings):

il braccio (arm)	**le braccia**
il ciglio (eyelash)	**le ciglia**
il corno (horn)	**le corna**
il dito (finger)	**le dita**
il frutto (fruit)	**le frutta** (**i frutti** may be 'results')
il ginocchio (knee)	**le ginocchia**
il labbro (lip)	**le labbra**
il lenzuolo (sheet)	**le lenzuola** (uncommon **i lenzuoli**)
il miglio (mile)	**le miglia**
il muro (wall)	**le mura** (city walls) (**i muri** as 'barriers', etc.)
l'osso (bone)	**le ossa**
il paio (pair)	**le paia**
il sopracciglio (eyebrow)	**le sopracciglia**
l'uovo (egg)	**le uova**

Remember also that there are certain nouns that do not vary their form in the plural. You should know the following categories:

(a) nouns stressed on the final syllable: *la città, le città*.
(b) monosyllabic nouns, *la gru* (crane), *le gru*.
(c) nouns ending in a consonant, *il filobus, i filobus*.
(d) composite nouns, *il portacenere, i portacenere*.
(e) nouns ending in *-i, l'analisi, le analisi*.

Up to now we have been thinking about the plurals of nouns. There are however also a number of difficult points connected with the formation of the feminine. In the following list, the feminine is distinctly different from the masculine:

il babbo (father)	**la mamma** (mother)
il bue (ox)	**la mucca** (cow)
il cane (dog)	**la cagna** (bitch)
il fratello (brother)	**la sorella** (sister)
il genero (son-in-law)	**la nuora** (daughter-in-law)
il marito (husband)	**la moglie** (wife)
il maschio (male)	**la femmina** (female)
il padre (father)	**la madre** (mother)
il re (king)	**la regina** (queen)
l'uomo (man)	**la donna** (woman)

There are others, but these are the most important, and although some of them are ridiculously easy, you would perhaps be surprised to hear how many times I have heard people who ought to know much better referring to *una fratella* and so on. Be on your guard.

It is worth making one further point, as so many people become confused when they are referring to animals ('But I don't mean the female, I want to say the male!'). Some animal names have no feminine form: *delfino* (dolphin), *coniglio* (rabbit), *topo* (rat), *tordo* (thrush). Others, on the other hand, have no masculine form: *aquila* (eagle), *balena* (whale), *pantera* (panther), *rondine* (swallow), *scimmia* (monkey), *tigre* (tiger), *vipera* (viper), *volpe* (fox). In the event of having to specify the masculine or feminine when the form is lacking, you say: either, for example, *la scimmia maschio* or *il topo femmina*, or else *il maschio della scimmia* or *la femmina del topo*.

Allow me to point out, in conclusion, what you have possibly already noted for yourself, that differentiating between words having either gender snags or just one letter different from another word causes considerable difficulty at times. See, for instance, *capello* (hair) and *cappello* (hat), *dita* (fingers) and *ditta* (firm), *copia* (copy) and *coppia* (couple).

English-Italian
Cross-Reference Index

N.B.

In using this index, it is very important to bear in mind that the Italian word against the English one merely indicates under which entry one should look in the main section of this volume. It may or may not be an actual translation of the word in question. It must be remembered that several different points may be mentioned under a single entry. By way of example, against 'advice' we find the word *mancia*; this is definitely not a translation of 'advice', but under *mancia* in the main section we find not only the translation of it (i.e. 'tip' in the monetary sense), but also mention of 'tip' in the sense of 'advice'; hence the cross-reference. You are therefore advised to tread with care in using this section.

A

able, capace
about, pressappoco
about time, ora
absolutely, addirittura
absolutely incredible, pazzo
absolutely right, giusto
accident, accidente, disgrazia
accident at work, morte
accident insurance, assicurazione
according to size, SG
accountancy, accountant,
   ragioniere
ace, fuoriclasse
action (legal), processo
actual, attuale
actually, invece
adapt, accomodare
adapt to, adeguarsi
address, indirizzo, recapito
adjust, accomodare
adjust to, adeguarsi
adulterate(d), sofisticato
advice, mancia
advisability, opportunità
afford, mezzo

affront, offendere
after all, resto, definitiva
again, ancora
agenda, odg
agree, agreement, accordo
aim, metà, tendenza
air, aria
air lift, ponte
air mail, via
all ears, orecchio
all grist to mill, brodo
all in all, conto
all right, accordo, andare, bene
All Souls' Day, morto
all the better/worse, tanto
already, già, ora
alsatian, lupo
amateur, professionista
amuse oneself, amusing,
   divertirsi
anchor, ancora
ancient times, antichità
and so, ebbene
and so on, così, via
angry, incavolato
animal husbandry, zootecnia
announcement, partecipazione

annoy, fastidio, noia, scocciare,
    seccare, stufo
annoying, dispetti
another question, discorso
answer, rispondere
antiques, antichità
anxious, preoccupare
anyway, comunque, insomma,
    resto
apart from, oltre
apology, scusare
appear, risultare
appearances, figura
apple (tree), oliva
application, istanza
apprehensive, preoccupare
approximately, su
aptitude, atteggiamento
arc, arch, arco
argue, argomento, polemica
argument, argomento
argumentative, polemica
armchair, poltrona
armed robbery, rapire
army, esercizio
arrange, combinare, provvedere,
    sistemare
arrangement, sistemazione
arrest, fermare
arrogant, superbo
art director, direttore
artful, furbo
articles of association, sociale
articulation, articolato
ashamed, vergogna
ask, rispondere
assistant, assistere
as soon as, come
assumption, ipotesi
assurance, assicurazione
astride, astraddle, cavallo
as usual, solito
at all, affatto
at a loss, smarrire
at any rate, caso, comunque,
    modo, resto
at best, ipotesi
at heart, fondo
athletics, atletica
at last, ora

at least, meno
atomic pile, pila
at once, subito
at pleasure, volontà
at present, attuale
at stake, ballo
attack, attaccare
attend, assistere, attendere
attendance check, gettone
attend to formalities, pratica
attic, attico
attire, attirare
attitude, atteggiamento
attract, attirare
at the usual time, solito
at will, volontà
at wits' end, santo
audit, verificare
auditor, sindaco
automatic vending machine,
    distributore
autonomy, autonomia
available, availability,
    disponibile
average, ordinario
award, coppa
away, via
away match, trasferta

B

baby's napkin, panno
back, back stroke, dorso
badger, tasso
bad business, faccenda
bad impression, figura
bad luck, scarogna
badly, male
bad manners, educato,
    mancanza
bad-tempered, fegato
bag, borsa, sacco
bag-snatcher, bag-snatching,
    scippo
balaclava helmet,
    passamontagna
balance of payments, bilancio
balance sheet, bilancio,
    patrimonio

ballerina, ballo
ballot box, urna
bandwagon, carrozzone
bank, banca, cassa
banker's draft, assegno
bank holiday, Ferragosto
bank rate, sconto
bargain, affare, negozio,
  occasione
barman, bar, barista
baron, barone
barrel, fusto
barrister, barista
bash someone, menare
batch, partita
bathing, balneazione
battery, batteria, pila
beach guard, stabilimento
beach stations, stabilimento
be acquainted with, corrente
be all the rage, fare
bean, fagiolo, fava
bear (hold), reggere
beard, barba
bear up, su
be ashamed, vergogna
beat, vincere
beat about bush, menare
be better/best to, convenire
be broke, verde
be careful, attenzione, fare
be cold, fare
become, diventare
be crazy, roba
bed-linen, biancheria
bedroom, camera, macchina
beefsteak, bistecca
bee in bonnet, chiodo
beer, birra
behaviour, costume
behind back, insaputa
be lacking, mancare
be missing, mancare
be off, tagliare
be of use, valere
be on order, arrivare
be on strike, scioperare
be present, assistere
be quiet, zitto
besides, oltre

beside the point, entrare
best wishes, auguri
be taken in, cascare
betray, corno
better half, metà
be warm, fare
bewilder, smarrire
be worth, valere
beyond (the), oltre
beyond compare, paragone
beyond control, caso,
  volontà
bidet, bidè
bid farewell, salutare
bidonville, baraccati
big, grosso
big-headed, presuntuoso
big name, big
big shot, big, grosso
bill, conto, disegno
billion, miliardo
binding, impegno
bird in hand, uovo
birth certificate, nascita
birth control, nascita
birthday, nascere
birthplace, nascita, paese
birth rate, nascita, natalità
bit, pezzo
bitter end, oltranza
black, nero
black eye, nero
blackguard, mascalzone
blackleg, scioperare
black list, libro
black market, borsa, nero
black sheep, nero
bleak, squallido
bless you, salute
blind thing, cavolo
blitzkrieg, lampone
block of flats, palazzo
blonde, bionda
blotting paper, carta
blow, colpo
blue collar, impiegato
blunder, papera
blunt, pelo
board, tavola
board (bus), salire

boarding school, collegio, convitto
body corporate, persona
bogus, fasullo
bon voyage, buon giorno
book, libro
bookcase, bookshop, libreria
bookstall, edicola
bore, noia, rompiscatole, scocciare, seccare, stufo
bored, annoiato
boredom, noia
bored stiff, stufo
boring, annoiato, noia
born, nascere
borrow, borrower, mutuo
boss, capo
bother, fastidio, noia, scocciare, seccare
bottom, fondo
bow, arco
box, boxing, box
bracket, parentesi
brainwashing, lavaggio
branch (bank), sportello
brave, bravo
brawn, coppa
brazenness, faccia
break (vow), voto
breakdown, guasto
breakdown lorry, carro attrezzi
breakfast, fare
breed, razza
bribe, bustarella
bridge, ponte
bright, lucidare, lucido
broad bean, fagiolo, fava
broadly speaking, grosso
broke (moneyless), soldi
broth, minestra
budget, bilancio, preventivo
bugbear, nero, scogliera
building, palazzo
bulb, lampadina
bump into, tamponamento
bump off, fare
burn, bruciare
bus, mezzo
business, azienda, faccenda, firma, negozio

business consultant, commercialista
business deal, affare
bus-stop, fermare
busybody, ficcare
but, ma, però, pure
butter, burro
by a hair's-breadth, pelo
by chance, caso, occasione
by dint of, forza
by end of, entro
by land, via
by-law, leggina
by now, ormai
by-pass, tangenziale
by sea, via
by the way, parentesi, proposito
by way of example, mò

C

cabbage, cavolo
café, bar
calcium, calcio
call (for tenders), gara
call-up, leva
camera, camera, fotografo, macchina
camping ground, lift
camping place, camping
can, bidone
cancel, cancellare
candy floss, fila
canteen, cantina, mensa
can't go on, avanti
can't wait, ora
can you beat that? capirai
capable, capace
car, macchina
carabinieri patrol car, gazzella
caravan, carrozzone
carbon paper, carta
card, scheda
card-index, scheda
care, impegno
caretaker, portiere
car-park attendant, abusivo
carry (bear), reggere

carry out, realizzare
cartoon, fumetti
case, caso, cassa, ipotesi
case-history, casistica
cash-desk, cassa
cash grant, contributo
cash in hand, fondo
cat, gatto, micio
catch (cold), pigliare
catch (fish), pesca
catch fire, pigliare
catch hold, addosso
cause, provocare
cause trouble, grana
caught red-handed, sacco
cave, cava
ceiling, attico
cellar, cantina, mensa
centre, centro
century, novecento
Chamber of Commerce, camera
champion, fuoriclasse
chance, occasione
change, cambiare
change (money), resto, spiccioli
change (subject), discorso
Channel, oltre
chap, tizio
charity, carità
chat, argomento
chauffeur, autista
cheap, ordinario
cheat, fregare, imbroglio
check, controllare, verificare
cheeky, dispetti
cheer, tifo
cheerio, ciao
cheers, cin cin, salute
cheer up, dagli, su
cheese, formaggio
cheque, cheque-book, assegno
chest, cassa
chewing gum, gomma
chock-a-block, pieno
choose between devil and . . .,
    finestra
chop, braciola
Christmas cake, panettone
CID, polizia
cigarettes, bionda

city, urbe
city council, comune
city planner, urbanista
city planning, urbanistica
civil proceedings, processo
claim, inquadramento,
    pretendere
clean record, incensurato,
    pregiudicato
clean sweep, piazza
clear, lucido, risultare
clearance sale, liquidazione
clear up (fix), sistemare
clergyman, clergyman
clerical grade, impiegato
clerk, impiegato
clever, bravo, dritto, furbo,
    spiritoso
cliff, scogliera
climb, scalata
clockwise, orario
clodhopper, burino
close, afa
close relation, parente
cloth (rag), panno, straccio
clothes, attirare, panno
cloverleaf, svincolo
clutch disc, disco
coach, carrozza, pullman
coalition, bicolore
coat of paint, mano
coffee, bar, caffè, espresso
coincidence, coincidenza,
    combinazione
cold, raffreddore
collective agreement, normativo
college hostel, convitto
collision, investimento,
    tamponamento
column, palo
combination, combinazione
combine, combinare
comedy, commedia
come in, accomodare, avanti
come near to, mancare
come on, dagli, forza, su, via
come round, ricovero
come to nothing, sfumatura
come to point, definitiva
comic, fumetti

comical, buffo
commercial traveller, piazza
commitment, committed, impegno
common, ordinario
common cold, raffreddore
commotion, commozione
commuter, pendolare
company, company policy, azienda
compare, confronto
comparison, confronto, paragone
competition, gara
competitive examination, raccomandazione
competitor, vincere
complimentary copy, omaggio
compliments, omaggio
composed, sconosciuto
compromise, mezzo, via
compulsive liar, mitomane
conceited, presuntuoso
concentration camp, campo
concern, azienda, interessamento, toccare
concussion, commozione, concussione
condensed milk, latte
conditional discharge, incensurato
conductor (orchestra), direttore
confection, confectioner's, confectionery, confezione
conference, conferenza
confetti, confetti, partecipazione
confidence man, foglia
confiscation, sequestro
confront, confronto
confuse, smarrire
connection, combinazione
conscription, leva
consequently, quindi
consignment, partita
consolidated act, unico
consommé, brodo
constituency, collegio
constitution, fisico
consultation, consultazione

contemptible, inqualificabile
contest, gara
continent, continente
contractor, impresario
contribution, contributo
control, controllare
controversy, polemica, sindacato, vertenza
convent, convento
conversation, discorso
cooker, cooking, cucina
cool, fresco
coordinated, coordination, articolato
cork, tappo
corner kick, calcio
corporate entity, persona
corporate saving, autofinanziamento
corpse, cadavere
corpus delicti, delitto
corruption, costume, malcostume
cost-of-living bonus, contingenza
cost the earth, patrimonio
costume, costume
cottage, villino
couldn't care less, menefreghista
couldn't help, meno
country, paese
country house, villa
coup d'état, colpo
coupon (football), schedina, tredici
court, campo
court of appeal, istanza
coward, vigliacco
crafty, furbo
crane truck, carro attrezzi
crash, investimento
crazy, pazzo, toccare
cream, panna
create stir, rumore
crime, delitto
criminal, malavita
criminal trial, processo
crisis, crisi
cross, croce
crotchety, lunatico

crucial point, dunque
crude oil, olio, petrolio
crush, sbandata
crux, dunque
cuckold, corno
cufflinks, gemelli
cuisine, cucina
cunning, furbo
cup, coppa
cure, curare
currency, valuta
currency regulations, norma
current account, conto
custard, panna
custom, costume
custom built, fuoriserie
Customs Police, bionda
cut, tagliare
cut (rake-off), tangente
cut figure, figura
cut in half, metà
cut it out, fare, piantare
cutlet, braciola
cycling, cyclist, ciclismo

D

dad, papa
daggers drawn, ferro
damages, responsabile
damn, accidenti
damn it, managgia
dance, dance hall, ballo
dark, buio, oscuro
darkroom, camera, oscuro
dashed (hopes), sfumatura
date, dattero
date of birth, nascita
dead, rimanere
dead drunk, ubriaco
dead easy, forza
dead loss, bidone
dead tired, cascare
deal with, evadere
death, morte
death rate, mortalità
decade, decade
deceive, ingannare

decent sort, persona
decide, decidersi
decisive moment, dunque
deck, ponte
decline, tramonto
deduction, trattenuta
deficit, disavanzo
defraud, imbroglio
degree, diplomato, laurea
delay, ritardo
delight, delitto
delightful, suggestivo
deliver, recapito
delusion, delusione
demand, pretendere
demanding, impegno
demonstration, piazza
density, peso
department store, magazzino,
   rivista
deposit account, conto
depression, crisi
depth, altezza
design, disegno
desire, voglia
desk, banco
despicable, inqualificabile
detailed, capillare
detain, fermare
detective story, giallo, vigliacco
determined, grinta
devastating, inquietante
development fund, cassa
die, mancare
diesel oil, nafta
different, diverso
difficult, difficile, impegno
difficulty, imbroglio
diligence, impegno
din, chiasso
dinner, cena
diplomat, diplomatic, diplomato
direction, indirizzo
directions for use, norma
directly, addirittura
directly afterwards, subito
director, direttore
dirty trick, mascalzone
disagree strongly, polemica
disappointed, male, rimanere

disappointment, delusione
disaster, disastro
disclose, scoprire
disconcerted, sconosciuto
discount, discounted, sconto
discount rate, tasso
discover, scoprire
discovery, scoperta
discus, lanciare
discussion, discussione
disgraceful, disgrazia, inqualificabile, vergogna
disgust, schifo
dishwasher, lavare
dismiss, esonerare
displaced person, apolide
disposed, disposto
dispute, sindacato, vertenza
disquieting, inquietante
distributor, distributore
diving board, trampolino
do as he says, retta
doctor, dottore, professore
doesn't matter, niente
dogged, grinta
do it your own way, testa
dome, cupolone
Donald Duck, fumetti, papera
don't care, importare
don't forget, raccomandare
don't know, non so
don't mention it, niente, prego
door, sportello
dossier, pratica
double bed, piazza
dough, pasta
do without, meno
down and out, morto
draught, aria, corrente
draught beer, birra
draw (lottery), lotteria
drawing, disegno
dreary, squallido
drenched, bagnato
drifter, sbandato
drift to towns, urbanesimo
drink, bere
drinking water, acqua
drive, guida
drive me crazy, diventare

driver, autista
driving lessons, guida
driving licence, guida, patente
driving school, guida
drop, lasciare
dropout, sbandato
drum, bidone
drums, batteria
drunk, ubriaco
dryclean, lavare
drycleaning, lavaggio
dry wine, vino
duckling, papera
dud cheque, assegno
duffel coat, montgomery
dummy (cards), morto
dummy (pacifier), succhietto
duster, straccio
dustman, immondizia, netturbino
dying for/to, voglia

E

ear, orecchio
early, ora
early bird, pigliare
earth (elec.), messa
Easter egg, uovo
easy as pie, niente
easy-chair, poltrona
easy to get on with, mano
easy to influence, suggestionabile
economic planning, dirigismo
economic policy, dirigismo,
 politica
economics, politica
economic situation, congiuntura
edit, edited, curare
editor, direttore, responsabile
education, educato
effective, incisivo, valido
efficient, valido
effrontery, faccia
egg, uovo
eighteenth century, settecento
election, consultazione

electric iron, ferro
electricity, corrente, elettricità
electric shock, sciocco
element, elemento
emotion, commozione
employee, elemento, impiegato
employment, lavoro subordinato
empty, vuotare
empty wishes, velleità
end, fondo
enema, lavativo
engagement, impegno
enjoyable, divertirsi
enjoy yourself, buon giorno,
   divertirsi
ensue, risultare
enter, entrare
entertaining, divertirsi
entry, partita
envelope, busta, bustarella
erase, cancellare
eraser, gomma
escalator, scala mobile
escalator clause, adeguarsi
escapade, scappatella
escape, evadere
escort, traduzione
estate, patrimonio
estimate, preventivo
even, addirittura, ancora,
   neanche, pure
event, gara
eventually, eventualmente
evil, male
evocative, suggestivo
exacting, impegno
examine, visita medica
excellent, bene
excellent spirits, umore
exceptional, fuoriclasse
exceptionally, via
excuse me, dispiace, permesso,
   scusare
execute (order), evadere
exercise, esercizio
exercise book, quaderno
exonerate, esonerare
expected, sconto
expenditure, entrare
experience, esperienza, pratica

experienced, pratico
experiment, esperienza
exploit, sfruttare
expose, scoprire
express train, espresso, rapido
extensive, capillare
extortion, concussione
extraction (origin), oriundo
extremist, extraparlamentare

F

fabric, fabbrica
face, faccia
factory, fabbrica, fattoria,
   industria, stabilimento
fail exam, laurea
failure, guasto
faint, filo, smarrire
fair, giusto
fairly, piuttosto
fake, fasullo
fall, fall for it, cascare, foglia
falling star, fila
fall to, toccare
false, fasullo
fame, notorio
family allowances, assegno
fan (supporter), tifo
fancy, figurarsi
fancy dress, costume
fare, tassì
farm, azienda, fabbrica, fattoria,
   fondo
fasten, attaccare
fast train, direttissima, espresso
Father Christmas, papa
father's name, paternità
faute de mieux, mancanza
favour, gentile, piacere
fawning, ossequio
fed up, stufo
fee, retta
feeble, debole
feel done, naso
feeling, sensazione
feel in good form, gamba
feel like, voglia

fellow, tizio
felony, delitto
female, femmina
few, qualche
fickle, mobile
field, campo
field events, atletica
fifteenth century, Quattrocento
figure (body), personale
file (papers), pratica
filing cabinet, scheda
filth, immondizia
filthy, schifo
final design, disegno
financial year, esercizio
financier, finanziere
find, scoprire
fine (to pay), contravvenzione, polizia
fine thing, roba
finicky, pignolo
finishing touch, toccare
fire insurance, assicurazione
firm, azienda, bottega, firma, negozio
first offender, incensurato
first-rate, ordine
fishing, pesca
fish soup, minestra, zuppa
fishy, gatto
fit, adatto, giusto
five-year, quinquennio
five-year plan, lustro, quinquennio
fix, accomodare, sistemare
flabbergasted, cascare, rimanere
flag of convenience, bandiera ombra
flair, portato
flaky pastry, pasta
flamethrower, lanciare
flash, lampone
flatfeet, polizia
flat out, birra
flesh, carne
flight engineer, motorista
flirtation, scappatella
float, morto
floor, marciapiede, pavimento
floor polisher, lucidare

flop, disastro
flying saucer, disco
Flying Squad, mobile, polizia
focus, messa, mettere
foolish, sciocco
foolscap, carta
foot, piede
football, calcio
football match, partita
football pools, schedina, toto-calcio, tredici
force maieure, caso, forza
forces (armed), naia
forecourt, piazzale
foreign exchange, divisa, valuta
foreign policy, politica
for fun, scherzo
forget it, lasciare
forgive, scusare
for heaven's sake, carità
fork, forkful, forchettata
form, modulo
for some time, pezzo
fortuitous, occasione
fortunately, meno
forty winks, pisolino
forward, attaccare
forward (letter), evadere
foundation pile, palo
fraud, imbroglio
freckle, lentiggine
free, disponibile
free gift, omaggio
free kick, calcio
free will, volontà
fresh, fresco
fresh air, aria
fringe benefits, addizionali
from now on, avanti, poi
from time to time, tanto
fuel oil, nafta
full dress uniform, divisa
full marks, voto
full speed, gamba
full up, pieno
fully recovered, gamba
function, funzione
fund, cassa, fondo
fundamentally, fondo
funny, divertirsi

furious, incavolato
furniture, mobile
further, oltre
further on, avanti
fussy, fastidio, pignolo

G

game, calcio, partita
game (dogged), grinta
gangway, corsia
garage, autorimessa, box
garbage, immondizia
gas cylinder, bombola di gas
gay power, froscio
gazelle, gazzella
Gemini, gemelli
general conditions, normativo, trattamento
general election, consultazione
general strike, scioperare
genial, geniale
genius, geniale
get, diventare
get a move on, su
get better, cavare
get blind drunk, sbornia
get by, arrangiarsi
get hot and bothered, prendersela
get into trouble, combinare
get job for someone, sistemare
get money out of, cavare
get out of it, cavare
get out of way, mezzo, piede
get quite straight, intendere
get something back, ricovero
get to the bottom of, fondo, oltranza
get up to, combinare
gift, presente
gifted, portato
gift horse, cavallo
gift of gab, sciolto
give a lift (ride), passaggio
glass, bicchiere
gnaw, rosicare
goal, meta

goalkeeper, portiere
goalpost, palo
go away, fila
goddess, diva
go Dutch, romano
go for walk, fare, passeggiata
going concern, azienda
going to, andare
golden handshake, liquidazione
goldfish, rosso
good, bravo
good afternoon, evening, buon giorno
good impression, figura
good job too, meno
good Lord! o Dio
good luck, auguri, lupo
good manners, educato
good morning, night, buon giorno
good offices, interessamento
good will, buon giorno, disponibile, volontà
Goofy, fumetti
gooseberry, uva
go out, salire
gosh, capirai
go-slow, scioperare
gossip, chiacchierone
go steady with, fila
go to, recarsi
go to bed, andare
go to hell, paese
go upstairs, salire
governess, governante
government controls, dirigismo
government crisis, consultazione
governor (prison), direttore
graceful, gracious, grazioso
gradually, mano
graduate, laureato
graft, concussione, malcostume
grammar school, ginnasio
gramophone record, disco
grandchild, nipote
grant, borsa
grapes, uva
green, greenish, verde
greet, salutare
grill, arrosto

grocer's, drogheria, salsamenteria
grotto, grotta
ground, campo
grounds, motivo
grow, diventare
growth rate, tasso
guesswork, naso
guide book, guida
guidelines, indirizzo
guts, fegato
guy, tizio
gymnasium, ginnasio, palestra

H

had better, convenire
had its day, arrivare
hair, capellone
half, metà, mezzo
half truth, halfway, metà
hamlet, borgata
hammer, chiodo, lanciare
hand, mano
handbag, borsa
hangover, sbornia
happen, capitare, successo,
verificare
hard-boiled egg, uovo
hardly ever, mai
hard nut to crack, filo, torcere
hat, capellone
haughty, superbo
have cake and eat it, cavolo
have feeling of, provare
have good time, divertirsi
have money on you, addosso
have on tip of tongue, lingua
have to, forza
have tooth filled/out, dente
head, testa
headed paper, carta
head in whirl, girare
headmaster, direttore
head office, sede
head of state, capo
head physician, primario
headquarters, sede

heads or tails, croce, testa
health, salute
health insurance scheme, mutua
heap, mucchio, pila
heaps of, sacco
hear, sentire, udire
heat (sports), batteria
heavy cold, raffreddore
height, altezza
hell, cavolo, managgia
hello, ciao, pronto, salve
help, assistere
he-man, fusto
hereafter (the), oltre
here is, ecco
here we go again, risiamo
heritage, patrimonio
hide and seek, nascondino
hiding place, nascondino
highness, altezza
high school, ginnasio
hijack, dirottare, pirata
hit-and-run driver, pirata
hit nail on head, centro
hold (support), reggere
hold water, acqua, fila
hole, buca
Holy See, sede
homage, omaggio
homosexual, froscio
honeymoon, miele
hoodlum, teppista
hoodwink, ingannare
hooligan, hooliganism, teppista
hope for best, santo
hope so, auguri
horn, corno
hors d'oeuvre, antipasto, pasto
horse, HP, cavallo
hospitalization, hospitalize,
ricovero
hot line, filo
house, villa, villino
household chores, faccenda
housekeeper, governante
how, come
how clever, forza
how do you do, piacere
however, comunque, mai, però
humour, umore

hunger strike, scioperare
hurt, male, rimanere
hut, baraccati

I

identity card, tessera
idiotic, scemo
if, eventualmente
if only, magari
if possible, possibilmente
ignore, ignorare
imagine, figurarsi
I mean, anzi
I mean to say, o dio
immediately, addirittura, subito
immorality, costume, malcostume
imposing, superbo
impresario, impresario
impressionable, suggestionabile
impressive, suggestivo
in advance, ora
in agreement, rimanere
in any case, comunque, modo
in case, mai
inclined to, disposto, portato
income tax, imposta
in conclusion, definitiva
incur debts, chiodo
indeed, anzi, davvero
in-depth, capillare
in detail, filo
Indian ink, inchiostro
indictment, capo
individual, tizio
industry, industria
in fact, anzi
ingenious, geniale
inherit fortune, patrimonio
injection, iniezione
ink, inchiostro
inland revenue, fisco
in-laws, parente
inner tube, camera
in no way, modo
in one ear, orecchio
in person, persona

in practice, praticamente
in short, insomma
in short while, poco
installation, messa
instead, invece
instructions, norma
insult, offendere
insurance, assicurazione
interchange, svincolo
interest, interessamento
interesting, suggestivo
international player, azzurro,
  nazionale
interrelated, articolato
intervention, intervento
in the dark, buio, oscuro
in the lead, testa
in the way, piede
in this way, modo
invalid chair, carrozzella
investment credit, investimento
irksome, fastidio
iron, ferro
isn't it? vero
itching to, ora
it's a pleasure, mancare
it's a question of, trattare
it's no trouble, mancare

J

jam, marmellata
janitor, portiere
jargon, gergo
jerry-can, bidone
job, posto, sistemazione
job classification, inquadramento
jobs for boys, lottizzazione,
  raccomandazione
joke, scherzo
judge by appearances, ingannare
judgment, sentenza
jumbo tanker, petroliera
jumper, maglia
juryman, giudice popolare
just, appunto, giusto
just about to, lì lì

just as well, male, meno
just imagine, capirai, guarda un pò, però
just in case, caso, mai
just listen, cosa
just look, guarda un pò
just now, ora
just take a look, poco
just tell me, cosa
just the thing, fagiolo, fare
just you dare, provare
Juventus F.C., bianconeri, neroazzurri

K

keep mum, acqua
keep up appearances, figura
keep up with, testa
keep vow, voto
keep watch, palo
kerosene, paraffina
kick, calcio
kidding, scherzo
kidnap, kidnapper, rapire
kidnapping, sequestro
kill, fare
kill two birds, fava
kind, kindness, gentile
kiosk, edicola
kitchen, cucina
kitchen sink, lavabo, lavello
knit, knitting needle, ferro, maglia
knitwear, maglia
knock around, girare
knock head against wall, buca
knock off (steal), fregare
know what's what, sapere

L

laboratory, laboratorio
lace, pizza
lack, mancanza
lakefront, lakeside, lungomare

lame, zoppicare
lamppost, palo
landed property, fondo
landing stage, palo
land use, indirizzo
lane, corsia
language, lingua
lap, ciclismo
large, largo
lash out, menare
lastly, ultimamente
last straw, mancare, volere
Last Supper, cena
late, ritardo
lately, ultimamente
launderette, laundry, lavanderia
lawsuit, processo
lawyer, barista
lay (secular), laico
lay about oneself, menare
Lazio F.C., biancoazzurri
lazybones, lavativo
leaders, direttivo
leading (question), suggestivo
lead merry dance, filo
lead up garden path, menare
leaf, foglia
league table, calcio
least bit, affatto
leave, lasciare, permesso, tagliare
leave in lurch, piantare, rimanere
leave no stone unturned, oltranza
lecture, conferenza, lettura
lecturer, assistere
left over, disavanzo
leg, gamba
legal tender, valuta
lend, lender, mutuo
let, let be, lasciare
let oneself in for, gatto
let's, vediamo
let's go, andare
let's hope so, più
letterbox, buca
level crossing, passaggio
lever, leva
liable, responsabile

Libra, bilancio
library, libreria
licence, patente
licence plate, targa
lie, bugia
life insurance, assicurazione
lift, liftboy, lift
lift (ride), passaggio
light, accendere, luce
lighter, accendere
lightning, lampone
lightning strike, scioperare
like, dispiace
like this, così
limp, zoppicare
line, fila
linen, biancheria
line of country, campo
liqueur, bicchierino
list, elenco
list (to port, starboard),
   sbandata
little, poco
live, campare
liver, liverish, fegato
livestock, zootecnia
loan, mutuo
logical, logico
long, lungo
longer, oltre
longhaired, capellone
longing, voglia
long shot, campo
look, guarda
look after, look after yourself,
   curare
look for trouble, grana
look out, attenzione
lookout, palo
loose, sciolto
loose stable, box
lose, smarrire
lose bearings, tramontana
lose face, figura
lose head, testa
lose way, smarrire
Lost Property Office, smarrire
lot, mucchio
lots of, sacco
lottery, lotteria

lousy, schifo
lout, cafone
lubricant, lubrication, lubrificazione
lucid, lucido
luckily, meno
lull, parentesi
lunatic, matto
lunatic asylum, lunatic fringe,
   lunatico

M

macaroni, pasta
machine, macchina
mad, matto
madness, pazzo
magazine, magazzino, rivista
magic touch, toccare
magnetic field, campo
magnificent, superbo
mailing list, indirizzo
mainland, continente
mainly, più
make clean breast of, vuotare
make ends meet, sbarcare il
   lunario
make mountain out of molehill,
   acqua
make mouth water, acquolina
make off, fila, sistemare
make provision, provvedere
make shift, arrangiarsi
make sick, schifo
make trouble, piantare
make up mind, decidersi
male, maschio
manage, arrangiarsi
manager, capocomico, direttore,
   impresario
manly, maschio
manner, modo
manual control, intervento
mark, pagella, voto
market, commercializzare,
   piazza
marmalade, marmellata
masculine, maschio

mass, messa
master mind, mente
match, fiammifero, gara
matter, faccenda, importare
mayor, comune, sindaco
meal, pasto
means of transport, mezzo
measure, intervento, provvedere
meat, carne
medical (exam, checkup), visita
  medica
meeting, riunione
melted, sciolto
membership card, tessera
mess, guaio, macello, messa,
  pasticcio, pizza, roba
messenger, fattorino, messaggero
metre, metro
Mickey Mouse, fumetti
middle, mezzo
middle managers, quadri
might, capace
military service, militare, naia
milk, latte
minced meat, carne
mind, dispiace, mente
mind own business, affare
mind you, intendere
minor offence, contravvenzione
minutes (of meeting), processo
mirror, bicchiere
misdemeanour, delitto
miserable wretch, disgrazia
mishap, disgrazia
mislay, smarrire
miss, mancanza, piede
missile launching pad, lanciare
mitten, mezzo
mixed grill, arrosto
mixed marriage, school,
  promiscuo
mix-up, imbroglio, pizza
mocking, sfottere
monastery, convento
money, grana, quattrini, soldi,
  valuta
money order, vaglia
mood, umore
moody, lunatico

morality, morals, costume
morbid, morbido, morboso
more, ancora
more dead than alive, morto
more or less, meno
moreover, più
more than, oltre
more than ever, mai, più
morning coat, tight
mortgage loan, mutuo
mostly, più
motive, motivo
motorcycle, moto
motorcyclist, pilota
motorist, motorista
motor mechanic, motorista
motor scooter, motoretta
motorway, corsia
mountaineering, alpinismo
muck, immondizia
muggy, afa
mumps, orecchioni
municipality, comune,
  municipio
must, bisognare, forza
my! accidenti, capirai, però,
  uffa
mystery story, libro

N

nail, chiodo
namely, cioè, ossia
nap, pisolino
naphtha, nafta
narrow escape, pelo
nasty cold, raffreddore
national anthem, inno
national service, naia
naturally, capire, senza
nature, ordine
naughty, dispetti
necessarily, forza
necessary, occorrere
need, bisogno, occorrere, volere
negative, controproducente
neither, nor, ne, neanche
neo-fascist, missino

nephew, nipote
nerve, faccia, fegato
nerves, crisi
never again, mai, più
nevertheless, eppure
never too late, mai
new-laid eggs, uovo
news, attuale
newspaper, carta
news stand, edicola
nibble, rosicare
nice, carino, gentile, simpatico
nice mess, guaio
niece, nipote
night club, lift, night
nightwatchman, polizia, vigile
nineteenth century, ottocento
no business of yours, entrare
no flies on, gamba
noise, chiasso, rumore
non-aligned countries, impegno
non-denominational, laico
nonsense, bugia, discorso,
    sciocco, stupidaggine
noodles, pasta
normal, ordinario
northerner, meridionale
nose, naso
not all there, scemo
not at all, figurarsi, mica, prego
not be up to, not be capable of,
    altezza
not catch me, cascare
note, appunto
not get hang of, cavare
not give a damn, cavolo, corno,
    fregare
not help doing, fare
nothing, niente
nothing venture . . ., rosicare
no thoroughfare, passaggio
notice, accorgersi
notification, partecipazione
not in slightest, mica
not keep (promise), mancare
not know, ignorare
not know which way to turn,
    capo
not make sense, reggere
not my cup of tea, dente

not notice, caso
notorious, notorio
no trouble at all, mancare
not so bad, male
no use, niente
novel, novella
now, attuale, mò
nowadays, oggigiorno
now and then, occasione
now then, allora
nuance, sfumatura
nuclear reactor, pila
nuisance, grana, noia,
    piantagrane, rompiscatole,
    scocciare
number, numero
number plate, targa
nurse, curare
nursing home, curare

O

obscure, oscuro
obstacle, scogliera
obstruction, ingegno
obtain, procurare
occasion/ally, occasione
occur, mente, occorrere,
    verificare
of course, capire, certo, come,
    intendere, senza
off, via
off beaten track, mano
offence, offendere
offended, rimanere
office, studio
office hours, orario
off one's head, numero
off one's rocker, suonare
offputting, fastidio
oh! uffa
oh no, oh yes, via
oil, benzina, olio, petrolio
oil-fired, nafta
oil stove, petrolio
oil sump, coppa
oil tanker, petroliera
oil well, petrolio

O.K., andare, bene
olive (tree), oliva
olive oil, olio
on ball, gamba
once in blue moon, papa
on contrary, accordo, anzi, invece
one-man show, personale
one swallow does not . . ., rondine
one-way street, unico
on feet, on foot, piede
on lookout, attenzione
only child, unico
on other hand, invece
on point of, lì lì, pelo
on purpose, proposito
on spot, posto
on the whole, insomma
on time, orario
open door, apertura
operation, intervento
opportune, opportunità
opportunity, occasione, opportunità
or, oppure
orange squash, bar
orbit, orbita
orchestra stall, poltrona
organization, inquadramento
orphan/age, orfano
other fish to fry, gatto
otherwise, oppure
outboard, fuoribordo
out of breath, grosso
out of date, dattero
out of order, guasto
outspoken, lingua, pelo
outstanding, fuoriclasse
overawe, soggezione
overbearing, prepotente
overdrawn, assegno
overseas, oltre

P

pack, ficcare
packaging, confezione

packed, pieno
packing paper, carta
pain in neck, lavativo, scocciare
palace, palazzo
panel doctor, mutua
panther, pantera
paper, carta
papers, pratica
paraffin/wax, paraffina
paraffin lamp, petrolio
parade, rivista
parent, pagella, parente
parenthesis, parentesi
parking apron, piazzale
parochialism, campanilismo
parquet floor, marciapiede
partial to, debole
participation, partecipazione
party, partita
party bore, guasto
pass, valico
passage, corsia, passaggio
pass exam, laurea
pastrycook, pasticcio
patent/medicine, patente
patience, pazienza
patrol cars, polizia
patrolman, questurino, vigile
patronage, clientelismo, raccomandazione
pavement, marciapiede, pavimento
pay, salario
pay envelope, busta
pay visit, fare
peach, pesca
pear tree, però
peasant, burino, cafone
pea soup, minestra
pedantic, pignolo
pedestrian crossing, passaggio
penalty kick, calcio
penthouse, attico, servizi
performance, spettacolo
perhaps, magari
permission, permesso
permit, patente
person, persona
personal, personale
personal allowance, assegno

personal assets/property, mobile
personnel, organico, personale
pest, rompiscatole
petition, istanza
petrol, benzina, petrolio
petroleum, olio, petroliera,
   petrolio
petrol pump, benzina,
   distributore, petrolio
phew! uffa
phone call, colpo
phoney, fasullo
photograph, photographer,
   fotografo
physicist, physics, fisico
physique, fisico
piccolo, ottavino
pickle, marinare
pictures, quadri
picturesque, suggestivo
picture story, fotografo
pie, pasticcio
piece, pezzo
pier, palo, pila
pigeon, pigione
pile, palo, pila
pile-up, tamponamento
pilfer, rubare
pilot, pilota
pimp, ruffiano, sfruttare
pinch (steal), fregare
pinch of salt, beneficio
   d'inventario
pirate, pirata
pitch, campo
pits, box
pit stall, poltrona
place (room), posto
plain as pikestaff, uovo
plain words, povero
plank, tavola
planned economy, dirigismo
plant, piantare
plant (works), stabilimento
plant out, messa
play, commedia
play (music), suonare
play about, dispetti
playing field, campo
play tricks, dispetti

play truant, marinare
play up, forza
play with fire, scherzo
pleasant, simpatico
please, gentile, piacere, prego
pluck, fegato
plucky, grinta
plug, tappo
plumber, idraulico
point, caso
point duty, polizia
point out, presente
poke fun at, sfottere
pole, palo
polemic, polemics, polemica
police, forza
police car, pantera
police chief, polizia
policeman, agente, polizia,
   questurino, vigile
police record, scheda
police surgeon, polizia
policy, indirizzo, politica
polish, lucidare, lucido
polite, educato, gentile
politician, politica
politics, politica
polls, urna
poodle, barba
pools coupon, schedina,
   totocalcio, tredici
poor, povero
pope, papa
Popeye, fumetti
porter, portiere
possibly, eventualmente,
   possibilmente
post, imbucare, palo
postal order, vaglia
power station, elettricità
practical, pratico
practically, praticamente
practice, esercizio, pratica
pram, carrozzina, passeggiata
prattle, chiacchierone
precisely, appunto, proprio
prejudiced, pregiudicato
premium petrol, benzina
prepared, disposto
presence, partecipazione

present, attuale, presente
press photographer, fotografo
pretend, fare, pretendere
pretend not to know, niente
pretty, carino, grazioso
prevent, togliere
preventive, preventivo
previous offender, pregiudicato
process, processo
processed cheese, formaggino
procuress, ruffiana
producer, impresario
product, production, productivity, prodotto
professional, professionista
professor, professore
project, intervento
promenade, lungomare
promiscuous, promiscuo
proper, adatto, giusto
property, property tax, patrimonio
prostitute, mondana, passeggiata
protest/er, contestazione
protest strike, scioperare
proud, superbo
prove, provare
prove right, verificare
prove to be, risultare
provoke, provocare
public school, collegio
public utilities, servizi
public welfare, assistere
puff pastry, pasta
pull leg, gamba, girare
pull out, tendenza
pullover, maglia, pull
pull through, cavare
pulp, pasta
pump, benzina
punch, menare
punctually, orario
pupil, elemento
purse, borsa
pushchair, passeggiata
put foot in it, papera
put in order, sistemare
put it plainly, povero
put on (light), luce

put on airs, aria
put out (offended), rimanere
put out (switch off), spegnere
put right, accomodare
put shot, lanciare, peso
put yourself in another's shoes, panno

Q

quads, gemelli
quarrel, argomento, litigare
quarry, cava
Queen Anne's dead, scoperta
question, questione
quibble, sofisticato
quins, gemelli
quite, piuttosto
quite a turn, colpo
quite crazy, matto
quite well, bene
quit it, piantare

R

race, razza
racing driver, pilota
racket (noise), chiasso
radiator, elemento
radio link, ponte
rag, straccio
rainbow, arco
raisin, uva
rake off, tangente
ramp, piazzale
rape, rapire
raspberry, lampone, pernacchia
rate, tasso
rate of exchange, cambiare
rather, indifferente, piuttosto
readiness, disponibile
reading, conferenza, lettura
readjust to, adeguarsi
ready, pronto
ready cash, cassa
ready-made clothing, confezione

real, pizza
real estate, mobile
realize, accorgersi, conto,
    realizzare, rendersi conto
really, addirittura, davvero,
    proprio
rear window, lunotto
reason, motivo
reasonable, trattabile
recently, ultimamente
recommend, raccomandare
recommendation, raccomanda-
    zione
record (sport), primato
recover, ricovero
red, rosso
Red Cross, croce
reef, scogliera
referee, arbitro, calcio
reference books, consultazione
refuge, ricovero
refuse (garbage), immondizia
regain consciousness, ricovero
regards, ossequio
region, regione
regional planning, assetto
register, raccomandare
registered office, sede
Registry Office, Anagrafe
regular petrol, benzina
regulation, norma
relation, relative, parente
relaxation, relax
reliable, attendere
remain, rimanere
remainder, disavanzo
rent, affittare, equo canone,
    pigione
repair, accomodare
reply, rispondere
request, istanza
required, occorrere, volere
resolute, grinta, incisivo
respectful, ossequio
respects, omaggio, ossequio
responsible, responsabile
result, risultare
return ticket, andare
reveal, scoprire
revolting, schifo

ride, passaggio, passeggiata
ridiculous, buffo
right, adatto, ragione
right away, subito
rightly or wrongly, ragione
ring, suonare
riot squad, Celere
rip-roaring drunk, sbornia
rise, lievitazione, salire
road, via
road accident, accidente
road conditions, viabilità
roast, arrosto
rob, robber, robbery, rapire
rocks, scogliera
romantic, suggestivo
Rome F.C., giallorossi
room, camera, posto, stanza
rot, stupidaggine
rough sea, grosso
round the bend, numero,
    suonare
row (line), fila
row (noise), chiasso
rubber, gomma
rubber dinghy, gommone
rubbish, bugia, chiacchierone,
    immondizia, netturbino,
    stupidaggine
rub out, cancellare
ruffled, sconosciuto
rule, norma
rule of the road, vigile
rumour, rumore
run away, running, fila

S

sack, sacco
saint, santo
St Peter's, cupolone
salary, salario
salesman, piazza
salute, militare, salutare, salute
sandwich, tramezzino
satisfied, rimanere
savings, disavanzo
savoury, saporito

scales, bilancio
scholarship, borsa
school report, pagella
scotch-tape, Scotch
Scotland Yard, polizia, scientifica
scoundrel, mascalzone
scram, piede
scrambled eggs, uovo
scrape, imbroglio
screen, vaglia
scrounge, scrounger, sbafare
seabed, fondo
seafront, lungomare
season ticket, tessera
secondary school, ginnasio
secondhand, occasione
secret service, SID
sectional furniture, mobile
secular, laico
see how things stand, punto
seeing that, tanto
seems to me, sapere
seethe (with anger), fegato
see through, fondo
see to, provvedere
self-esteem, proprio
semi-official, ufficioso
sensation, sensazione
sensible, sensibile
sensitive, sensibile
sensitize, sensibilizzare
sentence, sentenza
sequel, sequence, sequela
serious, impegno
serves you right, bene
service flats, residence
servile, ossequio
set (hair), messa
settle, conto
seventeenth century, seicento
several, diverso
severance pay, liquidazione
sewing machine, macchina
shade of meaning, sfumatura
shake hands, mano
sham, fasullo
shambles, macello
shame, disgrazia, vergogna
shameful, vergogna

shanty town, baraccati
share, partecipazione
sheer madness, pazzo
sheet, foglia, lenzuolo
shelter, ricovero
shelved, oltranza
shocking, sciocco
shoe polish, lucido
shop, bottega, negozio
shop window, finestra
shortage, crisi
short distance away, due passi
short of cash, quattrini
short story, novella
short time ago, poco
short walk, due passi
show (performance), spettacolo
shut up, zitto
shy, vergogna
sick of, stufo
sidecar, carrozzino
sieve, sift, vaglia
sign, fermare, firma
silent, zitto
silly, buffo, sciocco
simultaneous, contestuale
single, unico
single bed, piazza
single ticket, andare
sink, lavabo, lavello
sink or swim, minestra
sit-down strike, scioperare
situated, rimanere
size, numero
skid, sbandata
ski-jump, trampolino
skilled, pratico
skimmed milk, latte, panna
skin diver, sub
skin of teeth, filo
skyjacker, pirata
slab, lastra
slang, gergo
sleeping car, carrozza
slice, fetta
slick, dritto
sliding scale, scala mobile
slimming cure, curare
slip of tongue, papera
slot machine, distributore

slow train, espresso
slump, congiuntura, crisi
small hours, ora
smart (crafty), dritto, furbo
smell a rat, foglia
snapshot, fotografo
snub nose, naso
so, dunque, quindi
social charges, fiscalizzazione
Socialist party, partita
social life, mondano
social work, sociale
society gathering, mondano
so far, ora
soft, morbido
soldier, militare
sole, unico
so long, ci
something in wind, gatto
sometimes, qualche
so much (better/worse), tanto
sophisticated, sofisticato
sorely tried, provare
sorry, dispiace
sound, suonare, rumore,
  valido
soup, brodo, minestra, zuppa
southerner, meridionale
south Italy, Mezzogiorno
spaghetti, pasta
span, luce
sparkling wine, spumante, vino
special delivery, espresso
specific gravity, peso
speech, discorso
spill beans, sacco, vuotare
spin, filare
split hairs, pelo, sofisticato
spoilsport, guasto
sponge, sponger, sbafare
spoon, spoonful, cucchiaio
spot of bother, guaio
sprint, ciclismo
squalid, squallido
square, piazzale
square metre, metro
squatters, abusivo
staff, organico
staggered strike, scioperare
standardization, unificazione

stand someone up, bidone
star, diva
stark staring mad, matto
start from scratch, capo
start up (car), messa
stateless person, apolide
state planning, dirigismo
stay on feet, reggere
STD, interurbana, teleselezione
steal, fregare, rubare
stick, attaccare, ficcare
stick-up, rapire
still, ancora, comunque, eppure
stimulus, leva
Stock Exchange, borsa
stop, fermare
stopper (plug), tappo
store, bottega, magazzino,
  rivista
stove, cucina, stufa
straight, addirittura, dritto
straight line, retta
stranger, sconosciuto
streamer, fila
street, via
street sweeper, netturbino
strength, forza
stretch, tendenza
strike, scioperare
strike (clock), suonare
strike oil, benzina
striking, suggestivo
stringed instruments, arco
strip cartoon, fumetti
stroll, lungomare, passeggiata
strong breeze, fresco
student, elemento
studio, study, studio
stuff, cosa, roba
stumbling block, scogliera
stupid, scemo, sciocco
stupidity, stupidaggine
subdivided, articolato
subject, materia, pagella
subjection, soggezione
success, successo
succession, sequela
sugared almonds, confetti,
  partecipazione
suggestive, suggestivo

suitable, adatto, giusto
suit down to the ground, fagiolo
sultry, afa
summary trial, direttissima
summer time, ora
sum things up, punto
sunset, tramonto
sunstroke, insolazione
suntan, tintarella
superb, superbo
superstition, scaramanzia
supper, cena
support, disponibile, reggere
supporter, tifo
supposing, supposition, ipotesi
surely, certo
surface, pelo
suspect, foglia
swallow, rondine
sweater, maglia
sweet (wine), amabile, vino
sweet dreams, sogni d'oro
sweetish (wine), amabile, vino
sweet pastry, pasta
swimming, balneazione
swindle, bidone, imbroglio
switch, elettricità
switchboard, centralino
switch off, spegnere
switch on, accendere
sympathetic, simpatico
sympathy strike, scioperare
systematic, articolato

T

table, tavola
table-linen, biancheria
tablespoon, cucchiaio
table wine, pasto, vino
tactful, diplomato
take, pigliare
take advantage of, sfruttare
take a joke, scherzo
take care of, curare
take for granted, sconto
take hint, capire, foglia
take hold, reggere

take mickey, girare, sfottere
take notes, appunto
take notice, retta
takeoff, decollo
takeover, scalata
take place, verificare
take seat, accomodare
take steps, provvedere
take stock, punto
take to heels, gamba
take (something) wrong way,
  prendersela
talk, discorso
talk nonsense, sciocco
tangle, imbroglio
tape measure, metro
target, metà
tasty, saporito
tax, imposta
tax dodger, evadere
tax haven, paradiso fiscale
taxi driver, tassì
tax reform, imposta
tea, bar
teacher, professore
team, calcio
telegraph money order, vaglia
telephone, apparecchio
telephone directory, elenco,
  guida
telephone exchange, centralino
tell me, poco
tell truth, vero
temporarily, momentaneamente
tenacity, grinta
tendency, tendenza
terminus, capo
terra firma, firma
terrible, disastro, roba,
  tremendo
terribly, morire
terribly fond of, matto
thank heavens, male
thank you, grazie
that is, ossia
that's all, ecco
that's enough, così
that's right, appunto, giusto
that's that, ecco
that's to say, cioè, valere

then, allora, dunque, poi
the point is, punto
therefore, quindi
there is, ecco
thing, cosa, roba
thingummy, coso
thin on top, piazza
third party insurance, assicurazione
thirteen, tredici
thirteenth, tredicesima
though, invece
thoroughbred, cavallo
thoroughly, filo
threshold agreement, contingenza
thriller, giallo, libro
through train, espresso
throw, lanciare, buttare
throw weight around, prepotente
ticket office, sportello
ticking off, lavata
tight (drunk), orbita
tights, tight
till, cassa
time signal, orario
time to, ora
time zone, orario
tip, busta, conto, mancia
tiresome, fastidio
today, oggigiorno
toilet paper, carta
token (coin), gettone
tongue, lingua
too, pure
too big for boots, prepotente
too smart for words, scoprire
tooth, dente
toothpaste, pasta
topic, argomento
topical, attuale
torch, lampadina
torpedo tube, lanciare
toss up, testa
touch, touched, toccare
touch wood, corno, ferro
tour, giro
Tour de France, ciclismo,
maglia
town council, comune

town hall, municipio, palazzo
town planner, urbanista
town planning, urbanistica
tracing paper, lucido
track, ciclismo
track event, atletica
trade balance, bilancio
trade policy, politica
trade union, sindacato
trade-union dispute, vertenza
trade unionism, -ist, sindacato
traffic duty, polizia
traffic jam, ingorgo
traffic light, rosso
traffic police, polizia
train, trainer, training, allenare
tramp, barba
translation, traduzione
transvestite, costume
travelling expenses, trasferta
treasury, fisco
treat, trattare
treatment, trattamento
tremendous, tremendo
tremendously, morire
trend, tendenza
trial, processo
trick, trickster, imbroglio
trifle, minestra, sciocco,
stupidaggine, zuppa
trigger, contingenza
triplets, gemelli
trouble, grana, guaio, interessamento, noia
troublemaker, grana, piantagrane
truly, davvero
trunk call, interurbana
try on, provare
try to be clever, furbo
T-shirt, maglia
tube (railway), metro
tune up (car), messa
turn, girare
turn deaf ear, fare, orecchio
turn off/on, elettricità, luce
turn out to be, risultare, verificare
twentieth century, novecento
twins, gemelli

twist, torcere
type, dattilografa
typewriter, macchina
typhus, tifo
typist, dattilografa
tyre, gomma

U

ultimately, ultimamente
umpire, arbitro
uncover, scoprire
under control, controllo
underdone, dente
undergo, subito
understand, intendere
undertaker, impresario
undertaking, impegno
underwear, biancheria
underworld, malavita
undesirable, persona
undistributed profits, auto-
    finanziamento
unemployment, disoccupazione
unfaithful, corno
unfortunately, purtroppo
unification, unificazione
uniform, divisa
uninterruptedly, senza
university college, collegio
university professor, ordinario
unknown, oscuro, sconosciuto
unknown to, insaputa
unless, meno
unlikely, difficile
unofficial, ufficioso
unrest, conflittualità
unruffled, sconosciuto
unveil, scoprire
upbringing, educato
upright, dritto
upsetting, fastidio
upstart, burino, cafone
up to a point, punto
urbanization, urbanesimo,
    urbanizzazione
urbanize, urbanizzare
urban planner, urbanista

urban planning, urbanistica
urn, urna
usage, costume
utilities, impiantistica

V

vacuum cleaner, aspirapolvere
vain hopes, velleità
valid, valido
vanished, sfumatura
variety show, rivista
various, diverso
VAT, imposta, IVA
vegetable soup, zuppa
Venice, Serenissima
verify, verificare
very nearly, praticamente
very thing, volere
vest, maglia
via, via
vice squad, costume
victory, vincere
vigorous, incisivo
villa, villa
village, borgata, paese
vintage, vino
viola, violet, viola
VIP, notabile, pezzo
vision, visione
viz., ossia
vote, urna
vote of confidence, voto
votive offering, voto
vow, voto
vulgar person, cafone

W

wag (tail), menare
wage claims, rivendicazione
wage earner, salario
wages, salario
wagtail, ballo
wait, attendere
walk, passeggiata, piede

walk streets, marciapiede
want, volere
ward, corsia
ward off evil eye, scaramanzia
wash, lavare, lavata
washbasin, lavabo
wash dirty linen, panno
washing, lavaggio
washing machine, lavare
wash up, lavare
waste paper, carta
water supply system, acquedotto
way, modo, via
weak, filo
weakness, weak spot, debole
wedding announcement,
   partecipazione
weighing machine, bilancio
weight, peso
weigh up, vaglia
welfare worker, assistere
well, allora, dunque, ebbene
well-balanced, articolato
well-knit, articolato
well-known, notorio
well-mannered, educato
well now, well then, allora
we'll see, vediamo
wet, bagnato
what, cosa
what a . . ., razza
what a bore, barba
what a shame, vergogna
what's-his-name, coso
what's more, più
what's the matter, pigliare
what's up, prendersela
what's wrong, male
what's yours? pigliare
wheelchair, carrozzella
when, come
when in Rome, paese
while away, ingannare
whipped cream, panna
white collar, impiegato
white paper, libro
who knows? boh!
why on earth, mai
why's and wherefores, perchè
wide, width, largo

wildcat strike, scioperare
wildfire, bruciare
will, volontà
willingness, disponibile
winding up, liquidazione
window, finestra
window envelope, busta
wine, vino
winner, winnings, vincere
wire, filo
wish, auguri, voglia, voto
withholding tax, trattenuta
within ace of, pelo
without doubt/fail, senza
with pleasure, volontieri
with regard to, ordine
witty, spiritoso
wolf, lupo
won't hold water, acqua
wood pulp, pasta
work, funzione
worker classification, inquadramento
working class, salario
working hypothesis, ipotesi
work permit, carta
works, stabilimento
workshop, laboratorio, ufficina
work-to-rule, scioperare
worn out, straccio
worried, worry, preoccupare
worrying, inquietante
worrying problem, capo
worth, valere
worthwhile, buttare, convenire,
   valere
wretch, disgrazia
wring, torcere
writing paper, carta
wrong, ragione

X

X-ray, lastra

Y

yardstick, metro

yarn, fila, filo
yellow, giallo, vigliacco
yes, eh, già
yet, ancora, eppure, però, pure
yew tree, tasso
yokel, burino
yolk, rosso

you never know, sapere
you're welcome, niente

Z

zeal, impegno
zip fastener, lampone